Consciously Embrace Your True Personality

Life's Little Secrets Book Series
Book Two

Consciously Embrace Your True Personality

Spiritual Transformative Education

TERRANCE G. SWEJKOSKI

Conscious Clarity Center, Inc.
Traverse City, Michigan
49684

Copyright © 2024 Terrance G. Swejkoski; also commonly known by the name, Terry Swejkoski.

Trademark: *The Train of Life™* and *Conscious Clarity Energy Process™* by Terrance G. Swejkoski

Published and distributed in the United States by: Conscious Clarity Center, Inc.: https//consciousclaritycenter.org

Editor: Karen Swejkoski, Traverse City, Michigan

All rights reserved worldwide. No part of this book may be reproduced by any mechanical, photographic, or electronic process, or in the form of a phonographic recording; nor may it be stored in a retrieval system, transmitted, or otherwise be copied for public or private use—other than for "fair use" as brief quotations embodied in articles and reviews—without prior written permission of the publisher.

The author of this book does not dispense medical advice or prescribe the use of any technique as a form of treatment for physical, emotional, or medical problems without the advice of a physician, either directly or indirectly. The intent of the author is only to offer information of a general nature to help you in your quest for Spiritual well-being. In the event you use any of the information in this book for yourself, the author and the publisher assume no responsibility for your actions.

The events related to the author's experiences, including conversations that occurred, have been re-created to the best recollection of the author. Some situations have been modified, compressed or expanded; and names and identifying details of certain individuals have been changed for confidentiality purposes.

FIRST EDITION
First Printing, 2024
ISBN-13: 978-0-9994399-3-7

Printed in the United States of America

Dedication

Dedicated to everyone who said, "There must be something greater to this life than seen on the surface."

Acknowledgments

I send a special thank you to my wife and editor, Karen, who reviewed this spiritual discourse. I am grateful for her talents and understanding to keep my "write as you speak" writing style in place without changing the contextual meaning. Karen's infinite love, energy, patience and support with me during the moments I check out of society to follow my path are greatly appreciated.

Another person I must thank for her love, energy and patience is my darling daughter, Sage, whose old soul teaches me to be present daily. Her understanding of the importance of this discourse, even at the age of nine, is deeply appreciated.

Reminder

"Meditation is not some *'thing'* you do; it is the experience of Being that which you are."

"You are a Spiritual Being having a human experience guided by Source Energy daily."

- Terrance G. Swejkoski

This Spiritual Discourse is a work of channeled energy brought to light by Source Energy during infinite moments of silence!

Table of Contents

Consciously Embrace Your True Personality 1

Dedication 5
Acknowledgments 5
Reminder 5

- Table of Contents 7
- Introduction 17
- Part One 19
- Understanding Super-ego 19
- Preface 21

Chapter 1 23

- Live Your Life Purpose Every Day 23
  - Is It Possible to Live Purpose Daily 23
  - What Are Some Steps for a Purpose-Driven Life 25
  - If Old Ego Is Gone, Am I Living My Purpose 27
  - What Happens If I Slip 29
  - When On Purpose, Are You Aware 31
  - Does Awareness Dissolve Temptations 34
  - Am I on My Own in this Life Experience 39
  - What Is a Life Situation 42
  - What Is Life 44
  - Is All Life on Purpose 46
  - Where Did Life Originate 49
  - Where Do the Questions Originate 52

- Do We All Have the Same Questions ... 55
- Are We Here Only for Purpose ... 57
- What If We Never Find Our Purpose ... 59
- Chapter 1 Suggestions - Live Your Life Purpose Every Day ... 62

Chapter 2 ... 67
- Assistance from Spiritual Guides ... 67
  - Do We Always Have Spiritual Guides ... 67
  - Who Are Spiritual Guides ... 70
  - Can Anyone Be a Spiritual Guide ... 72
  - How Do I Connect with Spiritual Guides ... 74
  - What Are Historic Lessons ... 78
  - Once Aligned with Spiritual Guides, Does It Get Easier ... 81
  - Who Keeps Asking These Questions ... 83
  - If I Know I'm Doing Wrong, Am I Judged ... 85
  - Do Spiritual Guides Come To Everyone ... 87
  - Do Dreams Count As Spiritual Guides ... 90
  - Are We All Together - Or Separate ... 93
  - What's the Balancing Life Force ... 95
  - What Does Energy Vibration Do for Connection ... 98
  - Do Humans Know How to Love ... 100
  - Can a Spiritual Guide Be Defined ... 102
  - Chapter 2 Suggestions - Assistance from Spiritual Guides ... 104

Chapter 3 ... 109
- Keeping the Faith During Life Challenges ... 109
  - Why Is It So Hard at Times ... 109

If I Give Up, Did I Lose My Purpose 111

How Can You Have Faith During Overwhelming Challenges.114

Can I Really Accomplish All Spirit Tells Me I Can 116

Does Life Need to Have Peaks & Valleys...............................118

If I Keep My Faith, Will Life Be Easier....................................121

When the Guidance Comes, Do I Get Confused...................123

How Do I Know It's Not Super-ego Tricking Me 125

Who Defines My Feelings About Spirit Anyway 127

Do Affirmations Help 130

Why Do Challenges Seem Easier Than Problems 132

Is It Reality Only Based Upon How I Think 135

Can I Change My Thoughts to Change My Life....................137

What Does All This Have to Do with My Happiness 140

Can You Define Your Self-Limiting Challenges 142

Chapter 3 Suggestions - Keeping the Faith During Life Challenges 144

Chapter 4 151

Ask Better Questions 151

So What's a Better Question 151

Flowing In Spirit Produces Better Questions........................153

How Do I Know My Question Was Poor 155

Do All Answers Lead to More Questions 157

What Happens When Questions Are in Conflict 159

Does Super-ego Always Want Control of My Questions 161

Does Separation from Ego Lead to Better Questions 163

- How Many Times Have You Questioned the Answers 165
- If Answers Confuse Me, What Do I Do 167
- Who Said It All Has to Make Sense Anyhow 169
- Are My Beliefs Guiding My Questions 172
- Do Questions Come from Mind or Spirit 173
- How to Handle the Answers 176
- Always Live From the Higher Self Questions 178
- Methods for Better Questions 180
- Chapter 4 Suggestions - Ask Better Questions 182

Chapter 5 187

- Know What You Deserve 187
  - What Do I Deserve 187
  - How Do I Define What I Deserve 189
  - Why Do I Challenge My Worthiness 191
  - Does Life Hold Me Back or Does Ego 194
  - Is Ego Tricking Me Again 196
  - Why Do I Feel Confused When Ego Comes Knocking 198
  - If I Knew My Authentic Self, Would I Still Question My Worth 199
  - How Is Getting in Touch with Authentic Self Imperative for Happiness 201
  - How Do I Stay Focused 204
  - When Does It Get Easier 205
  - Do I Need This Book 207
  - If Everything Is In Proper Order, What's Taking So Long 210

Will Spirit Always Guide Me 212
How Do I Know It's My Highest Self Communicating 214
What Is the Purpose for This Conflict of Thought 216
Chapter 5 Suggestions - Know What You Deserve 219

Part Two 225
Super-ego Falls Away 225

Chapter 6 227

Understanding the Voice Inside 227
What Is My First Step to Understanding the Voice Within ... 227
How Do I Keep Inner Voice Active in Daily Life 229
Is It Important To Always Listen To Inner Voice 232
Has Inner Voice Ever Let You Down 234
Why Do Most People Live in Ego 236
What Can Happen If I Only Listen to Inner Voice 239
Why Is Inner Voice Quiet at Times 241
What Happens When Thought Takes Over 243
Can True Essence Be Explained in a Way Everyone Will Understand 244
Why Do the Number of Questions Seem Too Much to Tolerate at Times 246
If Inner Voice Is Unlimited - Am I 248
How Do I Thrive with Conflict All Around Me 250
Why Does the Spiritual Realm Seem So Natural 252
Is "Being" Part of the Process 254
Is the Process All Part of the Bigger Plan 256

Chapter 6 Suggestions - Understanding the Inner Voice 258

Chapter 7 263

Aligning Through Love 263

How Does Love Fit with All This Spiritual Learning 263

The Power of Love Will Always Overcome Any Negativity ... 265

Why Is It That When We Love, We Are Living Our True Self 267

How Has Love Influenced Your Life 269

When You Are in a State of Loving Energy, How Do You Feel
.... 271

If You Feel So Good in Love - Why Choose Differently 274

Does Drama Have an Effect on Love 276

Why Is Love So Easy 278

How Do We Keep Love the Constant in Our Daily Life 280

Do You Believe Love Conquers All 282

Is Love the Focus of Your Life 285

Why Isn't Love the Focus of Your Life 287

Why Do We Have Free Will 289

Can You Remember Times When Love Helped You 291

Why Do We Question Love 294

Chapter 7 Suggestions - Aligning Through Love 296

Chapter 8 301

Giving and Receiving 301

What Is the Power Behind Giving and Receiving 301

Why Should We Give First Before Receiving 304

What Is Your Natural State of Being 306

Do You Live Your Life Based Upon Rules 308

Are You in Touch with Your Highest Self 310

Does Giving Only Help Others 312

How Do You Feel When You Give 314

How Do You Feel When You Receive 317

Why Is It Important to Feel the Same Both Giving and Receiving 319

Have You Tried Volunteering 322

What Does Connection with Others Do for You 325

Is It Really All About You or Everyone Else 327

Can You Have Your Cake and Eat It Too 329

Do You Live Your Life Based Upon Sharing 331

What is the Universal Law of Attraction 333

Chapter 8 Suggestions - Giving and Receiving 335

Chapter 9 341

A Life of Abundance 341

Just What is Abundance 341

Can You Live a Life of Abundance without Money 343

Most People Are Shackled to Possessions, Are You 345

Do Your Possessions Define You 347

How Can You Minimize Stuff in Your Life 348

Would You Consider Yourself Abundant with Less 351

How Much Time Do You Spend Worrying About Your Stuff . 353

Can You Justify Every Material Possession Honestly 355

Have You Ever Given Away Something You Love 357

Does Having a Lot of Material Items Make You Happy 359

How Does the Cycle of Money Work for You 362

Do You Believe in Giving and Receiving............................... 364

Can You Equate Purpose with Possessions.......................... 366

Are You Happier with Love or Material Things 368

How Does Your Life Blueprint Determine Your Wealth 370

Charter 9 Suggestions - A Life of Abundance...................... 373

Chapter 10 379

We Are a Body of ONE! 379

What Does - We Are a Body of One Mean 379

Does How We Think Make Us Who We Are 382

How Do You Fit into the Body of One Philosophy................ 384

Without Thinking, Can I Identify Myself As Being One with All 387

Do You Believe in Letting Go and Letting God 390

Do You Believe There Is a Greater Power Than Yourself...... 392

How Do You Define Your True Self....................................... 394

Was There a Time You Felt Connected with Everything 396

When Was the Last Time You Connected with Nature 399

How Do You Feel When You Are in Nature 401

Are There Simple Steps for Connecting with Source Energy 403

Do You Believe in Life after Earth Lifetime 407

Can You Explain How You Got Here 409

Do You Believe in Miracles 411

You Are a Body of One 414

Chapter 10 Suggestions - We Are A Body of ONE! 416

   Illustrations 421

Illustration A 423

Illustration B... 425

Illustration C... 427

Illustration D 429

Illustration E... 431

Illustration F 433

Introduction

When you finally accept that all of life has a specific vibrational frequency, you will understand that peaks and valleys are nothing but changes in energy vibration. You will constantly vibrate at the energy level you are putting out each moment, aligning you with similar energies based on your choices. Therefore, you can choose to be in Harmony with Source Energy or in Harmony with others that are vibrating at other lower frequencies of energy vibration.

Remember, all final decisions are made only by you – but only after listening to all opinions of others attempting to influence you and based upon their own beliefs. Therefore, you ultimately increase or decrease your energy vibration based on your free will choice. So, is it necessary to have peaks and valleys of energy vibration? The answer is – it depends on what you agreed to before you took possession of the body you are currently using. Your energy vibration may lower if you harmonize with someone needing your input at a given moment. Allow the vibration to adjust to the present moment, and you will never go wrong.

You are currently at the exact energy vibration level you need to be! The proof is that you are vibrating at that frequency - NOW.

- Terrance G. Swejkoski

Part One

Understanding Super-ego

Preface

Excerpt from Book One – Consciously Live What You Feel

You are not a human being; you are a Spiritual Being having a human experience. Let that sink in for a few minutes before continuing. Don't think about it, just sit with it. My goal is to assist you in remembering who you really are and to realign you with your true Highest Self.

Beginning the moment you were conceived, the essence of which you really are began to be clouded by the good intentions of your parents, teachers and society as a whole. This is no one's fault; it is simply a statement of fact. And so it is…read on…change is coming!

- Terrance G. Swejkoski

Chapter 1

Live Your Life Purpose Every Day

Is It Possible to Live Purpose Daily

Now that you have learned to merge Personality with Soul, the answer is YES; everyone can live their purpose daily. It's simply a matter of choosing to do so. Once the heart is guiding the choice, it is merely a matter of staying on track by not allowing the desires of the ego to fog the reality of purpose. If you can live one minute, one hour, or one day aligned with the true meaning of being here, you can do so anytime. And remember, consciousness is the key to the fulfillment of purpose.

We already know the force behind the ego will do whatever it can to keep you from your purpose. As we progress in our ability to keep our ego in check, it will become easier each time a choice comes. Anchoring the heart's energy in place allows us to focus on what is essential. The more profound knowledge that comes from the Higher Self will always be there to guide you. Check in directly with Higher Self energy anytime you feel unsure about what is happening externally - check in by simply sitting silently in a meditative state of Being and observing your feelings.

If you are experiencing days when your energy is low, it may have come from some external factor that you allowed to permeate your true essence. Always remember that the force of negative emotion is trying to produce a smokescreen to diminish your Conscious Clarity. No matter how often you are living in total awareness with the Spiritual Body at the forefront of your life, a misaligned Emotional Body will always be attempting to overshadow your bliss.

If you are feeling negative emotion for some reason, allow the feeling to arise, but quickly choose to see it for what it is and nothing more. For example, if you feel tenseness in the body, this is a clue that you are out of Harmony with the Higher Self energy. Just smile and acknowledge the ego's presence. Then, quickly dive deeply inward for guidance from the Higher Self; it will never fail you.

As was learned at the Soul Merge level of the *Conscious Clarity Energy Process*™, there will always be well-meaning individuals attempting to influence your path. We now know from experience that most of these individuals are still firmly connected to third-dimensional realities, which only allow lower energy (sensory perception) of what is to guide their lives. By staying aware of this smokescreen and the constant bombardment of ego-driven influence, the effect of these illusions will be minimal. Remember, although the Soul Merge progress is complete, the Super-ego will still attempt to bring unnecessary challenges to your life.

Remember, the Conductor is always the One truly in charge of which path The Train of Life™ follows. If you have difficulty staying on a proper course, raise your energy to a higher level of Conscious Clarity. Then, you can take easy steps immediately.

What Are Some Steps for a Purpose-Driven Life

The mind, which is part of the Physical Body, wants you to believe that you must be "doing something" at all times. It wants you to think there must be a particular sequence of steps to stay on track and live a purposeful life. In reality, the only thing you need to do is nothing. Yes, you read that correctly: do nothing and feel the energies that guide your purpose-driven path begin to flow within you. Constant connection with Source Energy is all you need to live the life of your dreams.

Meditate (consciously bring yourself to your essence) each time you feel out of alignment with your Higher Self. The only step necessary to stay connected with Source Energy is to sit in the moment's bliss. Allow your body to fall away and bring your attention to the intention of being joined with Source Energy in each moment. Just as you are doing nothing to cause your breathing to take place, the same is true for your connection and constant conversation with Source Energy. Once you bring your awareness of Source Energy to the level of daily understanding that the True Personality knows how to communicate, you will patiently wait for guidance from within to move you forward in your life experience.

Stay connected with Source Energy in each moment. It IS possible, but you must bring pure silence to your awareness to fully energize the moments of light that are constantly available to you. You have learned to keep the Spiritual Body at the forefront of your daily life to stay on track. To fulfill your Divine Purpose for being here, you must consciously train your mind to stay connected with the Source Energy. The True Personality is always connected, but the brain may veer off track if you allow it to. The Universal Level of the *Conscious Clarity Energy Process*™ is a stepping stone to the final level of awareness, the Monadic level. To experience that level, you must bring your attention to light each moment.

Use your time wisely each day and begin to feel how easy life can be. By staying connected with Source Energy, you can hear the subtle messages beckoning you to stay alert and ready to take action on what Source Energy is directing you to do at each moment. If you feel uneasy or not in a constant state of peace, it is a message being transmitted to you to let you know you are not following the path laid out for you.

The old ego is still sitting in the background, waiting for a time when you are weak (not connected at a conscious level with Source Energy) to pounce back into your life. However, your Spiritual Body is stronger than the Physical Body, so stay connected to the Source Energy which allows you to witness what the old ego is up to. Remember, the ego is very clever and will be a constant nuisance, so keep Conscious Clarity at the forefront of your Mental Body and just BE!

The only step you need to take to stay on track is to consciously stay connected to Source Energy by living in a meditative state of Being.

If Old Ego Is Gone, Am I Living My Purpose

If you are feeling peaceful, it is a good bet that you are fulfilling your purpose for being here. The Abundance of Love, Peace, and Light can only be found within you. If you align with this Abundance, you will hear the messages from Source Energy. You will move forward lovingly in that awareness of Self, benefiting everyone who experiences your pathway. So allow yourself to breathe calmly and embrace the Divine power of Source Energy.

Your True Personality is about to blossom into reality as you continue to raise your energy vibration to be in complete Harmony with Source Energy. By keeping your Spiritual Body at the forefront, you will live a life of Joy that cannot be equaled in any other way. You are ready to experience the True Purpose you agreed to long ago before entering your body.

Keep in the back of your mind that your old ego is very clever and will always be there in the background, ready to pounce back into your life. However, you have been reprogrammed to live from a state of surrender, where you can always check back in with your Kundalini energy flow to check for blockages. If you feel a blockage, this is a sign that your old ego is rearing its ugly head, and you should immediately begin clearing the blockage. Step through all the chakras and feel the energy of each one. If questions arise from this review of your energy flow, sit in silence until the solution to removing the blockage manifests itself.

One of the most challenging aspects of this human life is to stay connected with the Spiritual Body at the forefront of reality. Until you overcome the insanity of living with the Physical Body at the forefront of your life, it will be a frequent task for you to consciously check in with Source Energy. Sometimes, the silence of checking in with Source Energy can be deafening when the Super-ego attempts to bring you back into Physical Body control. You will hear false messages that do not align with your True Purpose. False statements happen when you feel superior because of your spiritual teaching awareness. Once you witness this Super-ego and its cleverness, you can consciously dismiss its attempts to corrupt you back to the old illusion of Self, which always feels superior to others. This superiority complex disorder is a powerful tool in the ego's arsenal of weapons to attack your true nature. Many spiritual seekers are corrupted by its clever advances and fall out of Spiritual Body alignment.

Always remember that you are still inexperienced at being in the beautiful state of Being consciously connected to Source Energy. Your life is now moving in the direction you want, but sometimes you feel like you are slipping backward.

What Happens If I Slip

In follow up to the last question, as to whether or not you are living your True Purpose for being here, the matter of slipping or not living your True Purpose comes to the surface. First, make no judgments as to whether or not you are living your purpose. If you are flowing with the natural energy of God-realization, you will always be living your purpose, even if you allow your Super-ego to bring you out of awareness of your True Self. It's all in balance, and Source Energy always brings you to where you need to be; whether you or others judge them is irrelevant. Even momentarily slipping back into ego's control is in alignment; it's sometimes a paradox.

Allow yourself to grow Spiritually at your own pace and accept what aligns with your Original Source Energy Agreement. Never forget that no matter your life situation, you are always aligned with what you agreed to before coming here. Therefore, the mistakes or missteps you make always align with some part of the life plan you agreed to for yourself with Source Energy.

As long as you live consistently with the Spiritual Body at the forefront of your reality, you are ahead of the game compared to most people. You are responsible for only one person; that person is you and no one else. By understanding who you are, you have taken a quantum leap forward in the illusions brought before you daily. Others will always attempt to control you by using their influence of illusionary power over you. Never allow the true essence of your Spiritual Self to influence your life through these manipulations. You are not here to please anyone or to stay in alignment with another life plan. You are here to grow spiritually, and the way is not always straightforward due to the strength of the illusion before you.

You are a Spiritual Being having a human experience. The spiritual growth you will achieve for yourself is your only mission completed through serving others. This mission does not mean adhering to their plan of what's best for the world. It means you will follow your Higher Self perspective by being spiritually here for everyone. Therefore, never get lost in someone else's idea of what is best for you. You will know what is best for you by constantly checking in with Source Energy. The feelings that resonate with Love, Peace, and Light will show you the way. Stay connected with Higher Self awareness, and you will be just fine.

When On Purpose, Are You Aware

When living your True Purpose, you are most definitely aware of it. Conscious Clarity is all about awareness, aligning with your Original Source Agreement so that you are living a purpose-filled life. When you are in a peaceful state of Being, you are alert and conscious of what is manifesting in your life. No explanations are necessary to satisfy the ever-thinking mind. You are simply in a state of Grace where you are always in direct contact with Source Energy.

As you continue to flow with life, you no longer need to understand why everything unfolds as it does from a Physical Body perspective. Now that you are living your daily life situations in a conscious state of Being, aware of your true identity as a Spiritual Being having a human experience, you can allow life to unfold naturally. You are no longer fighting the ego, as it has merged with the Soul, and now the Spiritual Body brings forth all that is necessary for you to thrive in this human or form-based world. There's no need to force anything; visualize what is needed to fulfill your purpose and then sit back and allow the Universe to bring it into reality.

You no longer need to work hard to be what you thought you wanted to be. Stop the clever ego from manipulating you. You are now in vibrational Harmony with Source Energy, and the moments needed to plan and re-plan, over and over, based upon a strict set of goals, are not necessary anymore. You have grown spiritually to the point where your "Knowing" guides your actions. You live from a state of pure Grace and allow the flow to bring you into conscious awareness of what is unfolding for you. Your Kundalini energy is flowing, and you are One with Source Energy.

Your life is no longer about "what's in it for me." Now, it is about how I can serve to bring Harmony to the entire world.

What you do now comes from Source Energy, manifested into a reality. So you know without a doubt that as long as you are in Harmony with Source Energy flow, you will live an abundant life.

Release any doubt arising from the mind's old tapes and bring your true vision (Original Source Agreement) to light. You have grown to the point where you can now enjoy the lessons you have learned the hard way. There's no need to rush or be anxious about anything. You awaken when you understand that knowing your path based upon listening to the guidance flowing through you is different from planning everything based on some ego-centered goals. The Universe works its magic in the cosmic realm of reality, where timelines are no longer essential to you. This realization should always keep you in peace and gratitude for everything and everyone that comes your way.

Enjoy the ride and allow yourself the luxury of knowing you are way ahead of the typical dance of life. You have grown to the point of consciousness, which most people never achieve in many lifetimes. Yes, the Super-ego will test you; however, there will be a difference in the outcome compared to where you were just a few years ago.

Does Awareness Dissolve Temptations

The ego uses temptation in a negative sense, whereas you desire to do something pleasing to the ego, but in truth, it is unwise or something that you know will not positively serve your well-being. On the surface, the temptation will give you some form of pleasure typical of a physical body alignment. However, conversely, a spiritual attraction will bring you closer to Harmony with Source Energy. The spiritual interest could be anything with a higher energy vibration invisible in the physical world. For example, it may be the temptation to generate or manifest a feeling of Joy based upon attending some spiritual event that you know will increase your vibration.

In each scenario, the actual negative or positive effect of fulfilling the temptation will bring about some form of satisfaction depending on how your Four Body System is aligned. Now is an excellent time to review the difference between a Four Body System that is spiritually or physically aligned. If you consistently live with the Spiritual Body at the forefront of your reality, this review will be straightforward because you learned this lesson in Book One: *Consciously Live What You Feel*.

If you did not read Book One, I recommend doing so before continuing this book. Everyone should read the book series sequentially to ensure completion of the Soul Merge process before continuing. If you are reluctant to go back to read Book One, this is your Super-ego playing tricks on you again and a sure sign that your vibration level is not at a state of awareness for you to appreciate the importance of the Soul Merge process.

The following alignment comparison will be one of the most critical lessons in this book.

We all consist of a Four Body System. How deeply we integrate into the various parts of that system determines how we approach our life situation daily. If you could discover how to acknowledge that you have these multiple aspects of the Body without allowing them to control you, your life would be much happier. Through meditation, you can consciously stay connected with the highest power of this system, the Spiritual Body.

The actual order of the Four Body System is of the utmost importance concerning our perceived level of happiness. Therefore, it is naturally aligned when in the sequence below.

<u>The natural Four Body System alignment consists of the following:</u>

1. Spiritual Body

2. Mental Body

3. Emotional Body

4. Physical Body

Example – Typically Out of Alignment:

Most humans live based upon having the Four Body System reversed, where control is first perceived at the Physical Body.

- Physical Body - When the Physical Body is first, it identifies as situations happening to me (identity) or physical reality.

- Emotional Body - This, in turn, excites the Emotional Body, and a feeling is generated and perceived as done to my physical identity.

- Mental Body - These emotions then excite the Mental Body into thinking about what has happened to me (my story), usually based upon thoughts of the past and false beliefs that lead to some reaction to the life situation experienced.

- Spiritual Body - After much self-inflicted torment, the Spiritual Body sends a message that you may be overreacting to the situation. Then, an inner dialog or discussion within the Lower Self begins, and a decision is consciously made to either build on the story (which the Mental Body created) or to drop the issue in acceptance.

The difficulty with this type of pattern is it usually leads to fear-based action unless you have learned to catch yourself when you see this destructive pattern emerging.

Example – Naturally in Alignment:

If we analyze the same situation and reverse the control mechanisms of our Four Body System, there is an entirely different result.

- Spiritual Body - When the Spiritual Body is in control, and when a life situation occurs, it is first acknowledged, and acceptance is immediately allowed. The perception is mere "this happened"; it did not happen to me. It simply happened.

- Mental Body - Then the Mental Body activates to confirm; yes, this happened, and some action may be required.

- Emotional Body - Next, the Emotional Body ignites a feeling of empowerment to the challenge; it creates positive, solution-based emotions and provides action to resolve the issue rather than focusing on the challenge as a perceived problem.

- Physical Body - The result is that the body feels peaceful and excited about a challenge to resolve. The Physical Body remains stress-free, and the solutions appear from a higher knowledge base.

The beauty of this type of pattern is that the Four Body System works in Harmony without fear and feels peaceful, knowing that love through Divine power and wisdom can bring light to any life situation.

In the above examples, the resultant actions will vary dramatically depending on whether you live in Love or Fear. This result may sound somewhat unrealistic to some of you. However, focus on realigning yourself with the Spiritual Body (through meditation). Your life will be more balanced and aligned with the higher understanding experienced through Love, Peace, and Light.

As you should understand from the examples above, a misaligned Four Body System will have a different outcome for the same circumstance. The key here is to always be in Peace or Grace as you continue with this lesson plan.

If you are misaligned, you will feel a sense of discontent as you attempt to move forward. The feeling of uneasiness means a chakra is blocked somehow, and you are not experiencing the vibrational frequencies of this lesson due to the Super-ego regaining control of you.

However, you are not alone on this journey, and the Universe has all the time and resources available to bring your vibration up to a level of understanding that allows you to always feel at peace.

Am I on My Own in this Life Experience

Source Energy is always with you, the one constant you can rely on. We are all One with Source Energy, and each person is here to fulfill their purpose based upon the Original Source Agreement made before becoming human form. Life is merely a dance we enjoy with other participants while Source Energy watches over us.

All human life is cyclical, meaning it has a beginning and an end. The one thing guaranteed with human life is the gift of change. From the Physical Body perspective, you can feel a sense of aloneness at times, but this is merely a physical reaction to being in a state without someone or something accompanying you in that present moment. However, from the Spiritual Body perspective, being without other physical beings in your immediate presence is a time of pure Joy. It is time to consciously connect with Source Energy without disruption or interference from other physical beings.

As a child, I was often alone and sometimes even felt lonely because I questioned my Source Energy due to the false influences in my environment. Being told that I was only the Physical Body, I had no reference to the truth of who I was, a Spiritual Being having a human experience. Even though I would sit in silence and talk to God, eventually, the overwhelming lies well-meaning people were telling me took its toll on me, and I began to believe the adults. As a result, I sometimes became disconnected from Source Energy and felt that God had abandoned me; in fact, I left God for the false reality of the Physical Body and misunderstood who I am.

When we are children, we are vulnerable to false programming by adults because we have been trained not to question their beliefs. Incorrect programming is one of the greatest disservices and blatant disregard for the true essence that we can experience! Being influenced into believing you are something you are not is not the act of an enlightened person. Influence based on reference is nothing more than a continuation of false programming from adults before them. And the cycle continues until someone dares to step up and say NO MORE!

On many occasions, I would get into trouble for questioning so-called authority or those in charge of me in the societal control system. I would repeatedly ask, "How do you know," and await the response. Most of the time, I would get a reference reply, not a fact. If you did not experience something, you did not have a truth to back up your statement, and I would question anything other than first-hand experience. My questioning was especially disconcerting to the people in the religious realm of the false reality being hard-pressed upon me.

To this day, I still question those who believe they have authority over me because of what the authority figures believe is true. Most of the time, it's simply a reference from someone else's experience or another reference consideration. How absurd!

Never forget Source Energy is always with you; therefore, you are never truly alone and can always go directly to Source Energy for guidance. Source Energy watches your life situation unfold, whether awake or asleep. Nothing will if that doesn't give you deep knowledge and peace.

What Is a Life Situation

The mind can empower you to live a life in alignment with the Spirit, or it can cause a separation based upon the Super-ego and how you can use others to provide a false sense of happiness in the human illusion called life situation. Any thoughts from a Physical Body alignment perspective will give you a false sense of who you are. You will focus on living a life of "what's in it for me" rather than "how may I serve."

Life situation refers to human existence, the illusion of what life is about on the surface. Most people live life situations believing that this is all there is. They can't comprehend eternal life. Most of humankind is locked into the false belief that when the Body dies, that is the end of life. This birth and death scenario is a reality for a person swimming on the surface of the pool of life. In other words, there is no depth to their life, and it is typically lived by simply following the rules of others.

However, with the Spiritual Body at the forefront of daily life, a different perspective exists to view how life unfolds. By living from this meditative state of Being, you allow yourself the gift of remembering your Original Source Agreement, and you flow through life situations by being an active observer. You set an example of what it means to be a silent leader without actually doing much yourself. Instead, guidance comes from within during the quiet moments spent with Source Energy. Then, you share those lessons for the benefit of all. You allow those that you are to guide to make their own choices while at the same time imparting your recommendations subtly. You never force your viewpoint on matters of life; instead, you allow others to see the example you are setting to raise the world's mass consciousness.

The Super-ego will play tricks on you in this leadership role. It will attempt to make you believe you are better than others vibrating at lower frequencies or swimming on the surface of life. Watch yourself closely as your energy level begins to rise. The Super-ego will make it a real challenge to stay an active observer. However, your true Higher Self will prevail if you do not listen to the Super-ego. Bring your vision to light by allowing others to be who they are and know they are doing their best based on their current vibration level.

We grow spiritually at our own rate. Some people prefer a slow and gradual increase, which keeps them in a comfort zone. Other people choose to take quantum leaps and bypass the slower learning curve. This bypass can be both a hindrance and a blessing in disguise.

Once you learn that the life situation reality can be a spiritual experience rather than a human experience, you will be ready to live your life from the conscious choice of knowing your life is eternal. From this perspective, quantum leaps become the norm rather than the exception of this state of Being.

What Is Life

Life is the infinite energy or connectedness to Source Energy, the essence of who you are – a God-realized droplet within the same ocean united in Oneness of Self, the eternal messenger of Love, Peace, and Light!

If you read Book One, *Consciously Live What You Feel*, of the *Life's Little Secrets* book series, you already know the difference between lifetime and life. However, for those who may have skipped ahead or felt they could read the book series out of sequence (not recommended), I will again summarize:

Lifetime relates to your current life situation in this human form or Physical Body. The state of limited awareness uses the interconnection of form-based material entities or objects to bring happiness or sadness into your life. For example, a person's belief system on reference material is taught based upon a so-called authority on a subject or other people's belief system. Therefore, whether you are living this lifetime aligned with your Spiritual Body or Physical Body at the forefront of your life determines your level of happiness because happiness is an external thing subject to the outside influences around you to create the emotion of happiness.

Life is your eternal God-realized Self that requires no input or reference from any other entity or belief system to be fact. Life is your complete understanding of Source Energy and your deep understanding of actual knowledge. When living in this state of Being, the occurrences around you in the form-based vessel called the Physical Body matter very little in the big picture or your Original Source Agreement. You were brought into this incarnation for a specific purpose, and once you accomplish that purpose to its fullest potential, the Physical Body will be left behind, and you will move on. Moving on is the most challenging fact for the old ego and Super-ego to understand because there is always an underlying part of the Human Self that believes they are only the Physical Body.

As you release more and more of the old false programming you received from well-meaning people in your lifetime, you will continue to grow in realizing the Highest Self or God-realization. The fact that you are part of God is a Spiritual Truth, a fact that is considered blasphemy by low-vibrating, form-based thinking individuals. These people are typically misinformed about their true identity, which is taught in group-think mentality schools as dictated based upon a ruled or fear-based reality. As you grow spiritually, you will release your negative fear-based emotions. Some negative emotions may be lingering in the background of your mind. However, you will experience Conscious Clarity the more you live your current life, based upon a blissful existence centered in Joy through Love, Peace, and Light in Harmony with Source Energy (God).

Every part of your life is based upon the Original Source Agreement you made before your residence in your current form-based vessel. Yet until you truly realize who you are, you will continue to live at the vibration level of lower-self reality. The more you grow spiritually, the more you will understand how powerful you are and how little the life challenges surrounding you are in the big picture. It's all reasonable and aligned, even when your old or Super-ego interferes by not accepting what is.

Is All Life on Purpose

Most people believe they (the lower self) are in charge of their life plan and are unaware of the underlying Source Energy. They think their Physical Body is running the show and do not relate to the most extraordinary power in the Universe, which is operating beneath the surface of their life experiences. They go about their day in an unconscious state of awareness, where others lead them with perceived higher goals than themselves. They use thinking as their guide and believe doing has greater power than Being. This limited perspective is the underlying reason for all dis-ease in the world today. Mindlessly following someone else because they are perceived to have more power or authority than you do is living a life imprisoned in the beliefs of those in power.

Perhaps this book series will be the stepping stone for you to awaken to the level of Conscious Clarity that God has always meant for you. When the student is ready, the teacher will appear. Until then, understanding Spiritual Transformative Education remains a mere fantasy of the Physical Body imagination because the Mental Body (mind/ego) does not want you to evolve to your fullest potential. Instead, it wants you to stay locked into the academic education, societal system based primarily on limited fact and reference matter that the mind judges as truth. This control system keeps you locked into a narrow perspective of life based upon what is only seen on the surface by the five senses. Anything other than this limited belief system is considered fantasy by the ego-based Mental Body perspective or control mechanism.

However, when you live Knowing the inner power of Source Energy, you begin to dismiss the aggressive actions of others attempting to influence your life. You can say thank you for sharing and then move on to the state of Being, the essence of Source Energy, within for guidance. The Source Energy of Knowing, a sixth sense, is anchored in Being.

Being anchored in Knowing allows you to see yourself for the God-realized energy you are. When you shift your perspective to this Cosmic Intelligence, you know what IS in life with the Conscious Clarity of Universal fact. The experience of this limitless force in your daily life brings about all the synchronistic events necessary to live a life filled with Abundance. The realities shift, and you begin to witness the facts available to you from within.

Religions state that consciousness is only available to those who "think clearly" based upon some entity or force to worship. Yes, this is what most religions teach: we should idolize some form-based entity created by an organization's belief system. This religious falsehood says that if you do not worship this ego-perceived perception of God, judgment day will come at the end of your life, and God will punish you. This false belief is a continued control mechanism of the Super-ego and cannot be even slightly authentic in the Spiritual understanding of life. Once you escape this mentally-imprisoning manipulation, you will begin to see the God-realization aspect of your Being.

You are part of the Cosmic Intelligence or force responsible for all creation, the invisible power of Source Energy responsible for whatever was and will always be. You are far more powerful than your old ego or Super-ego will allow you to witness. Therefore, if you stay locked in this small-minded understanding or lower vibration of life, you will always strive for more but will be limited to the false beliefs in your false sense of the reality of who you think you are.

It is time to release this control mechanism and enter your actual reality. By removing any thoughts of negativity or false statements by others that measure the wrong dualistic and judgmental aspects of this false reality, you will witness the scam placed in front of you in this lifetime. You do not need anyone outside yourself to tell you who you are or how you should act. Your inner moral guidance will move you in the right direction without the need for any form-based rules or regulations.

You are a droplet of the eternal ocean of life and can never be anything less. You are the God-realization of all that IS, and your Cosmic Intelligence KNOWS this Spiritual fact.

Where Did Life Originate

When you live daily situations or your life from the perspective that Cosmic Intelligence is the Source Energy of all that is, all that was, and all that ever will be, you remain in a relaxed state of awareness. This flexible awareness allows you to live your life to its fullest potential. It will enable you to stay beyond thought and stories and instead open to the wondrous possibilities that open up to you each day through silence. You only need to remain embraced in the silence to stay connected with this flexible awareness. All the answers to the layers of belief systems that create solutions to each challenge lie in this silence. By being in the meditative state of silence, you will bring in the energies that allow you to observe life situations from a flexible awareness perspective. This perspective will enable you to experience life as planned for you.

If life is truly eternal, does it not then make sense that all that ever was, currently is, and ever will be is already available for you to experience? Can you see the value in staying flexible when witnessing something opposite to your ego's opinion? What if all views are merely stepping stones to awareness and flexibility? Is the quantum leap energy forced on all solutions? Are you willing to stay contented with the silence in each present moment so that when storms arise (and they will) in your lifetime, you can have the flexibility to bend beyond the storm's force? By gently swaying from your typical rigid opinion, you will hear Source Energy whispering to you.

Human life comes from nothing, created into the energy of something, on multiple levels of awareness simultaneously in the present moment! The present moment is all there is and cannot be exhausted or recreated. Do you understand how powerful that statement is? All there ever IS is the present moment, so why would you be so influenced by the past and future? The past never equals the future when you live life from the perspective of present-moment awareness because there is no past or future. Then why be upset when your current moment appears to be challenging?

Most lifetime societal beliefs come from the false idea that the past and future matter. In Spiritual reality, only the present moment is vital because Cosmic Intelligence is only NOW or present moment awareness. The ego needs to measure everything based upon some past or future and usually based upon false beliefs that have influenced your life experiences. It's no secret that most people walk through life with an urgency attached to every step, creating unnecessary stress in their minds. They live by unrealistic goals, typically implanted in the mind by an impractical idea of what life is. Once again, time or lifetime is the all-important measurement of Source Energy of their limited perspective of what life is.

By opening up to the unlimited possibilities available in each flexible moment, you can experience your current life situation based on endless possibilities. Rather than staying rigid to the influence of your opinion or belief, you can bring awareness to the soft voice of Source Energy whispering to you in silence where all the solutions to your questions are patiently waiting.

Why are you so rigid in your opinion regarding what life is? Do you have other questions that appear to be unanswered on the surface of life? If so, ask yourself why.

Where Do the Questions Originate

To understand where the questions originate, you must first be aware of the Spiritual truth that every answer or solution is already available to you and is simply waiting for you to ask the question. *Cosmic Intelligence knows all, sees all, and is omnipresent in every life situation you encounter during your Earth journey.* Therefore, the questions that arise (including all the questions in this book) are part of the spiritual learning process, known here as the *Conscious Clarity Energy Process*™.

You are gifted a fantastic tool to use for communication while participating in this Earth school, the gift of the Mental Body. In truth, the Mental Body is the second most powerful aspect of the Four Body System. Now you are correctly aligned with the Spiritual Body at the forefront of everything you do daily, it should be apparent how important the Mental Body is to fulfill your highest potential. Furthermore, you now understand that you are not the Physical Body; therefore, you no longer use the Mental Body inaccurately as when it was misaligned.

Because you are aligned properly now, you are using the Mental Body for its true intention. By observing everything around you, you can now use the information that comes into each life situation to its fullest spiritual potential. You now understand the Spiritual Body's purpose and how it interacts with truth rather than false beliefs.

Your Physical Body is merely a vessel to move you from Point A to Point B. The Mental Body is the tool you use to observe the happenings that may or may not require some form of action on your behalf. By staying connected to Source Energy, you can now understand the difference between false beliefs and what is actual reality or spiritual knowing. The energy field used to guide you comes in many forms on the surface of life situations. However, the existing guidance system is the Kundalini energy, which flows through your Chakras. You are now consciously monitoring this energy flow within the Body and understand that it is the key to consciously embracing your true Personality.

Now that you are always consciously connected with Source Energy, it's easy to separate spiritual truth from false beliefs that used to cloud your Conscious Clarity. Using the Soul Merge process, you shift your awareness (Refer to Book One) in your Mental and Physical Body. The Spiritual Body energy is moving at an amazingly high energy vibration now, and you are witnessing the spiritual guidance more clearly.

This spiritual guidance is also known as intuition. Still, the ego typically misunderstands the Spiritual Body as some fantasy or a false representation of truth by those who have not yet completed the Soul Merge process. Most of humanity views spiritual energy fields as unknown because they are not at the forefront of their daily understanding of truth.

Therefore, you will ask many questions if you are unaware of the truth. These questions are necessary to assist in bringing awareness to the energy vibration of the planet. This energy vibration is also known as the mass consciousness or the general spiritual knowledge level of the human community. Spiritual guidance brings conscious awareness questions to the surface. Because Source Energy has already created all the answers or solutions to every question, the mass consciousness has complete solutions to perceived problems, illusions, or challenges. Still, the ego won't accept this fact. Therefore, questions are a remarkable training tool for bringing Conscious Clarity to the surface.

Each person can live with the Spiritual Body at the forefront of everything they manifest each day or live with the Physical Body in the forefront, creating fear-based, problematic illusions. Therefore, the questions asked will vary significantly depending on the alignment choice.

Do We All Have the Same Questions

The questions that arise at each energy vibration level will be in Harmony with that same energy vibration. Therefore, if you are currently vibrating at a low level of spiritual understanding, your life will agree with others living at the same vibration or level of awareness. Consequently, you will ask similar questions as those surrounding your frame of reference because you have chosen to vibrate at the frequency of those you surround yourself with. You will be content with your current life situation and the people you surround yourself with until you make a new choice to move forward at a higher energy vibration level – it's really that simple.

Each of us has a script or Original Source Agreement we created to follow in life. The spiritual awareness of who you think you are determines what aligns with others. If you ask questions related only to a Physical Body alignment perspective of life, you will still believe you are only the Physical Body. However, suppose you know without a doubt that you are a Spiritual Being having a human experience. In that case, you will vibrate at a different energy level, and your questions will harmonize with other people or groups you socialize with. It depends on your choice, and no one else knows better which path is right for you. It would help if you searched deep within to find your questions so that the answers moving you in an enlightened manner can surface within Conscious Clarity of Self.

While you will undoubtedly overlap with false belief systems or others vibrating at a lower frequency, you should never lose track of the fact that you are the only one responsible for your actions. By now, you have grown in your understanding, whereas you no longer linger in the negative aspects of false reality. You now understand the path you pick each day directly results from a faulty, egoistic belief system or a God-realized life of bliss. You are the best coach for staying connected with your Original Source Agreement. You have the whole Universe working in Harmony with you, providing Love, Peace, and Light to guide your steps as you develop a Spiritual Body alignment philosophy with your Mental Body.

Therefore, the people you associate with will either move forward with you in spiritual enlightenment, or they will be left behind to serve their necessary level of growth based upon what timeframe is best for them. Each of us grows harmoniously with our energy vibration and the situations that need attention. Remember, you are on a spiritual journey. The clever Super-ego refines challenges with each new phase of your life. So allow the questions asked to be what they may, and understand that you can always request a better question if Conscious Clarity is eluding you.

Until you bring your full vision or Original Source Agreement to Light, your ego will challenge you at every junction of the spiritual journey. You always have a choice when you come to a challenge or intersection on the *Train of Life*™; which track you select will determine your questions, reality and life accomplishments moment by moment. We are all growing. Are you growing in the direction of your ultimate purpose for being here?

Are We Here Only for Purpose

Evolution depends on you fulfilling your ultimate purpose here on this planet. No person is more or less important than another, but we are all responsible for fulfilling the obligation we each made in our Original Source Agreement. The beauty of it is that we have free will to make choices along the way and whether those choices align with our ultimate purpose or they are not. Source Energy doesn't judge! Therefore, you are always free to make a different choice than you may have in the past. Each new present moment can be experienced without any doubt or fear of judgment by others. In truth, it doesn't matter what other people think because you are the master of your Universe.

Your energy vibration is innately poised to bring you into Harmony with your Original Source Agreement, and Source Energy knows that you will veer off track occasionally. Why?

Because it's necessary to learn some lessons the hard way so that they anchor into your subconscious mind in a manner that will always stay with you. A mindset is a fantastic tool. However, how you choose to use it is vital to the evolution of this planet. A proper perspective is essential to stay aligned with feelings that serve your Emotional well-being.

Because we are all connected in Oneness or Spirit, it is essential to realize that each choice made by everyone influences the whole Universe or life itself. From a spiritual perspective, Oneness means being aligned with others to fulfill your ultimate purpose in life. It may not occur in one lifetime, but will align with an eternal True Life Perspective!

Allow True Personality to grow Spiritually at its own pace or speed. There's no rush to fulfill your ultimate purpose for being here. Everyone increases their vibration at their rate of comfort. Many times, it's better to go with the flow instead of planning everything out to the letter. Thinking and planning take a back door to Being when you walk a spiritual path.

By Being in Spirit, you will witness opportunities from a completely different perspective than if you are always "thinking" about what you should do next based on goals. Goals are part of the Super-ego system setup during Super-ego-perceived enlightenment. Always remember that the Super-ego is waiting in the background, ready to pounce when you are living a false illusion of reality. Therefore, take a few moments to reflect (in silence) each time you prepare to make a significant decision. Sit in stillness and feel the energy of what it would "feel like" if you had already fulfilled your intention. Then, if you truly feel peaceful and joyous, take massive action in the direction of the spiritual guidance moving through you.

By living your life with the Spiritual Body at the forefront of everything you do, you will discover that you can make decisions in a heartbeat that genuinely align with your ultimate purpose for Being here.

What If We Never Find Our Purpose

This question is from the ego because the ego is always doubtful and questioning every decision. It always wants to attach a timeframe to everything, including whether or not you will discover your purpose for being here in this lifetime. If you ask "What if I never find my purpose?", you are living your life based upon a Physical Body alignment perspective.

Higher Self has no doubt whatsoever about your ultimate purpose. A Spiritual Body alignment in the forefront of your life is the natural state of Being. When you live from the flexibility of a Higher Self perspective, you innately know you are always living a Purposeful Life. The proof is that you are now where you are supposed to be. How do you know this — simply because you are here now! Your purpose is never lost, even when you allow your Super-ego to guide your life based on false beliefs about being spiritually special. Your Original Source Agreement allows for every misstep along your path. Therefore, when you believe you know your purpose for being here, you follow the steps necessary to fulfill your ultimate intention.

We each have the power to fulfill a lifetime in alignment with the Love, Peace, and Light of a Purposeful Life. You know deep within you when you are moving in the right direction, and only you can "feel" what it's like to live your life purposefully!

Each reincarnation brings you closer to the Highest Self awareness. As a part of Source Energy, you are always in Harmony with your purpose. When the mind is silent, your ultimate objective reveals itself. The timeframe for discovering your ultimate aim is never-ending or eternal because as we grow spiritually, so does our purpose for Being here. Spiritual growth is the key to finding your ultimate purpose. Stay flexible, enjoy each moment, and learn from the moments that leave you feeling out of touch with Source Energy. Discover the beauty of living in the moment and allow your ultimate purpose to develop in its own time. In truth, we have all the necessary time because our authentic Cosmic clock is never-ending.

When you connect in Oneness to Source Energy, each moment is a Godsend. If you know you are part of Source Energy, you have already created the path for fulfilling your ultimate purpose. However, if you still believe you are merely the Physical Body, you have not released the Super-ego's control over you or your perception of reality. If your thinking is causing doubt, your Mental Body remains misaligned with the Physical Body in control. This misalignment is the Super-ego reacting to your false sense of reality. If you feel out of sorts or uneasy about any direction you take on your path to enlightenment, you are still living an ego-driven life.

Bring your vision to light by stepping into your essence each morning when you get out of bed. Say, "Thank you, Source Energy, for allowing my body to take the next breath so that I can continue my life here on Earth to fulfill my ultimate purpose every single moment of my existence!"

Ask for spiritual guidance to keep you on track so that you can bring about change to the mass consciousness of the world.

You are never alone!

Chapter 1 Suggestions - Live Your Life Purpose Every Day

Once the heart is guiding the choice, it is merely a matter of staying on track by not allowing the desires of the ego to fog the reality of purpose. If you can live one minute, one hour, or one day aligned with the true meaning of being here, you can do so anytime. And remember, consciousness is the key to the fulfillment of purpose.

- Meditate (consciously bring yourself to your essence) each time you feel out of alignment with your Higher Self. The only step necessary to stay connected with Source Energy is to sit in the moment's bliss. Allow your body to fall away and bring your attention to the intention of being joined with Source Energy in each moment.

- Use your time wisely each day and begin to feel how easy life can be. By staying connected with Source Energy, you can hear the subtle messages beckoning you to stay alert and ready to take action on what Source Energy is directing you to do at each moment.

- Allow yourself to grow spiritually at your own pace and accept what aligns with your Original Source Energy Agreement.

- You are not here to please anyone or to stay in alignment with another life plan. You are here to grow spiritually, and the way is not always straightforward due to the strength of the illusion before you. You are a Spiritual Being having a human experience. The spiritual growth you will achieve for yourself is your only mission completed through serving others.

- We all consist of a Four Body System. How deeply we integrate into the various parts of that system determines how we approach our life situation daily. Through meditation, you can consciously stay connected with the highest power of this system, the Spiritual Body. The actual order of the Four Body System is of the utmost importance concerning our perceived level of happiness. Therefore, it is naturally aligned when in the sequence below.

The natural Four Body System alignment consists of the following:

Spiritual Body

Mental Body

Emotional Body

Physical Body

- The mind can empower you to live a life in alignment with the Spirit, or it can cause a separation based upon the Super-ego and how you can use others to provide a false sense of happiness in the human illusion called life situation. Any thoughts from a Physical Body alignment perspective will give you a false sense of who you are. You will focus on living a life of "what's in it for me" rather than "how may I serve."

- Life is the infinite energy or connectedness to Source Energy, the essence of who you are – a God-realized droplet within the same ocean united in Oneness of Self, the eternal messenger of Love, Peace, and Light!

- You are part of the Cosmic Intelligence or force responsible for all creation, the invisible power of Source Energy responsible for whatever was and will always be. You are far more powerful than your old ego or Super-ego will allow you to witness. You are a droplet of the eternal ocean of life and can never be anything less. You are the God-realization of all that IS, and your Cosmic Intelligence KNOWS this Spiritual fact.

- To understand where the questions come from, you must first be aware of the Spiritual truth that every answer or solution is already available to you and is simply waiting for you to ask the question. *Cosmic Intelligence knows all, sees all, and is omnipresent in every life situation you encounter during your Earth journey.* Therefore, the questions that arise (including all the questions in this book) are part of the spiritual learning process, known here as the *Conscious Clarity Energy Process™*.

- The questions that arise at each energy vibration level will be in Harmony with that same energy vibration. Consequently, you will ask similar questions as those surrounding your frame of reference because you have chosen to vibrate at the frequency of those you surround yourself with.

- Until you bring your full vision or Original Source Agreement to Light, your ego will challenge you at every junction of the spiritual journey.

- We each have the power to fulfill a lifetime in alignment with the Love, Peace, and Light of a Purposeful Life. You know deep within you when you are moving in the right direction, and only you can "feel" what it's like to live your life purposefully!

Higher Self has no doubt whatsoever about your ultimate purpose. A Spiritual Body alignment in the forefront of your life is the natural state of Being. When you live from the flexibility of a Higher Self perspective, you innately know you are always living a Purpose Driven Life. The proof is that you are now where you are supposed to be. How do you know this – simply because you are here now! Your purpose is never lost, even when you allow your Super-ego to guide your life based on false beliefs about being spiritually special. Your Original Source Agreement allows for every misstep along your path. Therefore, when you believe you know your purpose for being here, you follow the steps necessary to fulfill your ultimate intention.

Chapter 2

Assistance from Spiritual Guides

Do We Always Have Spiritual Guides

We are always connected to Spiritual Guides to assist us. These may have once inhabited a physical form and had the same purpose as the physical beings they now guide. Now, they offer higher vibrational guidance from the Spiritual realm to enhance our Spiritual Education. Through intuition, feelings, and spiritual alerts, we can tap into this unlimited source of advice, all of the Universal Intelligence. Your feelings are directly related to what you are taking action on in life. Whether or not you pay attention to these feelings or spiritual alerts is based on your energy vibration level.

If your energy vibration is low, you will not feel (hear) the guidance from Spiritual Guides because pure spirits vibrate at an energy level much higher than your physical form. Therefore, you must first silence your mind and increase your energy vibration to communicate directly. By now, you understand that the path to enlightenment is merely a silencing of repeated thoughts that do not serve your overall well-being. When you meditate, the Mental Body is silent, and you are in Harmony with Spirit Guides.

Everyone has said from time to time, "Something told me" to do this or that rather than following the mind's planned idea. This guidance is when you should pay attention the most, as this is the feeling or intuitive guidance that is part of your Higher Self reaching out to you. You will not hear the advice clearly if you are all wrapped in thinking and doing. Stop doing and begin Being each time you "feel" your actions are not in Harmony with your Higher Self guidance. Pause for a moment and consciously observe your thoughts and feelings. And then, stop thinking and sit in the bliss of silence. Say aloud; *I feel you telling me something more important than what I am thinking; guide me – I am listening.*

By consciously connecting with your spiritual essence in this manner, you will find yourself turning left when you thought you were supposed to be turning right. You will remain silent and listen intently rather than offer an opinion or observe your surroundings, moving about unconsciously. This guidance is your Higher Self assisting you on your journey. This guidance is always available to you at every single moment of your life. You are part of Source Energy; only this Source Energy can bring you closer to Oneness. This connection is what life is all about assistance with coming into your greatness! You are not alone on your journey, as each water droplet is part of the ocean of life. You connect to this Universal Intelligence, which always knows what is best for your well-being.

If you continue to dismiss spiritual guidance, it will alert you in other ways that are not always pleasant. This alert is because your ego needs a shock to the Physical Body to awaken you from your clouded perception of life. If you are unwilling to connect with Spiritual Guides consciously, they will awaken you abruptly, if necessary, to get your attention. So pay attention and stop taking the Physical Body path today!

When you are in Harmony with Source Energy and your Original Source Agreement, your life will flow as smoothly as a gentle stream, slowly moving around objects that block its path. You will feel at peace and listen for gentle guidance with Conscious Clarity. When you are out of alignment or not in Harmony with Source Energy and your Original Source Agreement, you will feel anxious, stressed, and rushed and perceive life as a struggle. However, you can change that harmful lifestyle to one of Love, Peace, and Light at any moment by listening to the Spiritual Guides in silence. The choice is yours – what do you hear?

Who Are Spiritual Guides

You will discover in Book Three, *Consciously Live the Monadic Life*, of the *Conscious Clarity Energy Process*™ that a cosmic hierarchy or ascended entities are guiding you. These entities include what Society has labeled Angels, Cosmic Contacts, or Spirit Guides. Of course, what you call a Cosmic Contact will vary depending on your culture, but it's all the same – they are Spiritual Guides!

Spiritual Guides come in many forms. They may include past spiritual partners, other intimate relationships, family members who have transitioned out of the body, and teachers who may have profoundly impacted you. Additionally, Spiritual Guides could be Celestial Beings whose primary purpose is to guide a particular astrological category of humans (for example, Capricorns, Sagittarius, etc.), your own Guardian Angel, and Source Energy itself.

All guided souls have learned to express assistance through intuition or feelings when needed or when a choice is ready to finalize. Your actions are always assisted by Spiritual Guides when you pay attention. You will hear this guidance with a higher level of understanding as you raise your energy vibration. You can naturally do this by surrounding yourself with other spiritual seekers. These groups are formed for peaceful, loving interaction with others, participating in spiritual seminars, spiritual gatherings such as Satsang Meditation events, Spiritual books, and courses related directly to Spiritual Transformative Education. Each of these tools is available to you in many different forms of media.

If you look upon past teachers who have written books as Spiritual Guides, you will realize that guidance comes in many forms with many different presentation methods. Always be conscious of your surroundings and begin to realize that Spiritual Guides are just around the corner of your awareness, just waiting for you to ask for Conscious Clarity of spiritual fact. Do what you know is right for you, and don't fear those egoist critics who want to block your greatness. Forgo thoughts that you are not good, educated, intelligent, or strong enough to fulfill your highest potential in this lifetime.

You are an extraordinary droplet of water in the ocean of life, part of Creation itself, and you have the God-given right to claim your greatness. Let your Spiritual Guides assist you when questioning the steps needed to fulfill your Original Source Agreement. You have more Spiritual Guides than your limited mind will allow you to comprehend. So stay alert and consciously bring your vision to light with the assistance of those created at the exact moment you were. It's all good, and the experiences of others can help you achieve even far more extraordinary things than our spiritual guides did before us.

Can Anyone Be a Spiritual Guide

"Can anyone be a Spiritual Guide?" is more of a statement than a question because we are all One, and each one of us channels spiritual messages to one another in the spiritual realm of reality. We are all teachers and students, as well. By consciously focusing our energies on the spiritual aspects of this lifetime, we can experience the spiritual wisdom of Light!

As you grow in spiritual awareness of your True Self, you will understand the meaning of life and align yourself with only those on the same path as you are, as both a spiritual seeker and spiritual teacher. Spiritual awareness will empower you to move forward with your Original Source Agreement from a level of understanding observed as Knowing. When you know the spiritual truth about life, you begin to understand the futility of what the ego attempts to present as truth.

The mass consciousness of this human existence has just started to glimpse at the actual reality of life. Therefore, it is up to all of us as Spiritual Beings to continue to bring the Spiritual Light to the forefront of human existence. By allowing yourself to channel the messages that come through you from the Cosmic Intelligence of Source Energy, you will bring new wisdom to the mass consciousness of the world. You and I are One – never doubt this fact.

The next time you see someone acting out from a position of ego, send them Love, Peace, and Light. Sending Love, Peace, and Light is part of being a Spiritual Being. When you align with others spiritually, primarily when they act out a false reality of fear, you increase their energy vibration without them knowing it. Because most people live from a physical plane of understanding, they are spiritually ignorant of who they indeed are.

Your spiritual power never diminishes by sharing it; it grows to a higher vibration every time you send Love, Peace, and Light to someone living a fear-based illusion of life.

When you act as the Spiritual Guide for someone who needs Light, you automatically receive additional Spiritual Guide guidance from the spirit world. Your advice is a magnet to Cosmic Intelligence and your Highest Self awareness of reality. When you observe an adverse action in someone and then send them Love, Peace, and Light, you receive a surge of energy from Source Energy. There is no need to think, as there is always a connection with the Source Energy of all Creation. By now, you know this to be the truth!

Therefore, each of us is a Spiritual Guide! If you ever feel depleted because of sharing energy with others, understand that the Physical Body feels this drain, not because it is weak, but because Source Energy is overpowering. When you consciously connect with Source Energy for long periods, it creates a surge in your Kundalini energy flow, and the body reacts to it. This surge is also known as Shakti energy or feminine energy. It is the root of Love, Peace, and Light. As you understand your Highest Self, you will discover your Physical Body will be able to handle these extreme energy surges better because you are increasing your energy vibration and bringing awareness to the surface of life.

Connecting with a Spiritual Guide as a go-between reduces the amplitude of the Source Energy surge, allowing the Physical Body to increase the connection timeframe with this energy without feeling drained.

How Do I Connect with Spiritual Guides

Silence is always the doorway into the Light! When we remove the external chatter from our presence, we allow ourselves the gift of the Highest Self awareness. There's no better place to be than in silence. Silence reduces the outside world to a lower resonance frequency so you can make direct conscious contact with Spiritual Guides.

You should begin all prayer and meditation with the presence of silence. Most people pray rather than sit in a meditative state of Being. Prayer is typically a one-way conversation with some entity outside one's Self. Religions usually teach prayer as direct communication with the spirit world. Religion teaches us to pray to a saint, a family member who has died, an outside entity, or God when we feel we need assistance with our *life* situation in some way. Prayer is usually some form of a request to improve our life situation or reduce pain and suffering of the mind and body. When living from a Physical Body perspective of what the Four Body System offers you, prayer is usually the best means of communication with the Spiritual Guides. To go beyond this level of understanding is more than that ego will allow you to accomplish.

However, if you now understand living in a state of meditative *Being* is indeed a direct connection with Source Energy, you will no longer pray to a God outside you. Instead, you will have an ongoing conversation with God within you. This ongoing conversation means you will feel God speaking directly to you through the voice of silence, feelings, or whispers. You will ask questions, and answers will be immediate. You will no longer wonder whether or not God hears what you are saying through this Highest Self direct communication.

God or Source Energy is not some separate entity that requires you to worship him. God is the Highest Self, the part of you that is collectively part of all Creation. Yes, that's right; you and God are the same. God never intended you to worship him as a separate entity. Therefore, if you are part of God, which means you are God, why would you believe you must worship him as some "thing" outside yourself? Sit and ponder that question for a while; it's vital.

Stop reading this book right now and take that question for a walk. "If you are part of God, which means you are God, why would you believe you must worship him as some 'thing' outside yourself? Get out in nature and feel your surroundings; don't just look around and see or hear your surroundings from a five-sensory perspective – BE PART OF YOUR SURROUNDS IN NATURE!

Source Energy is the entirety of the Universe! Direct connection with Source Energy is far more rewarding to your Highest Self than any prayer could ever be. You see, prayer is typically considered communication with something outside yourself. This false belief is backward from what Source Energy intended you to experience in life. You are a direct descendent of Source Energy and capable of all that aligns with this energy commonly known as God.

Listening to Spiritual Guides is an excellent way to connect with Source Energy while transitioning from Physical Body to Spiritual Body alignment. They allow you to step up your energy comfortably as you progress in your spiritual understanding of Self. You are the essence of the creative force for good brought to awareness through Love. You are the essence of the meaning of Love. You are the Peace created through Love. You are the Light manifested through Peace. Understanding this is an enlightening experience or stepping stone into the reality of the Highest Self and spiritual connection with the creator of all this is, was, or ever will be.

Love brings Inner Peace, and Inner Peace brings a direct connection with God, which is light. Once you enter this Light, you will no longer return to falsely worshipping or praying to an entity outside yourself. Instead, you will understand that you are a guiding Light to those around you. You will better understand those stuck in the false historical lessons of Physical Body alignment and allow them to experience their lessons fully. You will be a conscious observer and stop trying to force your opinion on others by allowing others to control their own lives without your interference unless they ask for your guidance. You will have stepped into self-mastery and learned to be a master of One – Your Self!

What Are Historic Lessons

Christ, Buddha, and other Spiritual Guides or channels better understand what a purpose-driven life can be. It is these masters of spiritual awareness that attempted to guide us into a reality of God-realization. We would be far better today if we only listened to their historical lessons. Unfortunately, most people do not understand that Spiritual Body alignment is God's intention for us to bring about a truly joyous life. These are the facts, but society has let these historic lessons come under the smokescreen of ego-based control dogma.

Our world remains manipulated by a few individuals calling themselves worldly scholars or leaders of society. From a self-centered perspective, these scholars function as masters who decide what is right and wrong. But then, they are given the power by unsuspecting people to rule over us by producing laws, rules, and false guidelines meant to keep society in control for the benefit of a few.

Our present-day world teaches academics and offers multiple degrees or diplomas of mastering academic text as the judgment of people's worth. This judgment is all based upon a Physical Body alignment mentality. This type of academic intelligence permeates the world as the guiding mechanism to falsely produce a society that allows "a few" to control everyone else. This theoretical system erroneously judges humans as having higher or lower intelligence. Keeping this control mechanism intact, including its grading system, allows others to forcefully implement their opinions on others. This type of control system, accepted by society as the rule of the land, feeds big egos. It historically judges everyone based upon a Physical Body misalignment or ego-based system of fear and control.

Big egos falsely create this control-based idea of what we are to experience with a few at the top in charge of everyone else. The most prevalent masters of this false sense of reality are evident in corporations run by multi-billionaires who have mastered controlling others through the force of money dominance. The sad part of this story is that most people believe this control system is working; it is on the verge of a tipping point of self-destruction. This viewpoint may seem like a bleak picture of what dominates today's world, but the truth is not always easy for the ego to digest.

Controlling others has been a historic formula for success for those considered scholars or academically superior to people without degrees or other artificial, ego-based, judgmental measuring tools and grading systems that hold people back from life mastery. These false systems or illusions of reality are historical examples of what an ego-based society has to offer. Unfortunately, it's only a matter of time before the whole system collapses under the false rule of its controlling dictatorship.

We are taught in school that no one is above the law. In reality, based on what we have experienced throughout history, is that some can manipulate the law for their benefit. Those who create manufactured statutes and regulations in the first place are the ones manipulating them! We give our power over others to control us and then wonder why life is so challenging.

On the other hand, spiritual law or spiritual intelligence is the only accurate Universal guideline you must follow to produce a joyous life filled with Abundance and limitless growth. The spiritual masters of the past had one thing in common: they all understood self-mastery. They knew we require responsibility for our well-being, and no one else has power over us. These masters aligned with the Spiritual Body at the forefront of every moment of their lifetimes. They had mastered the cosmic ability of the Universe by living life through Spiritual Intelligence guidance. They could consciously see the illusionary form-based world for what it is, and they taught God-realization education.

You have a choice. Follow the direction of Spiritual Guides such as these spiritual masters or the fearful order of our contemporized world as we know it today. Each has historical lessons, but only one can provide you with everlasting Joy through the Power of Love, Peace, and Light!

Once Aligned with Spiritual Guides, Does It Get Easier

Once you truly understand what it means to align with Spiritual Guides, you will have a constant smile because you will be experiencing life as destined. The joyous Knowing that comes from within will be your focus, and you will no longer be a prisoner of worldly pleasures believed to bring happiness and Joy.

Most of humanity seeks happiness, which is a false sense of bliss. The mind is typically aligned based upon Physical Body alignment; therefore, it believes that something outside of the Self can bring Harmony with the Universe, providing all form-based things and formless, eternal ecstasy. Listening to those who teach happiness as something internal makes me smile, as it is a false sense of reality. Your happiness manifests by outside situations aligning with one's belief system. Conversely, Joy is never-ending and comes from the inner core of Self and Conscious Clarity of True Self awareness.

We are in a state of bliss when we are living the experience of Inner Peace and the never-ending Light that is with us at all times. Nothing outside of us will bring about Joy, as Joy is an eternal gift of Being One with the power of all that is, the Power of Source Energy surging through us at all times. Joy is never ending; no matter how much we use it, it can never end. Joy is the totality of all feelings, Knowing, and the simplicity of the one great gift bestowed upon us, and it is eternal. Source Energy continually gives and never asks for anything from us in return. It is the source of all Harmony and aligns with everything you could ever ask for to live in the blissful Divine elegance at the core of Spiritual Transformative Education.

Spiritual Transformative Education teaches us to stay consciously connected to the Source Energy of all that was or will be. As a result, you have the power to remain in a constant state of bliss. By simply living in a state of Gratitude, you will quickly learn that you are more compelling than your Mental Body could ever understand completely. But, first, you must shift your perspective to Spiritual Body alignment to even glimpse the all-encompassing beauty available to you at all times.

The Physical and Mental Bodies' need for external pleasure is outside what Spiritual Guides offer because they do not understand what it means to be anything other than the greatness you indeed are. Therefore, Spiritual Guides can only lead you closer to the Highest Self awareness – because that is all they KNOW!

Ask better questions, and Spiritual Guides will lead you to eternal Light!

Who Keeps Asking These Questions

You must first understand that all the answers or solutions to any questions came before the questions came into reality. Furthermore, you must realize that True Personality, being aligned in Harmony with Source Energy, is where the lessons are co-created. What does this mean? Can you begin to grasp the magnitude of this energy vibration? Everything has already been resolved or brought into Conscious Clarity!

The master does nothing, yet he leaves nothing undone.
– Tao Te Ching, Lao-tzu

True Personality provides the means to reconnect fully with your True Essence, God-realization. You are the co-creator of all that was or ever will Be. You are part of Source Energy, assigned to bring Light to the world. Your gifts are your tools, and your awareness is what is being brought to Light right now through Conscious Clarity of Self or True Personality.

Your True Personality is now at the forefront of your Being or life. In other words, you naturally align Spiritually.

You see our world (possibly for the first time in this lifetime) from the perspective of God-realization. You are not separate from Source Energy – you are an intricate part of the Oneness of all it IS!

Source Energy is always with you and always part of you at the same time. Remember, you are not the body – you are IN the body. Therefore, if you are in the body, as a Spiritual Being with a human experience, you can answer every question that could arise in this form-based world. You are the co-creator of each new moment and can change your perception to align entirely with Source Energy because you now see with an eternal perspective of reality.

When you discover how to regain Conscious Clarity by sitting in a meditative state of Being, you recognize that every question arises because of living in this state of consciousness. Energy vibration is an essential tool in your form-based body. You are the creator of your destiny because you have free will to choose Physical Body or Spiritual Body alignment in each moment.

If you live a life of illusion based upon Physical Body alignment, you believe you will be judged by some outside entity when the Physical Body dies. But, conversely, suppose you are living a life based upon Spiritual Body alignment. In that case, you KNOW that judgment is part of the false illusion and irrelevant to Spiritual Knowing.

If you do not comprehend this now, the Super-ego controls you with illusionary cleverness!

If I Know I'm Doing Wrong, Am I Judged

The secret to answering this question is interpreting who you believe you are. If you live by the false reality of being only a physical body, you still live in fear. You are still living in a state of mindfulness that has you locked in the Super-ego's grasp of duality. This conscious vibration of the Super-ego has locked you into a transcendent belief that you are greater than the whole of which you indeed are. But, then, this is "wrong-mindedness" and is judged by a limited perspective of this mindset.

This transcendent belief can be very confusing for someone who has increased their energy vibration to a state where they have begun to hear the higher vibration messages from Source Energy. The Super-ego can be very clever in how it attempts to implant "wrong thinking" into your consciousness. On the one hand, you are now vibrating at a level most of humanity will not experience in this lifetime, but your energy level is still low enough to be tricked by the Super-ego.

When you discover the "I" of your I-AM-Ness, you will release the Super-ego completely. It's a mistake to place yourself above others based on the comparison (competition) rather than cooperation with the entire Universe. Just because you are vibrating at an increased level of energy vibration does not mean you are better than anyone else. We are all One, and the energy vibration is merely a level of understanding – not comparison!

You are part of the entire package: the trees, streams, leaves, animals, atmosphere, and other human forms. Each is part of the whole. The totality of the Creation relates to how we each live our lives. Respect from this level of understanding is mandatory to understand forgiveness truly. It's not about forgiving others for their actions judged by your Super-ego or themselves. It's about not being a part of the separation that the Super-ego still needs to survive at the lower vibrations of the human form.

A true "I" knows only wholeness and always comes to the table of humility with an open heart. There is no judgment by the actual "I", which lives in I-AM-Ness of the whole, moment by moment. So likewise, your True Personality does not judge anyone else or your Super-ego. It simply observes and allows everyone and everything to Be. The moment you grasp this discovery's magnitude will be when you have released the Super-ego. Removing the Super-ego is the moment you have been waiting for – to begin your journey based upon an energy vibration in Harmony with Source Energy.

Remember, the Mental Body only understands what correlates to your Four Body System alignment. So it comes back to the question, How are you spiritually or physically aligned? The answer will put you in direct connection with Spiritual Guides to assist you on your journey, or you will be left outside this level of guidance, relying strictly on your Super-ego's cleverness to survive.

Remember, there is no judgment in the reality of Oneness!

Do Spiritual Guides Come To Everyone

Spiritual Guides most assuredly come to everyone – without exception! However, it is necessary to be diligent in your spiritual practice to take full advantage of the messages or assistance planned for you. Yes, it is all part of the Divine plan for you to receive this outstanding guidance; you are never alone, even during times of perceived turmoil or chaos. Therefore, let your feelings guide you to the messages that are always coming through, and never doubt that you are experiencing what you need to stay true to your Original Source Agreement.

As you increase in energy vibration, you will see that those who doubt your new way of living will begin to fall away from your consciousness because you no longer allow the ego to judge you falsely – move on. Remember, in the ego-perceived weakness rests all the Power of the Universe!

You do not exist on the surface of the form-based world. You are the Spirit that drives the physical body. So guided you are even when you feel alone in your quest for spiritual enlightenment. Sometimes, the Super-ego feels very powerful, but this is merely a false illusion of power in life situations. When you feel disconnected from everyone in society, you experience tremendous spiritual growth. The path of a God-realized person is not always easy. It would be best if you kept the fact that most of the planet, especially in the West, lives life from a false sense of reality.

Those who ridicule your Knowing live a life swimming on the surface and do not understand that Spiritual Guides are assisting you. Allow those who mock you to be as they are, as it is not your responsibility to even care what they think. Always remember, when people believe based upon reaction, they are prisoners in the false, illusionary world. But thinking comes before feeling emotion when aligned properly from a spiritual perspective. You are ready to act when you sense direction from Spiritual Guides. Allow your wisdom to shine through the smokescreen of the Super-ego, and you will never go wrong. Pay no attention at all to those that ridicule your Knowing. As Jesus stated, "Forgive them, for they know not what they do."

Those who choose to complicate life by judging others are not vibrating at a high enough frequency to hear the Spiritual Guides attempting to contact them. They are too busy with surface-based reality to feel the energy of these tranquil messages. Therefore, they judge what they do not understand and do not believe the guidance trying to nudge them to the truth. They are typically caught up in a frenzy, like a fish out of water, unconscious of actual reality.

Keep your life as simple on the surface as it is within you. The strength provided to you in that peace will allow you to stay aligned with the God-realized way of Being. Allow your vision to come into the Light and be ready to experience a life far beyond that of an ego-driven person. You co-create with Source Energy during the moments you are Being who you are. Enjoy the sweet nectar of these moments and allow the Power of Source Energy to flow through you by accepting the guidance provided by Spiritual Guides, especially during your dream state.

Do Dreams Count As Spiritual Guides

What is a dream? Nothing more than another dimension or state of awareness seldom found in the illusion of surface-driven thought or form-based life situations; it is the space between thoughts. The idea of non-thought is a paradoxical reality of life for most people. However, once you begin to experience the benefits found by listening to the guidance found in non-thought, you will start to understand that words do not matter. You can connect directly with Spiritual Guides and Source Energy in the dream state (altered reality). There are no limits when connected with life at this advanced state of Being.

Keep your conversations with Source Energy to yourself for the most part because most people will not understand what you are sharing anyway. The key to sharing is Knowing your audience; what is their energy vibration level? Connect with the energy vibrations of the audience and you will know what to say guided by Source Energy.

Have you ever been accused of daydreaming when you are supposed to be taking action based upon a societal-perceived reality? This daydreaming means you are off someplace else when others tell you to be present. This trance-like state is one of the most critical times when you momentarily disconnect from society and consciously feel the messages from Spiritual Guides. Don't allow the distractions of others to interrupt your conversation with the Spiritual Guides; these are Divine times.

This author is often accused of not listening or not hearing what someone says. I am temporarily unavailable during these times, as I am in direct contact with Spiritual Guides or Source Energy and do not hear the sounds of the form-based world. It's not that I don't care what is said; it simply means that I have checked out for a few moments. These are times when I feel a sense of connection that goes far beyond what is on the surface of life. When returning from one of these short trips into what I call "my private world", I feel peaceful, grateful, and energized.

Most of humanity would have you believe it is childish or self-indulgent to frequently return to the silence of an altered dream state during a time of awakened reality. However, a genuinely awake person is awake when others think they are disconnected from the illusion or surface-driven thinking in the false reality world. This awakening is a paradox for the mind, as it wants to separate us from those guiding us from our altered state of Being.

The idea that we can be present physically without thought is too much for the typical mind to comprehend. Humanity typically believes what is on the surface of life;

therefore, what is real and unseen by the senses is not natural to the ego. This false reality is entirely backward thinking in the actual existence of life. So here we are again, back to how our Four Body System is aligned, challenged to detach from any other form of reality if you live only based upon a perspective of Physical Body misalignment. Ego will attempt to halt your silent connection with Source Energy at all costs!

Keep the Spiritual Body at the forefront of your life, and you will begin to experience the Abundance that is your destiny. Source Energy is always with you, but you must be willing to discover the language of non-thought communication through feelings before you attain the rewards of Abundance Source Energy offers you. You can reach your full potential and satisfy your Original Source Agreement by listening to the silent messages transmitted at the highest levels of consciousness. Source Energy tends to speak directly to you at what may seem to be the most inopportune times - go with it!

When you reach this level of communication, the Super-ego would have you believe that you are more advanced than others. However, the reality of this backward thinking is your first clue that you are on track and beginning to fully understand that we are all connected through Oneness with Source Energy. Therefore, don't allow your Super-ego to place you above others from a comparative perspective. Instead, allow yourself the benefits of vibrating at a higher level of understanding, but remember we are all One and equal in actual reality.

Are We All Together - Or Separate

You are taught in the superficial, ego-dominated culture of the world to see with sensory eyes only. What is part of physical form is the only believed reality. This false reality separates you from the actual life you intended to live here in the Physical body. This mind-based idea of what is real is part of the ego-driven or conditioned mind and a false state of Being. To experience what is real, all you need to do is begin to allow spiritual guides to connect with you at the level of Oneness. At the level of non-thought, serious communication is found, and all the solutions manifest.

If you still believe you are separate from others, you will continue to judge everything, and your path will continue to be controlled by others. You will stay prisoner to the ego-dominated culture that holds most of the world, believing you are either better or less than someone else. This culture is an unconscious or conditioned life based upon a superficial level of judgment and limited awareness of truth. I suggest that you change your way of perceiving life entirely by making a 180-

degree course correction into the world of silent communication with Oneness.

What would you feel if you accepted everything seen in the external world as perfect? Would you still judge others based on your limited understanding of who they are? Would you continue to believe you are better than someone who may be less fortunate than you are financially? Would you continue to place yourself on a pedestal based upon academic achievements, awards, and certificates received because others are rating you? Would you continue to see other people's outward or physical appearances as lacking? Would you continue to ridicule others because of their beliefs? This self-centeredness is all a world of separation, a Super-ego-based dogma controlling your continued limited idea of reality. Even if you have merged the Soul and mind in alignment with actual reality, you are still vulnerable to the Super-ego's clever control tactics at this energy vibration level.

When you consciously dive deeply into the ocean of spiritual reality, you see the limited understanding of what life is on this superficial basis. When you experience life at the level of Oneness, you begin to see the beauty of every life situation moment as a beautiful dance guided by the hand of Source Energy. Source Energy does not make mistakes! You are in this world to experience the reality of perfection found at the level of non-thought and non-judgment of any life situation you may be privileged to experience. You are not part of the negativity of life situations; you are the Spiritual Being having the human experience of life itself.

Please stop trying to persuade others to be as you would like to see them. Instead, let everyone be who they are and bring a new Light to your vision. Open yourself up to the idea that all is perfect and that Source Energy has an exquisite plan in Harmony with your Original Source Agreement. Stop looking outside yourself for the solutions to mind-based problems – after all, what created these problems in the first place?

When was the last time you felt balanced? Where all your categories of life harmonized with Source Energy, and you thought that it couldn't get any better than the present moment? When was the last time you felt aligned with your Original Source Agreement? When you honestly answer these questions, you will be ready to turn your life around and become balanced with the life force of actual reality, and you will know the true meaning of contentment.

What's the Balancing Life Force

We are at a tipping point of destruction regarding how we view what is truly important in our Western Society.

Unfortunately, many of our government leaders oppose what God intended for us. This tipping point is due to ego-based leadership rather than life force or Source Energy's contentment. Source Energy has provided all we need to live a joyous life in Harmony with the Universal Intelligence responsible for all Creation.

So why are we so confused if Source Energy has given us free will to make our own choices, including electing the world's government leaders? Unfortunately, due to the manipulation of ego-based policies, government rules created by egos, and constituent spiritual ignorance, we are now lowering our energy vibration in Western Society rather than increasing it. The choices clearly show us that we are on a path of destruction, and we can only have faith that we will see an awakening before it is too late to reverse this mental insanity. One of my favorite quotes by Ralph Waldow Emerson clearly defines our current plight:

"When it is dark enough, you can see all the stars."

We have not experienced enough darkness or low-energy vibration in our government actions to bring Light to all available through the life force of Creation rather than destruction to guide our societal path in the Western world. During the Trump Administration, we witnessed the hard work of our past leaders wiped out piece by piece by an egotistical administration vibrating well below the level of a bully. This catastrophe is due to a population split or division based on Ego/Fear and Spirit/Love.

All ego-based dogma's false power is based on fear and driven by the low-vibration mentality of fear-based ideologies. Conversely, Spirit is rooted in love-based Universal Intelligence. Fear and Love are at opposite levels of the energy spectrum. It is time for our awakening through Spiritual Transformation Education to bring Light to darkness.

A life feared centers on chaos, confusion, and ego-based control mechanisms. Conversely, a life of Love centers on conscious awareness of who we are, Spiritual Beings. A human experience is supposed to be rooted in the life force energy of Source Energy or God-realization. If you believe your energy vibration doesn't matter, you are sadly mistaken and manipulated by clever egos, including your own.

It is your responsibility as a Spiritual Being to bring your understanding of the True Self to the forefront of your daily activities and to bring our Western Society back on track. When you surrender to this reality, you will begin to see the consciousness of the Western world shift back from the insanity of ego-based disconnection to the balanced life force of Spiritual Intelligence.

Source Energy has an amazingly joyous plan for us, but you must step up your energy vibration to truly understand how it aligns with your Original Source Agreement.

What Does Energy Vibration Do for Connection

Many levels of connection with Source Energy manifest at varying levels of energy vibration awareness. If you are in touch with your feelings, you are probably one of the few who genuinely understands the Knowing found at the level of Oneness with Source Energy. This vibration level is beyond that of the mind. Surrender to Knowing that Source Energy will always align you with your Original Source Agreement.

You have gone through the experience of Soul Merge, where you discovered how to properly align your Four Body System with the Spiritual Body in the forefront of your life. Doing so increases your energy vibration to the level of Knowing and sets you on a straight course without the clutter of Mental Body chatter most people live by.

Suppose you believe you are vibrating at a higher energy level than most of humanity. In that case, you either have already experienced a direct connection with Source Energy or have been tricked by the Super-ego into believing you are better than others. How you discern between the two will directly reflect your life situation outcome.

Genuine Source Energy connection comes from silent guidance, which is felt rather than heard. This form of communication is far beyond what the mind can understand in its current state of reality. However, once you discover that you can directly connect with Source Energy, it becomes easier for the ego to accept. The key is to stay meditative because this is the essential aspect of a direct connection with Source Energy. Until you surrender to the truth of acceptance of what it is, staying directly connected with Source Energy will be challenging because your vibration level will continue to vary.

Meditative connection is where spiritual guides come into play; a spiritual guide, whether a relative transition or the spiritual consciousnesses of a spiritual teacher like Jesus, will assist you with the energy vibration of your current understanding.

Stepped-down energy, which aligns with your present vibration, allows you to experience Spiritual Intelligence from an understanding level that the mind can discern without doubt or prejudice. Because we have been programmed or think based upon a false-conditioned sense, we must first remove the obstacle of doubt from our conditioning to receive the exclusive benefit of direct communication with Source Energy at the highest level of Love.

Do Humans Know How to Love

The definition of Love will vary based upon the perception of the ego-based (fear-based), conditioned mind, or spiritual-based Knowing and natural state of Being Love when living with the Spiritual Body at the forefront of your life choices. The ego-based mind is a result of false fear-based societal perceptions. Fear is the condition of separation implanted in us since birth. Until the shift occurs where spirituality is behind our decisions, we will continue to be a humanity based on judgment, fear, and separation. This ego-based scenario is sad, but we each have a choice to rise above this limited false reality.

Society teaches punishment as an antidote to all fear-based choices rather than the reality of right or wrong-mindedness based on the unity of Oneness. Therefore, the comparison of right or wrong-mindedness is not a judgment but a measurement or notice of whether we are reacting to fear or taking action based upon Love, Peace, and Light. Unfortunately, the ego doesn't understand this, and the Super-ego has taken this falsity to arrogance, making it almost impossible to discern by spiritual understanding. When we judge or place ourselves on a pedestal of being more spiritually intelligent than someone else, it takes our level of arrogance to the illusion of a false sense of spiritual reality.

This arrogance is because the Super-ego still clings to the Physical Body and form-based false reality of life.

As a Spiritual Being, Love is your natural state. By focusing on Love, Peace, and Light as your guidance system, you do not need the Super-ego's manipulations as a false tool to get what you want in life. Being a Spiritual Being means taking action when appropriate based upon "Knowing" what is right or wrong-mindedness in action. You release the ego's need to judge whether something is "good" or "bad", and you flow through life based upon acceptance of what is. You begin to see the Oneness in everyone and treat wrong-minded thinking differently.

To Love unconditionally is the true definition of what Love is. When you live your life based upon Being one that is Love, rather than trying to achieve Love or doing loving things, you will see the outcome of your life situation change. Love, acceptance, and kindness are the antidote to hatred, anger, and punishment (threats). Remove the ego-based FEAR of punishment and replace it with the Spiritual reprogramming of right-mindedness. This realignment will set you on a path of self-discovery that will assist you in understanding the true meaning of Love and how Spiritual Guides align with this Oneness of Spirit.

Can a Spiritual Guide Be Defined

Words cannot define Spiritual Guides. A Spiritual Guide is the embodiment of the Spirit, based on feelings, Light, and channeled messages of the Spirit!

When you truly understand who you are, you will begin to understand the Oneness that embraces your essence. You will flow through life knowing that you are never alone because you are part of the originating Source of all Creation and have nothing to fear while visiting the form-based world. Your Spiritual Guides are your brothers and sisters of the Universe, and this Cosmic power is your family. You are not of this world – you are merely in this world having a human experience. Suppose you have not yet anchored this reality into your belief system. In that case, you are still allowing ego to control your life by allowing your life situations to influence your True Self perspective of life itself.

By bringing to Light the understanding that the outside world of form can never harm you, your life evolves to the level of Monadic awareness of the Oneness that is your true essence. When you finally surrender to the fact that you are the invisible witnessing essence within the physical body, you will walk this Earth free of the constraints placed on a form by other form-based control dynamics. This awareness means that you are free to live your life based on what you know is best for you rather than what others have determined to be best.

Once you truly understand, without any doubt, that you can move through life based on your Original Source Agreement, you will realize that all the limitless scenarios that you co-created within that agreement are already available to you. So why hold yourself prisoner to a system outside yourself? Why allow others to dictate your reality when unaware of their spiritual greatness? Stop surrounding yourself with those who do not understand their true spiritual essence. Instead, bring your vision to light through the reality of Oneness. By escaping this ego-dominated physical world, you will open yourself up to the Power of Love and leave fear behind you.

When you view each person around you as a Spiritual Guide, you will understand what it means to have total freedom. Duped for far too long, it is time for you to finally escape the burden of the false Mental Body control dynamics. When you place faith or the Power of Source Energy at the forefront of your reality, you completely change the perspective of what once appeared to be a problem.

From this perspective, you realize that every person, present or past, is a Spiritual Guide moving you forward in Spiritual growth.

Chapter 2 Suggestions - Assistance from Spiritual Guides

We are always connected to Spiritual Guides to assist us. These may have once inhabited a physical form and had the same purpose as the physical beings they now guide. Now, they offer higher vibrational guidance from the Spiritual realm to enhance our Spiritual Education. Through intuition, feelings, and spiritual alerts, we can tap into this unlimited source of advice, all of the Universal Intelligence. Your feelings are directly related to what you are taking action on in life. Whether or not you pay attention to these feelings or spiritual alerts is based on your energy vibration level.

- Spiritual Guides come in many forms. They may include past spiritual partners, other intimate relationships, family members who have transitioned out of the body, and teachers who may have profoundly impacted you. Additionally, Spiritual Guides could be Celestial Beings whose primary purpose is to guide a particular astrological category of humans (for example, Capricorns, Sagittarius, etc.), your own Guardian Angel, and Source Energy itself.

- "Can anyone be a Spiritual Guide?" is more of a statement than a question because we are all One, and each one of us channels spiritual messages to one another in the spiritual realm of reality. We are all teachers and students, as well. By consciously focusing our energies on the spiritual aspects of this lifetime, we can experience the spiritual wisdom of Light!

- Silence is always the doorway into the Light! When we remove the external chatter from our presence, we allow ourselves the gift of the Highest Self awareness. There's no better place to be than in silence. Silence reduces the outside world to a lower resonance frequency so you can make direct conscious contact with Spiritual Guides.

- Christ, Buddha, and other Spiritual Guides or channels better understand what a purpose-driven life can be. It is these masters of spiritual awareness that attempted to guide us into a reality of God-realization. We would be far better today if we only listened to their historical lessons. Unfortunately, most people do not understand that Spiritual Body alignment is God's intention for us to bring about a truly joyous life.

- You have a choice. Follow the direction of Spiritual Guides or the fearful order of our contemporized world as we know it today. Each has historical lessons, but only one can provide you with everlasting Joy through the Power of Love, Peace, and Light!

- When you discover how to regain Conscious Clarity by sitting in a meditative state of Being, you recognize that every question arises because of living in this state of consciousness.

- When you discover the "I" of your I-AM-Ness, you will release the Super-ego completely. It's a mistake to place yourself above others based on the comparison (competition) rather than cooperation with the entire Universe. Just because you are vibrating at an increased level of energy vibration does not mean you are better than anyone else. We are all One, and the energy vibration is merely a level of understanding – not comparison!

- Keep your life as simple on the surface as it is within you. The strength provided to you in that peace will allow you to stay aligned with the God-realized way of Being. Allow your vision to come into the Light and be ready to experience a life far beyond that of an ego-driven person. You co-create with Source Energy during the moments you are Being who you are. Enjoy the sweet nectar of these moments and allow the Power of Source Energy to flow through you by accepting the guidance provided by Spiritual Guides, especially during your dream state.

- Most of humanity would have you believe it is childish or self-indulgent to frequently return to the silence of an altered dream state during a time of awakened reality. However, a genuinely awake person is awake when others think they are disconnected from the illusion or surface-driven thinking in the false reality world. This awakening is a paradox for the mind, as it wants to separate us from those guiding us from our altered state of Being.

- All ego-based dogma's false power is based on fear and driven by the low-vibration mentality of fear-based ideologies. Conversely, Spirit is rooted in love-based Universal Intelligence. Fear and Love are at opposite levels of the energy spectrum. It is time for our awakening through Spiritual Transformation Education to bring Light to darkness.

- Genuine Source Energy connection comes from silent guidance, which is felt rather than heard. This form of communication is far beyond what the mind can understand in its current state of reality. Because we have been programmed or think based upon a false-conditioned sense, we must first remove the obstacle of doubt from our conditioning to receive the exclusive benefit of direct communication with Source Energy at the highest level of Love.

- Society teaches punishment as an antidote to all fear-based choices rather than the reality of right or wrong-mindedness based on the unity of Oneness. Therefore, the comparison of right or wrong-mindedness is not a judgment but a measurement or notice of whether we are reacting to fear or taking action based upon Love, Peace, and Light.

Once you truly understand, without any doubt, that you can move through life based on your Original Source Agreement, you will realize that all the limitless scenarios that you co-created within that agreement are already available to you. So why hold yourself prisoner to a system outside yourself? Why allow others to dictate your reality when unaware of their spiritual greatness? Stop surrounding yourself with those who do not understand their true spiritual essence. Instead, bring your vision to light through the reality of Oneness. By escaping this ego-dominated physical world, you will open yourself up to the Power of Love and leave fear behind you.

Chapter 3

Keeping the Faith During Life Challenges

Why Is It So Hard at Times

We typically get so wrapped up in our big-picture plan for our life that we do not listen to the clues that come to us from Spiritual Guidance. When we align with Source Energy and the Divine Plan already in place, life flows effortlessly, and greatness is achieved.

We can achieve greatness by focusing on what we can do in each moment while listening intentionally to the guidance sent to us during the silent moments of meditative awareness. The mind is an incredible tool to co-create the big picture of our life, which is nothing more than the Original Source Agreement being fulfilled one moment at a time. If the Mental Body is adequately aligned, then it is used to produce the best results possible. If misaligned, your results will be directly proportional to the misalignment, and you could wander from one challenge to another.

Staying in the present moment is the key to achieving everything you ever need. If you break down immense achievements into small tasks, you will soon realize the present moment is the only time anything is achieved in life. By allowing yourself to be present and in a state of Love, Peace and Light, you can accomplish everything your heart desires, which means what aligns with Source Energy and your Original Source Agreement.

However, the Super-ego will constantly manipulate you into doing tasks out of alignment with your Original Source Agreement because the Super-ego still wants control over you! Don't be misguided by feelings of superiority to other people that may not be vibrating as high as you are now. Stay out of your Mental Body if you find it misaligned.

The Super-ego is truly clever; it will lead you to take action on whatever false messages it transmits through the misaligned Mental Body. You could spend years living a false reality just by listening to the false guidance of a Super-ego. It only wants one thing – to keep you locked in the prison of a false reality of what life is truly all about.

If you are taking action on thoughts from your Super-ego, you will notice that all this action is directly related to what's in it for me in the big picture. However, if you use the spiritually aligned Mental Body, you will notice that all actions taken are part of the alignment with the Source Energy that helps others. Only after you have successfully assisted others in achieving their purpose will you be rewarded with the realization that you are living a fulfilled life of service.

Do not doubt that you will achieve greatness and that greatness is found by staying aligned with your true purpose for being here. If you feel Love, Peace and Light in each moment, you are living your Original Source Agreement reality.

If you feel out of touch with Spiritual Guidance, you have slipped back into the control of the Super-ego. As you move forward up the ladder of energy vibration, you will soon realize when you are out of alignment. Your purpose will seem unclear again, and you will temporarily lose the peace that drives your actual spiritual reality. Please pay close attention to your feelings; they will never disappoint you.

If I Give Up, Did I Lose My Purpose

We live in a perceived world of limitation and duality that attempts to keep us locked in a control mechanism of false power. When, in fact, the only true power is the Spiritual power of Source Energy that guides the Universe. Once you discover your purpose for Being here, you will perceive your life from a completely different perspective based on Love, Peace and Light. If you fall below that vibration level, know that you have fallen below true self-alignment and allowed your Super-ego to slip back into the driver's seat of your life momentarily.

The only way you will ever momentarily give up on your purpose is if you are back under the control of the Super-ego. You have grown to understand that with the Spiritual Body in the forefront of your present moment, everything aligns with your Original Source Agreement and your True Purpose for being here. Suppose the Super-ego finds a way to bring your energy back down to the Physical Body level of limited understanding. In that case, it is simply part of the overall Divine Plan, and there is a lesson you are about to discover. Be gentle with yourself and pay close attention to your present moment circumstances.

Remember, there is a difference between giving up and surrendering to what is in the present moment. A person aligned with the Physical Body at the forefront of their life typically lives a life of duality and judgment. This duality brings about negative feelings when challenges arise, and they go into either defeatist or victim mode. They fall below the understanding that things only happen around them rather than to them. If you find yourself slipping to this level, rather than giving up based on the situation, acknowledge that Super-ego momentarily slipped into the forefront of your belief system. Just brush yourself off and get back on track!

Smile, bring your awareness back to proper Spiritual Body alignment, and realize there is a lesson to discover from the challenge. By surrendering to what is, you allow yourself to see the situation from a solution-based perspective rather than a defeatist, false reality. Acknowledge that there are times when you may feel uneasy or confused about a given situation, but that is merely a clue that a deep Knowing is on its way. Accept what is and ask for guidance as to whether or not some form of action is necessary to reinstate the inner peace which is your natural state of Being.

There are always multiple ways to perceive a situation mentally in the illusion of form-based reality. But when it comes to it, there is only one path to take from a Spiritual perspective. When aligned with Source Energy, challenges are met with open arms because the reality of a lesson coming is more potent than any adverse reaction the Super-ego may impose on you. Stay alert and see the spiritual beauty of every life situation on your path; have faith that a solution will present itself in due time.

How Can You Have Faith During Overwhelming Challenges

Faith is immeasurable when viewed with the eyes of Spiritual Knowing and connection with Source Energy. During periods of seemingly overwhelming challenges, it is faith that keeps us going. Yes, the physical life situation may feel way beyond your control (in the moment), but as long as you keep your spiritual Knowing at the forefront of your actions, you will get through any life situation that may seem too much to handle. When you truly "feel" the connection with Source Energy, there is a peace that overcomes all overwhelming questionable thoughts.

When we feel overwhelmed by life's situations and challenges, our faith stands out the most. Can you remember when you felt there was nothing more you could do during a seemingly overwhelming strife? Somehow, you got through it! When we get to the end of our rope and falsely believe all hope is gone, faith kicks into high gear and brings us to the realization that the only appropriate response to some challenges is surrendering to what is.

Having faith that the same Universal Intelligence that beats our hearts and causes breathing to happen is ready to take control of our life situation challenge hinges on our depth of Spiritual Knowing or energy vibration. When you can truly surrender to the fact that you have done everything within your control to alleviate an overwhelming situation – at that moment, Source Energy takes control.

We are all part of the Divine Universal Plan that Source Energy has in store. At our core, as Spiritual Beings having a human experience, we know this without doubt. If this experience were always blissful, then it would no longer be necessary for us to be here to heal to the level of enlightenment. In truth, each life challenge brings you closer to the reality of spiritual understanding experienced through the power of spiritual guidance and faith in that guidance. When you are at your lowest perceived point of dealing with overwhelming conditions, it is at that moment that you are beginning the journey of healing the story that the false Mental Body is telling you.

If you have slipped to Physical Body alignment, you will believe you are beyond hope of recovering from the challenge. This fear is an unnatural state of Being; it is the opposite of what you are here to learn. It is the Super-ego once again taking control of your life experience and the place the Super-ego wants you to dwell in. When you align with the Physical Body at the forefront of your life, comprehension is at the low energy level of unconsciousness and in alignment with a victim mentality.

However, if you are Spiritually aligned, you will accept what is and know that there is a lesson learned from the experience you are having. Allow your faith to bring you to that "this too shall pass" state of peaceful acceptance of what is. You will understand that you are not in control of every life situation and that there is a greater power than yourself moving you to your next step of evolution. What is happening around you today is necessary for your spiritual growth; the proof is that it is happening! No other explanation is required.

Can I Really Accomplish All Spirit Tells Me I Can

True Self, the Highest Self or God-Realized Self, will never lie to you. Purity is at the True Self understanding energy level, not the lower self level. Never question the awareness brought to you by listening to the guidance from Source Energy if you want to have an abundant life filled with a Spiritual Body alignment and balanced well-being.

The Super-ego will attempt to trick you into believing you are less than you are. There is an ego-based word for this called Psychosynthesis, which is new in the illusion of mental health psychology academic world. This mental gymnastics industry uses whatever it can to convince you that you are less than a Spiritual Being having a human experience. They continue to relate to many old paradigms still rooted in mind-based psychological academics. Remember, the psychology world is rooted in the mind and the false beliefs of a societal acceptance that this academic-trained industry is always right. Therefore, the mind will never fully accept the power of spiritual awareness because it has no way to measure or compare it other than the mental illusion of the physical brain.

I agree that those vibrating at a deficient energy have chosen to dismiss the morality of right-minded thinking. Right-mindedness thinking is nothing more than living in Spiritual Body alignment with the Highest Self guiding every thought, rather than wrong-mindedness, which is simply a life guided by egoistic, illusionary beliefs. When you are out of Spirit or aligned with the Physical Body at the forefront of your reality, you are under the ego's control.

Some psychologists will argue reality using Psychosynthesis to convince you you need their expertise to get back on track. Psychosynthesis providers target deficient energy vibration levels because of control at the Physical Body alignment level. Fortunately, once you shift to Spiritual Body alignment through Soul Merge, you can stop the psychotherapy and concentrate on the truth of a body living in a state of spiritual well-being.

How many industries would evaporate if the Spiritual Body alignment was at the forefront of all societal beliefs? How many ego-driven professions or careers would cease to exist if we just lived our lives with the reality of Oneness? Do you believe that all the diagnosed mentally ill people on the planet are receiving the care they should have by being medicated to where their energy level stagnated below the level of spiritual awareness is blocked? The medical industry would lose billions of dollars if everyone were to live a God-realized life of natural well-being. Whenever you have someone trying to convince you that you are only the Physical Body reality – run as fast as you can!

We all experience peaks and valleys in energy vibration levels. Be careful not to be misdiagnosed by a mental health professional who truly believes they are helping you when they are merely subconsciously saving their career from extinction.

If someone tells you that you have a mental illness because you do not follow their academic guidelines of an acceptable societal judgment of your mental state, say thank you and move on or ask them to explain their diagnosis in Spiritual terms.

Does Life Need to Have Peaks & Valleys

When you finally accept that all of life has a specific vibrational frequency, you will understand that peaks and valleys are nothing but changes in energy vibration. You will constantly vibrate at the energy level you are putting out each moment, aligning you with similar energies based on your choices. Therefore, you can choose to be in Harmony with Source Energy or in Harmony with others that are vibrating at other lower frequencies of energy vibration.

Remember, all final decisions are made only by you – but only after listening to all opinions of others attempting to influence you and based upon their own beliefs. Therefore, you ultimately increase or decrease your energy vibration based on your free will choice. So, is it necessary to have peaks and valleys of energy vibration? The answer is – it depends on what you agreed to before you took possession of the body you are currently using. Your energy vibration may lower if you harmonize with someone needing your input at a given moment. Allow the vibration to adjust to the present moment, and you will never go wrong.

One of the reasons we are here today is to continue the healing process; otherwise, we would no longer be here. We would not return to bring another lesson to the enlightenment of Conscious Clarity unless we meant to provide the lesson. You are currently at the exact energy vibration level you need to be! The proof is that you are vibrating at that frequency - NOW.

As we dance through life by living it through a "meditative state of Being", we discover that the current moment is the only one we have and honor whatever energy vibration is currently available. We don't question or compare one vibration to another. We live a simple life of service and understand that our energy vibration naturally aligns with that which requires our input to raise the world's mass consciousness (energy vibration).

The teacher is always ready to step into the current moment to impart the wisdom of the higher energies. Still, we must also understand that those needing the most assistance vibrate at a lower energy vibration. Remember, you are only here to serve others. You will bring increased Spiritual Light into the world by keeping that reality in the forefront of your mind. Allow yourself the flexibility of experiencing life as a Spiritual Being having a human experience. Spiritual Being Reality will serve you and those around you precisely as Source Energy intends.

Enjoy the journey and bring the Light of Source Energy to everyone you meet. Having faith that there is a higher power in control of all that IS will keep your energy vibration at exactly the level it needs to be at each moment.

If I Keep My Faith, Will Life Be Easier

Knowing that there is a Divine Master Plan, which you have agreed to before coming into this current body, will anchor your faith. You Know you are a Spiritual Being; following that wisdom, your daily life experiences align with Source Energy. By keeping your Four Body System aligned with the Spiritual Body at the forefront of every experience, you will learn to witness life as the observer and stay focused on this perception.

When doubt becomes a thing of the past, you understand how you approach life differently. It becomes so easy and relaxed that you no longer even consider the possibility that you will not have a balanced life. Knowing you are balanced, you begin to bring higher energy vibration action to every daily occurrence. This balanced life is effortless to do when you are correctly aligned. The ego doesn't understand that life is meant to be lived without conflict or worry. This lack of knowledge is mainly because we all have been brainwashed into believing that someone else is in control of our destiny. This control dynamic is a sham anchored into the subconscious by those in societal power.

Now that you know the truth, it is up to you to stay aligned with faith and bring the wisdom of this newfound energy to the surface of your daily reality. When you "Know" there is a better way, you begin to take healthy actions in life situations rather than reacting to them in fear. This action is one of the last challenges of eliminating the Super-ego from your life experience. By recruiting the mind to serve the Soul, you open up to the higher realms of reality. This perception of life is what spiritual enlightenment is all about. When you release the old control paradigm from your reality, you see how sacred life truly is, and the old control dramas disappear.

Indeed, you will be tested over and over again until you are fully entrenched in proper Spiritual Body alignment. This testing is just a method of anchoring in the truth. Don't allow the tests to overcome your knowledge, which is the proof you have experienced along the path of enlightenment. You can always think back to times when you doubted your faith, but miraculously found that the life situation you were experiencing at those times of doubt turned out for the best. Life situations on Earth are not always easy, but life itself always is.

Every experience has been set before you to bring your energy vibration up to a level that will allow you always to see each life situation for what it truly is. By staying aligned with Source Energy, you can easily discern what truth is when guidance comes and what is false based upon some Super-ego or false influence. If you stay focused on Spiritual Body alignment at the forefront of your life, these tests of faith can be overcome easily.

When the Guidance Comes, Do I Get Confused

As we move forward in our new consciousness, we may become confused when Source Energy guidance presents itself. You may question whether or not it is genuinely Source Energy speaking or the Super-ego playing another clever trick on you to move away from your True Purpose for being here.

There is an overlap from when you surrender fully to Source Energy and live a fulfilled spiritual life. The Super-ego is the master of disguise; it will bring false realities to you in many forms. However, you can always check in with Source Energy at your Highest Self level of understanding. At that energy vibration, all that is false reveals itself, and you will experience Conscious Clarity communication in its proper form.

At this level of Conscious Clarity communication, which is the Fifth Dimension of reality, you will begin to "feel" the difference between Super-ego communication and Source Energy. If Super-ego is speaking, you will experience an energy drop, and one or more of your chakras will block. You will experience an uneasy feeling within your energy flow and have doubts about who is speaking. When you feel this doubt, and the question arises, "Who is speaking?" that is a sure signal it is Super-ego. The Super-ego still wants to control but in a different way than the ego of the past.

Once you transition from the Physical Body to Spiritual Body alignment, the old ego is merged with the Soul forever. You will never slip backward to that lowest vibration once you taste the sweetness of Spiritual Body alignment. To be confused is a natural progression in the Spiritual Awakening you are experiencing.

Perhaps you have not yet accomplished consistent balance in your life. This confusion indicates you are not in sync with your Original Source Agreement. This misalignment is all part of the Divine Plan that Source Energy has for you; watch for a lesson coming. You will be tested along the path of enlightenment many times. Until you surrender fully to Source Energy without any doubt whatsoever, you will continue the testing process. Accept the confusion you are feeling and allow yourself the gift of inner peace that is your natural state of Being. Being with Source Energy always allows the energy vibration to build at the correct rate for you.

Turn your life over to Source Energy entirely and never look back – you are in Divine hands! When you only see one set of footprints in the sand, know that Source Energy is carrying you!

How Do I Know It's Not Super-ego Tricking Me

The keyword in this question, "How Do I Know It's Not Super-ego Tricking Me?" – is KNOW! When you receive guidance from Source Energy, you will be at peace, and the light of this sacred Knowing will shine through you with feelings of Joy. The energy vibration that Source Energy provides is like none you have ever experienced from form. This formless communication with Source Energy will lift you to a vibration level far exceeding anything from the Mental Body. Even if you are fully enlightened, your mind will always be a servant to the Highest Self reality of life. NEVER DOUBT THIS – SOURCE ENERGY IS ALWAYS WITH YOU!

There is so much openness that shines in the form of feelings when you are connected with Source Energy that you will find it impossible to put words to it. It will vibrate at a frequency that is so powerful you will have absolutely no doubt whatsoever as to the nature of what you are experiencing. Once you have touched the face of God in this way, you will never forget it. Then, in all future moments, when you are experiencing this sacred connection, you will feel the exact feelings that are unquestionably Source Energy speaking directly to you. It will be much stronger than any Spirit Guides working behind the scenes to assist you in life.

If there are any doubts, no matter how minimal they may seem, it is the Super-ego playing tricks on you again. When a misaligned Mental Body is involved in any decision-making process, thought will replace feelings, and you will experience a flood of questions that arise from doubt and manipulation of the Super-ego. These tests will stay with you until you completely surrender to Source Energy guidance. The Super-ego is strong and will control you until you can honestly tell the difference between it and Source Energy speaking through you. There's no magical way to explain the difference with words. The magic is in the feelings vibrating through you, the Kundalini Energy flowing freely without the manipulation of Super-ego.

As you continue on your life journey, you will find it more accessible and easier to distinguish between Source Energy guidance and Super-ego manipulations and trickery. When the Super-ego is involved, you will not feel peaceful and will say and do whatever the Super-ego wants if it controls your actions. I can tell firsthand that the difference between the two communications is like night and day. The light of Source Energy radiates feelings of Love that you can only experience through Divine Communication. Anything else is darkness or trickery of Super-ego.

Who Defines My Feelings About Spirit Anyway

The only person who can define your feelings about Spirit is your Highest Self, found in the pre-programmed Original Source Agreement life plan you created. By allowing yourself to stay in a meditative state of Being, you bring Love, Peace and Light to your journey. Your feelings are the non-word communication methodology of the enlightened Soul. If you are in touch with your feelings, you are walking a path of Joy because you know you are a Spiritual Being sent here to have lifetime experiences in Harmony with Source Energy and your Original Source Agreement.

That spark of bright light called your True Self is the essence of who you are and radiates the Highest Self (God-Self) energy vibration. When you truly realize you are a spark of white light within the Physical Body, you will understand that you are genuinely part of the Source Energy. By Knowing you are a part of this Divine Oneness of life itself, the conscious decisions you make throughout the day will align with the unlimited white light of a God-realized person. You will consciously listen to the inner dialog always available to you. When you discover you are automatically a God-realized Being, connected to Source Energy, your life will never be the same again. However, you have been trained/manipulated for so long that you have lost touch with this reality. Allow this inner energy process to unfold peacefully.

Religions typically teach that God or Source Energy is outside you and should be considered separate. The truth is that Source Energy is part of you or the internal, white light spark of Source Energy that permeates your very Being. Therefore, when you finally decide to live in this God-realized state of Being, you no longer listen to the Super-ego or other outside influences that distract from your Conscious Clarity of who you are. The question arises, why would religions teach this falsehood of Source Energy being something only outside you? The simple answer is control.

Monarchs created religions out of fear of losing control of the people. The primary basis for establishing the religion was an ego-driven, fear-based dogma that still controls a majority of the population today. When fear is the root of keeping people controlled, they follow the leaders without questioning the information. However, in Spiritual teaching, only Love is honestly presented. Many religions attempt to use both in a mixture of duality to satisfy the egoist control dogmas of the past. How arrogant!

Therefore, when you realize that this religious control system has duped you, you finally start asking better questions for Conscious Clarity. This questioning is not something misguided religious interpretations of the Bible can tolerate. The people defend these false narratives at all costs. The sad part of this whole circle of misunderstanding is that it will continue to cloud the Spiritual Body truth if it is not brought into the Light.

Jesus knew he was a Spiritual Being having a human experience and advocated this throughout his travels once he fully understood the Christ Consciousness of reality. However, the religious establishment of the time feared that the people would listen to this Spiritual message and had to end it before they lost control of the people. After the age of thirty, Jesus taught only Spiritual Christ Consciousness. The religious leaders wanted no part of that in their dogmatic control system. Therefore, the religious leaders did everything they could to suppress the truth of what Jesus was teaching the people and predictably put him to death to stop the truth from becoming the everyday reality.

Unfortunately, this is what many large organizations do. They create false stories they know can easily be embedded in the subconscious mind to control those they want to retain power over. Spend a few moments simply thinking about all the rules and regulations presented to you over your lifetime by ego-driven policies. Does it give you warm feelings of Love, Peace and Light?

Do Affirmations Help

When defining affirmations from a spiritual perspective, they are much different than you might expect. They are not just pleasant comments by someone outside yourself that compliment you or affirm that you are doing a good job or a parent giving a child an affirmation like, "What a nice picture you drew." Affirmations from a spiritual perspective are a statement from Source Energy, "a statement of truth" that you are on track or the correct path to spiritual enlightenment. This statement of truth comes in knowing that you are connected with Source Energy and bringing new visions to Light or awareness as you continue your journey.

There are unlimited resources to bring your visions to the Light of the world. You have many opportunities that are brought before you each day. However, most of them aren't visible unless you are vibrating at a frequency in alignment with the chance. The mind would not understand this without the Spirit guiding it. This spiritual ignorance is why your Spiritual Body alignment is so crucial at this phase of your spiritual discourse with Source Energy.

If we pay close attention, we will create many opportunities by living a Spiritually Conscious Life in Harmony with Source Energy. We already "know this awareness as truth" because, over the past few lessons, you have understood that you mostly manifest what you focus on. Being conscious of what you are thinking aligns you with the necessary events, relationships, specialty books and media to bring positive affirmation into your field of spiritual vision. Others may see the same opportunity as something absurd or unimportant, but from a spiritual perspective, what a Spiritual Being sees is relevant to their path.

Your Original Source Agreement becomes more apparent as you progress with your spiritual lessons or life experiences. As you follow your journey, you begin to have more of what are typically called "déjà vu" occurrences. Most people brush these off as a feeling that they have been somewhere or done something before and dismiss it without digging deeper into what it means. In truth, it is a sign from Source Energy that you are remembering a segment of your Original Source Agreement. Is this now an "aha moment" for you? It should be!

When you become aware or conscious of your Original Source Agreement by paying close attention to your intentions in your Mental Body, you will find Love, Peace and Light while others around you see fear, conflict and darkness.

This is an important lesson to bring to your consciousness. If you want to grow spiritually and exponentially, increase your energy vibration by listening closely to the Source Energy affirmations presented to you in the subtle ways you are now beginning to understand openly. When we finally "get it," the misconceptions of the old Mental Body that were once rooted in Physical Body misalignment and fear will drop away entirely, and you will begin to consciously tell the difference between a problem and a challenge in life.

Why Do Challenges Seem Easier Than Problems

When you observe something happening and view it as a problem, these so-called problems anchor in your mind as a negative story, aligning with the lower vibration of a victimization mentality. From this limited Physical Body alignment perspective, a challenge is typically viewed based on some old experience. Whatever resultant aspect was realized in the past is brought into the present; therefore, the person assumes the future will have the same problematic ending. This scenario is just another manipulation realized on the illusionary screen of the problematic mind that constantly lives in the past. Remember, the past never equals the future. The false idea that the future directly reflects the past is part of the unconscious mind and will not serve you well in the present moment.

As our vibration increases and we live from the Higher Self perspective of a Spiritual Body alignment, we understand without doubt that all challenges are nothing more than tests. Therefore, when a challenge (test) arrives, we can accept it for what it is and prepare ourselves for the solution to appear. When we consciously view a challenge from this spiritual perspective, we have the power of Source Energy within to bring a solution to the forefront of the facts as they indeed are, as opposed to the way it's believed to be by the false story of the mind. All challenges in life arise because of something that you or someone close to you needs to learn or experience to bring the positive higher vibration to the forefront of your reality. The typical Physically aligned person cannot understand this truth.

If you realize you are about to experience a part of life based on your Original Source Agreement plan, you have different thoughts about what actions are required to deal with the challenge. If you eliminate the word "problem" from your mental vocabulary, the mind will not cloud your vision for a solution. The smokescreen of the lower energy vibration idea that you have no spiritual control over any form-based manifestation is Super-ego attracting to you what will not serve your Highest Self perspective of life. There is no such thing as a problem; problems are in the mind!

By bringing the Light of Spirit to any situation, you understand what the statement "there is a spiritual solution to every problem" means. This reality can be very confusing for someone still bouncing back and forth from Spiritual Body to Physical Body alignment.

When you finally bring your true purpose to light and live a life based on your Original Source Agreement, challenges will no longer arrive to test your spiritual awareness. At this point of enlightenment, you will realize that nothing outside of your true Spiritual Self can affect you because you know without doubt that you are a Spiritual Being. Yes, the body may be affected by some other physical aspect of an event that is taking place in the physical realm, but it will not affect your true Spiritual Being. Spiritual Being realization is not something the Super-ego wants you to experience because that would mean you have transcended the physical body reality of life and embedded in the Divine Oneness of the Universe.

When you finally understand that you are the only one who can change the present moment, you will see how easy it is to change a negative thought into a positive action that will always serve your well-being at the energy level meant to experience it. Change your thoughts, and you will change the impact of life!

Is It Reality Only Based Upon How I Think

Strictly from a Physical Body perspective, how you see your life unfolding results from how you think. Now is an excellent time to remind you that the definition of life situation is living the illusion of a Physical Body or form-based reality known as your lifetime. This reality means the birth and death of the physical vessel during this incarnation. Conversely, your life is the Divine Spiritual Life, which is eternal and rooted in non-thought, the present moment. It is understood to be everlasting and about what the Mental Body can comprehend based upon your energy vibration.

Returning to the life situation you are currently living in this incarnation of physical form, you are living a societal reality of form-based thought with a limited perspective typically based on false beliefs and reference to what other egos have taught you to be true. It limits you to what is possible in your life situation and does not lend itself well to the idea of non-thought. Most of society would judge you as unstable or delusional if you were to tell them that you live in a world of non-thought to make all your decisions in life situations. I'm not saying you should not speak your truth; I am merely saying consider the audience before you attempt to take them on a journey of the Spiritually Enlightened Self.

We live in an ego-based society where everything and everyone is typically judged because of their beliefs rather than simply by their actions. This limited perspective is rather sad and is all rooted in the Mental Body idea of duality and separation. Keeping people locked into the false notion of being only the Physical Body ensures that the control mechanism remains in place and the rulers of the land can keep everyone locked in the prison of a rule-based society. If you disobey the rules, you are judged by a system of egos, sentenced and incarcerated for a time based upon whatever physical timeframe the same controllers have deemed sufficient for your punishment. This system is the perfect authoritarianism situation, where the people believe they are free but are only allowed a limited perspective of what life truly is.

One would say that we are free to do whatever we want, including choosing what religion we decide to follow. However, in truth, we are prisoners of the religious beliefs or rules of said religions. Therefore, if you are religious, you follow some combination of religious-based right and wrong, which is not always in Harmony with the governmental control structure that is in place based on your geographic location. This system is all rooted in separation and meant to give you the false impression that there is a those against them reality or a limiting rule-based reality of life. This separation is egotistic-driven and limits your life situation and accomplishments based on what others decide is best for you. Unfortunately, the world's mass consciousness or energy vibration has not increased to a level of spiritual understanding to dispel this false illusion, even though we now live in a Fourth Dimension reality of life.

Most societal government control policies still hold the old paradigm of Third Dimension reality at the forefront of their thinking. They use the Physical Body alignment of separation to control the masses. This limited perspective causes them to think there is a separation between political parties, and they don't know what Oneness means. This misunderstanding is absurd to the spiritual seeker looking for a way out of this egotistic control paradigm.

Can I Change My Thoughts to Change My Life

It's essential always to remember that your life situation is not your actual eternal life. In this incarnation or life situation you are now experiencing in human form, you are part of a mass consciousness that includes the world and the stories of the various societal or geographic influences that go along with any group-think manifestation. Life situation is merely the top layer of life that is experienced very much like swimming on the surface of an ocean. A Life based on this limited perspective is, at best, a false representation of reality.

When you are grounded in the level of Spirituality that allows you to experience the depths of your True Self and the pure Source Energy found at the deepest levels of reality, you step away from the limited perspective of life situation and live your life based upon the higher vibration of Spiritual Being realization. This Spiritual realization is the God-Self revealed to you in the present moment of silence or non-thought. There is no more extraordinary place to be than eternally connected to this life force of the Highest Self realization. When you are committed to living a lifestyle that allows you to truly feel the God-Self communication at this level of awareness, your perception of life shifts extensively.

When you recruit the mind to serve the Soul, you begin thinking based upon listening to the non-thoughts of the Highest Self and no longer rely on the influences outside yourself to make decisions. You are a Spiritual Being having a human experience, but never allow yourself to be arrogant about that realization of self. Therefore, even though the Super-ego will continue to test you to regain control of your Mental Body, you will vibrate at a high enough frequency to dismiss the mental urge to slip backward.

However, if you feel doubt creeping into your decision-making, it's because you have momentarily shifted back into Physical Body alignment. But, because of your spiritual practice up to this moment, you will be able to discern when the shift occurs, and you will be able to get back on track in a heartbeat.

By shifting your Mental Body to being a servant of the Spiritual Body, you can shift your perspective to the Highest Self realization in everything you choose to take action on. The shift or realization is different from simply changing your thoughts; it is embracing your True Personality to its fullest.

Most would argue that replacing a negative thought with a positive one is all that is necessary to stay centered in Conscious Clarity. However, this is a false reality of the Super-ego's final attempt to regain control. This manipulation can be very misleading to the young spiritual seeker. It's not replacing a negative thought for a positive thought that matters; it's more the message's intent and how it affects your perception of reality.

By aligning with the Spiritual Body at the forefront of every action you contemplate, you become aware of the limitless possibilities you have before you and the outside influences that bring perceived happiness. This spiritual awareness or Conscious Clarity of thought and action is essential for your overall well-being development.

What Does All This Have to Do with My Happiness

Joy is your natural state of Being and aligns with the Divine plan for the Universe. One of your purposes is to stay aligned with this Joy and spread happiness worldwide. Every human being is meant to be happy and fulfilled with limitless Abundance, but the mind, often controlled by the Super-ego, drifts away from the Joyful life of your destiny.

The way you experience life is a direct reflection of how you perceive your True Personality. The Higher Self realized state of Being is always in alignment with the higher vibrations of Joy and happiness. Even though outside occurrences influence happiness in societal life, they cannot change your inner natural state of Joy. The Spiritual Self understands this entirely and has no fear of outside influences. However, the Super-ego will continue attempting to cloud your Conscious Clarity of this fact.

By now, you are living most of the time with the Spiritual Body at the forefront of your life, but the Super-ego is strong-willed. It will not surrender as quickly as the lower self ego. It will try to control you; you mustn't fall for its trickery. When you feel the Kundalini Energy slowing, this is a sign that your Super-ego has in some way influenced you. It will be subtle but an effective distraction from truth or Conscious Clarity of Self.

Never doubt that the kingdom of Heaven is within you. You are the Joy of the Universe and have the Divine power to overcome any manipulations your Super-ego throws at you. The more you acknowledge the sneaky presence of Super-ego, the more you will raise your energy vibration. It is in the Kundalini energy flowing through you that suppresses the manipulations of the Super-ego. Therefore, keep Kundalini energy vibrating at the Highest Self level, and you will destroy the manipulations as quickly as they arise. By increasing your energy vibration to the level of Highest Self awareness, the Super-ego will surrender to your Highest Self reality and eventually phase out completely.

You have traveled far in your quest for Spiritual Enlightenment, and now is the time to allow what you have discovered to fall into place naturally. You have the power to overcome any perceived diversity in your life, and it will be evident to you that you can and will create a life of Joy and happiness destined to experience. Let your Spiritual Body guide your path and your old paradigm of self-limiting challenges will disappear forever.

Can You Define Your Self-Limiting Challenges

Even though you are now vibrating at a higher energy level than ever before, you will still experience the influences of Super-ego occasionally. These influences can be very challenging for someone not consciously pursuing Spiritual Body alignment daily. It's easy to fall back into self-limiting beliefs that challenge your life because you are sometimes unconsciously focused on what you do not want rather than what you do want. Unconscious behavior creates a clouded perspective and diminishes your spiritual awareness when you fall back into old paradigms that have controlled you most of your lifetime. JUST STOP IT!

Stop whatever you are doing manipulated by Super-ego and get back on track. Don't dwell on the fact that you momentarily lapsed back into the control of the Super-ego. If you do, you will satisfy the Super-ego's intention to revert you to Physical Body alignment. If thoughts stream through your mind that produce negative questions or uncertainty, you are indeed falling for this old trick of the Super-ego. Never question your Spiritual Body alignment based on the false illusion of what is happening around you.

Remember, at first, it will take a strong sense of True Self to align you with Spirit on a Conscious Clarity level of understanding. The proper alignment is not always easy, especially for someone older in Earth years, because the illusion has such a firm hold on your reality. Be patient and allow the Spiritual Body alignment to develop at its own pace.

There is always a hidden purpose for falling back into the Super-ego's control dynamic to strengthen your conscious awareness of the True Self. Just laugh it off and see the manipulation for what it is. Then, get anchored back into your Spiritual Body alignment awareness and continue your journey. Now is an essential time as you begin to experience the power of your Conscious Clarity reality. When you are conscious of what is happening around you and consciously thinking spiritually, you will find it only takes a moment to check in and bring awareness into the Light!

Earlier, I mentioned challenges arise when you unconsciously focus on what you do not want. When you focus in a manner not in alignment with your purpose, challenges will be presented to you that bring you back to your purpose.

Example: If you have focused on something with the benefits serving your ego first, you will surely be disappointed when the outcome is negative. However, if you focus the energy spiritually, where the action centers upon assisting or serving others first, you will be rewarded with assistance from

Source Energy. The action will have a positive outcome that aligns with your purpose and the Original Source Agreement.

Don't bring challenges to yourself by making the mistake of putting your needs in front of others while silently asking for assistance from Source Energy. Your purpose will be revealed to you at increased levels of energy vibration each time you take action based on how you may be of service to others. Remember why you are here!

Chapter 3 Suggestions - Keeping the Faith During Life Challenges

We typically get so wrapped up in our big-picture plan for our life that we do not listen to the clues that come to us from Spiritual Guidance. When we align with Source Energy and the Divine Plan already in place, life flows effortlessly, and greatness is achieved.

- We can achieve greatness by focusing on what we can do in each moment while listening intentionally to the guidance sent to us during the silent moments of meditative awareness.

- There are always multiple ways to perceive a situation mentally in the illusion of form-based reality. But when it comes to it, there is only one path to take from a Spiritual perspective. When aligned with Source Energy, challenges are met with open arms because the reality of a lesson coming is more potent than any adverse reaction the Super-ego may impose on you. Stay alert and see the spiritual beauty of every life situation on your path; have faith that a solution will present itself in due time.

- True Self, the Highest Self or God-Realized Self, will never lie to you. Purity is at the True Self understanding energy level, not the lower self level. Never question the awareness brought to you by listening to the guidance from Source Energy if you want to have an abundant life filled with a Spiritual Body alignment and balanced well-being.

- If someone tells you that you have a mental illness because you do not follow their academic guidelines of an acceptable societal judgment of your mental state, say thank you and move on or ask them to explain their diagnosis in Spiritual terms.

- One of the reasons we are here today is to continue the healing process; otherwise, we would no longer be here. We would not return to bring another lesson to the enlightenment of Conscious Clarity unless we meant to provide the lesson. You are currently at the exact energy vibration level you need to be! The proof is that you are vibrating at that frequency - NOW.

- Knowing that there is a Divine Master Plan, which you have agreed to before coming into this current body, will anchor your faith. You Know you are a Spiritual Being; following that wisdom, your daily life experiences align with Source Energy. By keeping your Four Body System aligned with the Spiritual Body at the forefront of every experience, you will learn to witness life as the observer and stay focused on this perception.

- Monarchs created religions out of fear of losing control of the people. The primary basis for establishing the religion was an ego-driven, fear-based dogma that still controls a majority of the population today. When fear is the root of keeping people controlled, they follow the leaders without questioning the information. However, in Spiritual teaching, only Love is honestly presented. Many religions attempt to use both in a mixture of duality to satisfy the egoist control dogmas of the past. How arrogant!

- When you observe something happening and view it as a problem, these so-called problems anchor in your mind as a negative story, aligning with the lower vibration of a victimization mentality. From this limited Physical Body alignment perspective, a challenge is typically viewed based on some old experience. Whatever resultant aspect was realized in the past is brought into the present; therefore, the person assumes the future will have the same problematic ending. This scenario is just another manipulation realized on the illusionary screen of the problematic mind that constantly lives in the past. Remember, the past never equals the future. The false idea that the future directly reflects the past is part of the unconscious mind and will not serve you well in the present moment.

- All challenges in life arise because of something that you or someone close to you needs to learn or experience to bring the positive higher vibration to the forefront of your reality. The typical Physically aligned person cannot understand this truth.

- We live in an ego-based society where everything and everyone is typically judged because of their beliefs rather than simply by their actions. This limited perspective is rather sad and is all rooted in the Mental Body idea of duality and separation. Keeping people locked into the false notion of being only the Physical Body ensures that the control mechanism remains in place and the rulers of the land can keep everyone locked in the prison of a rule-based society. If you disobey the rules, you are judged by a system of egos, sentenced and incarcerated for a time based upon whatever physical timeframe the same controllers have deemed sufficient for your punishment. This system is the perfect authoritarianism situation, where the people believe they are free but are only allowed a limited perspective of what life truly is.

- Most societal government control policies still hold the old paradigm of Third Dimension reality at the forefront of their thinking. They use the Physical Body alignment of separation to control the masses. This limited perspective causes them to think there is a separation between political parties, and they don't know what Oneness means. This misunderstanding is absurd to the spiritual seeker looking for a way out of this egotistic control paradigm.

- When you are grounded in the level of Spirituality that allows you to experience the depths of your True Self and the pure Source Energy found at the deepest levels of reality, you step away from the limited perspective of life situation and live your life based upon the higher vibration of Spiritual Being realization. This Spiritual Being realization is the God-Self revealed to you in the present moment of silence or non-thought. There is no more extraordinary place to be than eternally connected to this life force of the Highest Self realization. When you are committed to living a lifestyle that allows you to truly feel the God-Self communication at this level of awareness, your perception of life shifts extensively.

It's easy to fall back into self-limiting beliefs that challenge your life because you are sometimes unconsciously focused on what you do not want rather than what you do want. Unconscious behavior creates a clouded perspective and diminishes your spiritual awareness when you fall back into old paradigms that have controlled you most of your lifetime. JUST STOP IT!

Chapter 4
Ask Better Questions

So What's a Better Question

In the previous chapter, you consciously decided to leave the control dynamics of the Super-ego behind most of the time. Continue to consciously check in with your Highest Self daily to ensure you are now living with the Spiritual Body at the forefront of all actions you take in life. Anytime you feel that your Kundalini Energy is not flowing smoothly and that there is a blockage in one of your Chakras, stop your actions and ask yourself if you align with the Spiritual Body.

When you are Spiritually aligned, all actions harmonize with how you may serve others. You agreed to come here to serve others, and if you are not putting service to others first, you are not in alignment with your purpose and Original Source Agreement. When you stay focused on serving others, the challenges in life are minimal and always there to assist you in asking better questions. Questions aligned with "how may I serve" rather than "what's in it for me". You will be amazed at the resultant difference when you focus on asking Spiritually aligned questions.

When you are in complete Harmony with the cosmic potential of Oneness actions, you see how the Super-ego transitions into the Light of Cosmic Intelligence. By bringing your vision to the surface of the Spiritual Body perspective, the results align with spiritual solutions to every challenge you bring to yourself. Yes, you do indeed manifest each challenge that comes your way. This realization is a problematic awakening for most people because they spend most of their time attempting to please themselves first without realizing they are even doing it.

When you stop "doing" for yourself first, you will experience the Divine power of "Being" for others. Being here for others ensures rewards for yourself manifest at a greater level for actions aligned with a Spiritual Purpose. Rewards in Harmony with your Original Source Agreement at this energy vibration level will be abundant. However, the reward will be minimal if you continue flipping back and forth from Spiritual Body to Physical Body alignment. You will need to work hard to achieve the same unique spiritual result. However, when you shift to a "Being for others first" reality, your rewards will be exponential and in alignment with your Original Source Agreement. This Spiritual Body alignment means the resultant factors will also harmonize with a much higher energy vibration, and Abundance will come your way as you never thought possible with little effort on your part.

The next time you create a plan for any new endeavor, check in with your Highest Self before taking action. By checking in with the Highest Self, you ensure the goals you want to achieve come from a Spiritual Body alignment perspective. Remember, you are here to serve others first - your rewards will be miraculous. A quick check-in with the Highest Self will bring your True Purpose to the forefront of your thoughts, and you will experience what it means to have the mind serve the Soul.

Flowing In Spirit Produces Better Questions

The mind is a complex tool meant to serve the Soul first - period, end of story! However, as you discovered in Book One, *Consciously Live What You Feel*, the mind created the ego to serve a Physical Body alignment reality. This Physical Body alignment will do whatever it needs to do to serve the current mass consciousness level of reality; it can be very clever. This manipulation is especially true for someone living the false reality of desperation. The ego will move them to do things that appear to serve others, but the root intention is first to satisfy the "what's in it for me" scenario. Then, as the true hidden root intention is satisfied, the service to others is minimized. The manipulator justifies it by claiming those I served must go alone now without my service to assist them. This process is merely the Super-ego talking; it can be compelling for someone who started with a false intention.

When you are truly living a conscious connection with the Spiritual Body at the forefront of your actions, you will dissolve the Super-ego once and for all. By constantly living a meditative state of Being, you will quickly discover how to check in to ensure you are correctly aligned to achieve a spiritual solution to every challenge. This reality will always serve your Highest Self and others as well. It will bring to Light the true intentions of your attention. This focused attention allows you to ask better questions because your energy vibration is higher. If you recall, all solutions are always available; they are just waiting for you to increase your energy vibration to a level that resonates with the higher-vibrating solution. Therefore, as you discover how to ask better questions, you will naturally align with a resultant factor that is always in Harmony with the Highest Self perspective of what IS.

Through Conscious Clarity of intention and when you are aligned Spiritually, there is no need to be clever or concerned with any outcome. You will understand that you naturally align with your True Purpose and Original Source Agreement. This alignment will ensure you experience a life of Abundance and deep inner peace. And that realization of inner peace will inspire you to fulfill your True Purpose for being here on this planet.

This moment is a beautiful time for you, as you are part of the experience called humanity. You have asked to be here, and the only possible way to live this life situation to its fullest is to "Enlist the mind to serve the Soul." You will ensure a Joyful life filled with Love, Peace and Light by consciously aligning with the Spiritual Body at the forefront of your every action. What more could you ask for than to live a Joyful life daily? Align with this perspective, and you will learn to ask the right questions in Harmony with the best the present moment offers.

How Do I Know My Question Was Poor

The life you are experiencing now reflects the questions you have asked yourself thus far. If you are not experiencing pure Joy from within you, it is a sure sign that you have been asking poor questions or, instead, questions that vibrate at a very low energy vibration. The resultant factors of low-energy questions mirror a Physical Body alignment and a victimization reality. We already know that feeling as though you are a victim of circumstances surrounding you is nothing more than the clever manipulation of the ego.

When we allow ourselves to bring our True Purpose to the forefront of our Being, we begin to understand that we are capable of miracles in every moment of this experience we call life. By bringing our True Purpose to the forefront of our lives, our actions take on an intention aligning with our Original Source Agreement. Nothing is more rewarding than Knowing you are in Harmony with your Highest Self and that all your actions align with how you may serve.

Can you remember, as a young child, the most crucial question to you was WHY? This question was part of your human growth experience. However, how many of you can honestly say the answers to your question "why" was answered from a Spiritual Body perspective? Based on the mass consciousness of the world at the time, every one of you will have a different answer. But for the most part, I believe the answers centered upon a Physical Body or ego perspective of reality.

Most people are afraid to ask questions that have the best chance of changing their perspective on life because of training to believe the half-truths of an ego-based society anchored in Fear. As sad as this may be, rest assured that you have been part of the same illusion that believed the Earth is flat. Until you step out of that illusion and consciously embrace your True Personality, you will continue to experience a resultant factor of low vibrating reality.

When you finally decide to step up your energy vibration to align with the Divine Power of the Universe, your life will evolve in Harmony with your Original Source Agreement.

Do All Answers Lead to More Questions

Your True Personality is always in Spiritual Body alignment and is naturally in Harmony with questions meant to enlighten you to your highest potential. This highest potential is the Highest Self or God-realized perspective of understanding. Therefore, the answers to your Highest Self questions will always concern a Spiritual intention. A Spiritual perspective can be unclear for a person still shifting back and forth from Spiritual Body to Physical Body alignment reality.

On the one hand, Spiritual Body alignment will always guide you to ask questions that will satisfy the reality of Oneness. However, on the other hand, Physical Body alignment will always send you off in a never-ending story of disbelief and doubt, which is a fear-based reality. With this in mind, the questions asked have a low vibrating nature and can only produce another fear-based question. This thinking is typical of our current society and keeps you in a false reality. If you don't believe this is true, turn on your television and watch the news for a few consecutive days. Pay close attention to how everything, especially the commercials, is fear-based.

The mass consciousness of the world has not yet evolved past the limited perspective of a fear-based society. As sad as this may be, it is the reality most people experience because they have been duped into believing everything they see on the news or read in the media is authentic. The Physical Body perspective is all a vast conspiracy to keep people under the control of leaders who do not have their best interests in mind consciously. Right now, our world's progress operates upon a money-controlled philosophy of what is best for people based upon the low-energy vibration of a few corrupt individuals who control the money markets. The world is manipulated daily by these power-hungry tycoons who have a limited perspective of what life is truly all about.

When we allow ourselves to be manipulated and controlled by others, we sacrifice our Highest Self reality. We unconsciously will enable the control mechanisms of low-vibrating governments to make rules and regulations that only have the purpose of controlling the people. These rules and regulations control the reality of a fear-based society and group-think, group-follow mentality. From a spiritual perspective, you will discover that your questions produce a higher vibrating resultant factor when you ask questions based on what's greatest for everyone.

In truth, we all want to live in Harmony with Love, Peace and Light. However, we are discovering more each day about the societal control mechanisms meant to keep us in conflict and stuck within a fear-based society.

What Happens When Questions Are in Conflict

Conflict is always a clever manipulation of something that is outside of you. Never forget how clever the Super-ego can be; it will always attempt to cast doubt into the mind through the unconscious mind. As long as you stay consciously connected with Source Energy, you will see conflict for what it is. Just bask in the beauty of the true Highest Self and allow the low-vibration thoughts of the mind to fall away if they pop in from time to time. It's all part of your testing process to ensure you stay on track and keep the Spiritual Body at the forefront of all action.

If you take the time to consciously observe what is happening around you in your life situation, you will quickly be able to discern truth from illusion. As a Spiritual Being, you have so much to offer this world, so serving your True Purpose and those that have not grown beyond a Physical Body reality is essential. When we observe the actions of everything outside of us, it becomes easy to see that life on Earth is nothing more than a dance of form-based illusion playing out the next scene in a "drama-based" movie. Why not label it a "comedy" instead?

I often wonder how it will be when everyone on the planet awakens to the reality that they are Spiritual Beings having a human experience. In truth, if you are still predominantly focused on the conflict surrounding you, you have not grown to the point spiritually that it is no longer visible to your Spiritual Body awareness. This realization is interesting because those of us who have genuinely seen the Highest Self perspective of life know that everything outside of us is an illusion, but for whatever reason we have, we still choose to fall back once in a while. This reality can be viewed as nothing more than another test to keep us conscious of our reason for being here. So, if you feel your Kundalini Energy flowing freely but conflict is still visible, understand that it only means you need to increase your energy vibration.

Your Highest Self only knows Love; therefore, anything you see surrounding you that you can label as conflict is just Fear in disguise. As you rise above the false reality of Fear, you will find that the moments you spend observing conflict diminish because you no longer have a use for Fear in your life. By being open to whatever comes your way with acceptance and deep inner peace, you will understand the true meaning of enlightenment.

Bring your Highest Self to the dance of life through Conscious Clarity of thought, and you will always feel the Love of which you truly are made. Everything else is a test!

Does Super-ego Always Want Control of My Questions

Everything the mind controls through Physical Body alignment is Super-ego control, including the questions arising from that alignment. If you were to shift your perception of life to a Spiritual Body alignment, you would be vibrating at a Higher Self frequency and able to discern the difference in how questions arise from within you. The Spiritual Body alignment is nothing more than your True Self reaching out to you to guide you through life situations at the level of Conscious Clarity.

The alignment of your Four Body System is the most vital tool to diminish negative questions arising from Super-ego manipulation within the illusion you have placed yourself in. Yes, you have chosen to live the life you are currently living. Your decisions up to this moment have put you in the lifestyle you are presently experiencing, and only you can make a shift to remove the control dynamics of the Super-ego. You have the power within you to experience bliss in every moment of your life, and you decide to bring about change in your life situation at any moment you choose to do so.

If the Super-ego is still manipulating you, you have chosen to allow this in your life experience. There must be some lesson that you still need to learn from a Physical Body alignment. If this were not true, you would not be asking the questions you are currently asking. This reality is hard for the Super-ego to understand because it believes it is better than those surrounding it. It will always attempt to manipulate every life situation so that it is guaranteed to have the last word in every false action you take when you are aligned improperly. The choice is yours - make the permanent shift now! No more excuses; either get yourself appropriately aligned, or you may as well stop reading now and set this book aside until you experience the pain you still need to learn from based upon a Physical Body alignment perspective.

If you wanted to recruit the mind to serve the Soul, you would do so and stop the insanity you are living at this very moment. That which is outside you can never replace the guidance within you. If you are to understand the power within you, it must be brought to the surface of your life experience consciously. Nobody aligned with the Physical Body at the forefront of their actions can achieve true fulfillment in this human experience. The Super-ego wants your mind to continue to doubt and question all guidance from within you.

Never forget, you are not this body. So when will you stop believing the false reality that you are this body? What must happen to finally get you to realign your Four Body System to the reality of spiritual truth? Is it not dark enough for you as yet? Are you not experiencing enough self-imposed mental or physical pain to make the simple shift now? Why are you not ready to shift your perception to a reality aligned with why you came here?

The answer to the above questions is at your Highest Self reality level. So why not shift to Spiritual Body alignment to ensure your perception of life experiences leads to better questions and solutions that come directly from Source Energy rather than the limited perceptions of the misaligned mind?

Does Separation from Ego Lead to Better Questions

The goal is not to separate the Super-ego from your Higher Self. The goal is to consciously keep the Super-ego merged with the Soul so that you can experience life from this higher vibration. When the Super-ego merges with the Higher Self without shifting back and forth from Spiritual Body to Physical Body alignment, you will truly experience what it means to *Consciously Embrace Your True Personality.*

It's easy to say "Just stay Spiritual Body aligned", but the reality is that the older you are in Earth years, the more challenging it is to realign your life completely. This challenge is why shifting your outside relationships to a life situation that harmonizes with like-minded people is essential. As you learn to embody this wonderful world of Spiritual Body alignment into your daily life, you understand that you are not separate from anyone else – you are part of the same Oneness.

The Super-ego loves to place you on a pedestal of being superior to others around you and will place you in situations where you stand out from the crowd. Don't allow this feeling of spiritual power awareness to manipulate you into believing you are special. Yes, you are unique and have been given a set of skills from Source Energy that aligns you with your Original Source Agreement, but that doesn't make you more than anyone else. It makes you blessed with gifts and nothing more. It is your responsibility to develop your gifts to their full spiritual potential. When you realize how blessed you are and how to fulfill your True Purpose, you will understand gratitude's true meaning.

When you approach your life experience from a position of gratitude and acceptance of what is without embellishing it with false beliefs that make your Super-ego feel special, you live a humble life without the need to be in the "limelight" of society. You can accomplish much more by being humble, aware of your gifts, and sharing them with the world for everyone's benefit. You may by now be experiencing a level of energy vibration that aligns you with the Divine power of Source Energy or Highest Self reality. Still, the key is to keep it to yourself as much as possible so that you do not fall back into the control dogma of societal influence.

Often, people at the beginning of their conscious spiritual journey make the mistake of believing they are more than others surrounding them. However, suppose you take your newly discovered Divinity to the understanding level of Knowing who you are. In that case, you quickly find that you can just "BE" who you are and fulfill your Original Source Agreement without the approval of others outside you.

When Super-ego is still making its presence known, it simply means you are still living at some level of doubt, separation and Fear. This arrogance means you still believe you must let others know you are unique because of your gifts instead of simply continuing your Life Purpose mission to fulfill your Original Source Agreement.

By staying consciously centered in the Universal Intelligence's beauty that controls everything in life, you learn to merge your splintered parts of self in Oneness or the I-Am-Ness of life.

How Many Times Have You Questioned the Answers

Anytime you question the guidance you receive from the Highest Self, you bring the Super-ego back into Physical Body alignment. When you are Spiritually aligned, asking questions is followed by immediate action based on the guidance provided to you by Source Energy. There are no follow-up questions to confirm that the guidance received is worthy of action. If you attempt to confirm the guidance, you are simply bringing Super-ego back into the forefront of your current life situation.

Always remember, by aligning your life with the Spiritual Body at the forefront of every question, you live a purpose-driven life. All of life is energy, and your conscious actions to increase your energy vibration allow you to dive deeply into the reality of the Highest Self solutions to any question. Suppose you are second-guessing the solutions presented to you; you are not doing yourself or anyone around you any favors.

Source Energy wants you always to be joyous and have Abundance. It doesn't understand anything else. Joy and Abundance are your natural state of Being on your journey, and anything that diminishes this Divine state of Being is part of the Super-ego's continued testing process.

How many times have you questioned the solutions you received from the guidance from within? For example, think of situations where you have been guided to act but chose not to. It could be something as simple as guidance telling you to take a credit card off your desk and put it in your wallet; you decide to leave it because your Super-ego didn't believe you needed to take it. Then, you drive to town, and a situation arises where you need that credit card to pay for something unexpected. Well, let me assure you, what told you to take the credit card off your desk was guidance, intuition, the voice from within or whatever other label you choose to use for the Source Energy guiding you to take action.

Don't question the guidance when directed to turn left instead of right. Just bring conscious awareness to the forefront and take action based on what appears to be the opposite of what your mind wants you to do. There is a spiritual reason for everything; that reason does not need to be understood, explained or confirmed in the present moment – move quickly into the action presented to you based upon the guidance received.

By living life from a state of Being prepared to change direction at any given moment based upon guidance received, you will discover a realm of reality that brings you in Harmony with your Original Source Agreement and finally begin to fulfill your True Purpose in life.

If Answers Confuse Me, What Do I Do

Nobody is immune to the clever tricks of the Super-ego. Therefore, you must check in with your Highest Self regularly to be sure you are consciously aware of your current body alignment. If you think thoughts that are not inspiring or

Spiritually aligned, it is a good sign that you shifted back to a Physical Body alignment point of view.

Solutions or answers to your questions will never confuse you if you are Spiritually aligned. The solutions will be crystal clear and direct you to act with Conscious Clarity of thought. Yes, when we are correctly aligned, life becomes easy and relaxed, and we move forward without confusion. It's as if you are an artist who sees a vision in your mind and then begins to paint the canvas of life based on this clear vision. It's hard to explain in words; it's more something you need to feel or experience to Know you are on the right track. You will immediately know the difference when this feeling or experience embeds itself into your consciousness.

When we feel confused by the answers or solutions to our questions, the Super-ego always brings another test to ensure we stay on track spiritually and mentally. What you think about will eventually manifest into your life situation experience, so be careful about the thoughts behind your actions. Everything that is physically real was at one time a vision, and then that vision manifested into reality based on thoughts and actions.

The old saying "action speaks louder than words" is not always accurate because words can lead to actions that are misrepresented unconsciously or based on false beliefs. This paradox can be very confusing if you are still bouncing in and out of a Spiritual Body outlook on life. That is why constant conscious awareness of thought is so important. By bringing your awareness to a conscious state of reality, you allow spiritual guidance to manifest fully to its highest potential energy vibration.

At this point in the *Conscious Clarity Energy Process*™, you are less susceptible to the tricks of the Super-ego, but be aware that it is still there, just waiting for the opportunity to pounce. You will know when this lower energy vibration shows its clever face because you will feel confused and uncertain of the direction or subsequent actions you should take to bring your vision to Light!

Therefore, pay close attention to thoughts that continue to flood into your life situation, influenced by something outside your true Highest Self. As you continue to grow spiritually, you will experience less of a temptation to revert to old egoist actions. Focus on your alignment and allow the visions and guidance to keep you on track.

Who Said It All Has to Make Sense Anyhow

Whether or not Spirituality makes sense to you is crucial because it speaks to the reality of perception. It still comes down to how you are aligned, spiritually or physically. A misaligned mind or Physical Body alignment will have a completely different reality than a mind aligned spiritually, whereas it serves the Soul or Highest Self perspective of life.

If you are still "trying" to make sense of how life situations evolve around you, then you are not "Being" life; you are "doing" life. To truly experience life to its fullest, you must live from a Highest Self perspective that understands (without doubt) why you have the human experience you currently have. This Highest Self perspective only knows Love and the unlimited possibilities available when you are Spiritually aligned. From a Spiritual Body alignment perspective, there is no separation or judgment of what is. Each present moment IS what it IS; this acceptance is all part of "Being Love".

When you live a life of Love rather than Fear, you pay attention to the silence or space between the thoughts, also known as the gap, instead of overanalyzing everything around you. The mind wants to figure everything out because it needs to "make sense" of what is happening around you. However, the spirit accepts what it is and monitors feelings to bring an enriched spiritual perspective to each moment. Once feelings are accepted, the result is "Being" beyond those feelings. "Being" is also understood as living life based upon Knowing and ultimately brings about the Highest Self perspective in each moment.

When you stop "thinking" about each happening, you begin to experience the present moment for what it is and no longer associate a future resultant or judgment about what the possible resultant factor will be. You live a life beyond the constraints of figuring it all out! "Being" is truly difficult for a Physically aligned person. Each moment within a Physical Body perspective of life aligns with ego doing rather than simply allowing life to unfold as it is.

I don't mean you will enjoy each moment if it is challenging; it simply means let it BE what it is and then move into the Highest Self state of consciousness. By being conscious of what is happening around you, you quickly accept the facts for what they are and learn to deal with life as it comes to you. By staying connected with your Highest Self in this way, you allow the wisdom of each experience to bring you closer to the energy vibration of learning from experience. Therefore, by experiencing life, you no longer cater to the Super-ego's manipulation of the facts surrounding you in actual spiritual reality.

When you truly understand this spiritual perspective of "what is", you align your actions with your Original Source Agreement and step up your energy to the reality of facts rather than the illusion of a false belief system.

Are My Beliefs Guiding My Questions

If your beliefs still guide your questions, you are not living a life based upon the higher energy vibration of Love. A "fear factor" is still in the back of your mind. You may not be conscious of this, as the Super-ego is very clever and will do whatever it can to hold you back from the solutions always available to you in the spiritual realm of silence.

All beliefs are Mental Body based and the duality of fear-based dogma. Fear anchors the false perception of reality in life. When you focus on what you believe, you place a smokescreen around your KNOWING. Don't allow the outside influences of your life situation to cloud the truth from your consciousness. You are far more than even your Super-ego will ever allow you to "believe" you are. By limiting yourself, you do nothing to achieve the full potential of your life.

For example, you could look upon yourself as a leader who shows people how to get in touch with the true Highest Self, or you can remain a victim of those around you in the control dogma of our current mass consciousness idea of what life is. All I am saying is ask yourself "Where you are in life at this very moment?", then prepare to be honest with yourself when you realize how you got to this point in the first place. You may quickly find that those around you have influenced you and have held you back from your True

Purpose for being here. Conversely, you may have taken a step in the right direction by acting on those feelings that have always been there to guide you in spiritual truth. Remember, the past does not equal the future; make Spiritual choices!

When you live a life based upon Spiritual Body alignment, you don't need permission from anyone outside yourself to bring a new vision to the world. Do you think any great leaders or innovators of technology followed what others directed them to do? They don't care if they "fit in" to the status quo; they know deep within themselves that they are more than just a body existing in blind obedience to societal rules and regulations. The world is not flat; wrap your arms around your greatness, and you will experience a well-rounded life that steps up your energy to the God-realized Being you are. You can step out of your false "belief system" and bring in the Light of Universal Intelligence, which guides all of life from the inner beauty of Spiritual Body alignment.

Do Questions Come from Mind or Spirit

Whether your questions come from mind or spirit depends again on your Four Body System alignment. Alignment can be very confusing for the mind if it has not yet aligned fully with the Spiritual Body at the forefront of your life. It would be best if you anchored into the subconscious that ALL solutions to every challenge in life are available in the

Universal Intelligence of KNOWING. In other words, the solutions are ready and waiting for you to ask the questions!

If you have not yet brought Knowing to the forefront of your daily life, you will have difficulty answering whether questions come from the mind or spirit. From a misaligned Mental Body perspective, the questions come from the mind based upon the illusion of problematic thinking. Yes, the misaligned mind believes in problems. All problems are a false reality based upon false beliefs that have either been drummed into your subconscious by outside influences or a limited thought process of scarcity and Fear. Even though you may be vibrating at a higher frequency by now, Super-ego will always be ready to trick you into slipping back into the illusion of beliefs.

When you fully understand the difference between believing and knowing, you will align so your questions come from a Spiritual Body alignment perspective.

> Example: Negative results of an expectation can be measured in two ways if you anticipated a particular outcome in life. A misaligned Four Body System will bring the victim back, and you will feel bad and then create a story of how you were a victim of not having your anticipated result materialize. This scenario is Super-ego stepping down your energy to the victim's

level again. Don't let your life situation create a smokescreen around your Original Source Agreement destiny.

A Spiritually aligned Four Body System will view mental disappointment as a positive factor. Properly aligned, you will accept the outcome by saying, "Interesting - that's not the outcome I anticipated; there must be something better coming that I am not aware of right now." Accepting what IS allows you to ask better questions rather than making up a story about why the outcome differs from the anticipation.

When aligned Spiritually, you always accept what is and then decide whether or not additional action is necessary, which makes the better question a simple yes or no answer. Therefore, if you answer yes, additional action is required - you will guided by spirit in the form of a better question. If you answered no, you live with the result of your original question and learn from the previous actions. Whether more action is necessary or not does not change your inner peace and you go on with your life in the present reality of what IS.

All resultant factors of your life are merely tests for you to witness. Remember, nothing is ever happening to you. Life situations are simply happening around you. Your life is meaningful, not the illusion of your life situation. A spiritually aligned person always has a more profound understanding, which brings solutions to challenges differently than seen on the surface of life's situational reality.

How to Handle the Answers

An answer to a question is that Source Energy is bringing you to the solution of a challenge you should take action on. The Higher Self focus on life is always in alignment with solution-based reality. When you understand that every life situation is merely an opportunity for Spiritual Growth, you will consciously integrate the Original Source Agreement into your daily experiences. In other words, once the Light comes on – you will have the opportunity to stay grounded in the awareness of the reality of a Spiritual Being. Therefore, solutions present themselves miraculously without thought.

When Spirituality is at the forefront of every action you take in this Earth school, your reality blossoms into Conscious Clarity of Higher Self perspective. The questions change; therefore, the answers or solutions become crystal clear when Source Energy presents the solutions to you. Nobody is immune to the reality of Spiritual Growth; however, the Super-ego does not make it easy to make the final transition into the Spiritual Body alignment. Therefore, you must always stay conscious and live the observer's life to keep your Higher Self at the forefront of all actions you consider in each moment.

As you make the final shift into there being a "spiritual solution to every challenge", you will embody your True Personality and drop the Super-ego interference. If you are still experiencing the influence of the Super-ego in your life, perhaps it is time for you to take additional steps to bring the Conscious Clarity of your Higher Self to the surface so that everyone around you can see the Light that you are. Step up your energy vibration, and you will stop doubting the solutions or answers to the questions that arise from your current state of Being. OM Chanting is one of the extraordinary tools available to increase your energy vibration quickly.

OM is the reality of the Universe brought to you in the vibrational reality of Oneness or of all creation. By chanting the word OM, you bring all the cosmic powers of this current moment to the level of creation in Oneness. Oneness is not something to experience with doubt of the Highest Self; OM Chanting is the experience of anchoring in the Divine power of the Universal Oneness, which dominates a True Personality perspective of life.

When you chant OM, the body releases its physical reality, and Source Energy's Divine energy empowers you in Oneness.

Always Live From the Higher Self Questions

Each question brings you closer to the Highest Self reality or a life as a God-realized Being. The ultimate goal is to heal the fragmented parts of the Self that have been blocking your full potential. The Oneness of the Universal wants you to become whole again. Therefore, your energy vibration is about to step up another quantum leap in the Spiritual reality of living your True Purpose every day.

When you begin to experience life from the Higher Self perspective, you no longer ask as many questions. You make statements based upon the Highest Self KNOWING! Your focus is always on "how may I serve today" rather than what is my reward for assisting others on their journey. When you finally readjust your Four Body System alignment to the level of Higher Self vibration, you understand what it means to be both the student and teacher. You bring a deep Knowing to the vibration level or mass consciousness of the world, and you live each day in the service of others.

There will always be various methodologies of schooling that allow people to pick and choose what resonates with them mostly. However, all teachings collectively end at the same place of "God Realization", where you finally admit that you are part of the magnificence of Oneness. In this Oneness, we allow our full potential to blossom and bring Light to the lower vibrating aspects of Super-ego and the limited perspective of that lifestyle. When you Know you are part of the Divine Light of the Universe, simply having a human experience, you place all your energy on providing spiritual action to everyone on your path. This action brings about a feeling of empowerment, and you realize you can increase the mass consciousness of the world.

A Higher Self question is another step up the vibrational truth of the Highest Self reality. When you consistently live your life from this perspective, bringing in your Divine energy, you break away from the form-based limited perspective of the mind. By living centered in Being, you stop doing and begin to experience life as it has always meant to be in Harmony with your Original Source Agreement. You become the messenger and share the Cosmic Energy of all life and bring an understanding that allows you to make statements instead of asking questions; at this level of understanding, you no longer place limits on your Divine actions.

The Super-ego will always seek control over you; you created it, and it is not about to release you fully into your Original Source Agreement destiny. It wants you to always have doubt in the back of the unconscious mind and stay in a world controlled by others for selfish purposes. It will attempt to move you to take action on false realities that appear spiritual on the surface. However, when you dig deeply into the intention to take action, you will quickly feel the energy drop if you are not true to your Life Purpose for being here. Always pay close attention to the energy flowing through the body and embrace your *True Personality* by feeling the extraordinary peace and Joy that emanates from your Highest Self reality.

When you are Spiritually aligned, all fears disappear, and your True Purpose flows with Divine Light!

Methods for Better Questions

No matter how highly you are vibrating, you must remember that ALL questions are part of the illusion of either ego or Super-ego. If you are still asking questions, you do not realize that all the solutions await you. The solutions are merely lying dormant or in a state of Physical Body alignment at some level of lower energy vibration based upon a life situation and an illusionary reality.

You will no longer ask questions once you consciously live life from the Spiritual Body perspective. You will make statements of Spiritual fact when challenges arise in your life situation. Conversely, when the Super-ego controls your actions, your life will remain fragmented until you heal that part of your life based upon the separation of the Highest Self reality. In other words, you will stay a prisoner of the physically aligned Mental Body and live a life based upon the illusion of false beliefs that will continue to hold you back from becoming your true Highest Self.

Consciously act on what is holding you back from your True Purpose reality by continuously checking in with your Spiritual guidance reality. When you finally accept that your life situation is fragmented based upon a flawed or false belief system, you will open up your conscious awareness to a higher state of reality. Because you are still asking questions, the form-based human is driving your life. By at least asking better questions, which ultimately only means asking questions in Harmony with your current energy vibration, you begin to see patterns evolving in your life situation. Once you start to recognize the patterns from a spiritual perspective, you can dismiss the false beliefs from your Mental Body.

Remember, the basis for all healing is found deeply within the splintered part of you. When you step into the Light of the Highest Self reality, you see that you are merely a speck of the totality of the Cosmic Reality of all life. This Cosmic Reality is not someplace a physically aligned Mental Body can witness. With Cosmic Reality vibrating at a much higher frequency than the typical Mental Body, it's no wonder the latter cannot comprehend its existence. Therefore, when stuck in the false reality of a lower energy vibration, you are controlled by the five-sense perspective of life. You do not realize there is more to life than what you observe on the surface.

When you finally shift to an adequately aligned Spiritual Body reality, you release the mind only to serve the Spiritual Body guidance, which is in alignment with your Highest Self and begin to fulfill your True Purpose for being here. Never doubt that you are a Spiritual Being having a human experience. Feel the Knowing guidance that emulates through your Source Energy connection with the Universe. Anything less is a form of the Super-ego control mechanism holding you back from consciously embracing your True Personality. The True Personality is Spiritual, never Physical.

Chapter 4 Suggestions - Ask Better Questions

As part of the Spiritual Evolutionary Process, we discover that we see life differently as we increase our energy vibration. Questions that arise at a low vibration of the beginning seeker focus on lower vibrational awareness of what's important in life. As we grow spiritually, we discover how our life situations have either held us back or moved us forward. Only you know how much time you have wasted on poor questions. Being honest with yourself as you delve into the deeper aspects of self will be of the most significant value to you during your life of service to others.

- When you are Spiritually aligned, all actions harmonize with how you may serve others. You agreed to come here to serve others, and if you are not putting service to others first, you are not in alignment with your purpose and Original Source Agreement.

- The goal is not to separate the Super-ego from your Higher Self. The goal is to consciously keep the Super-ego merged with the Soul so that you can experience life from this higher vibration. When the Super-ego merges with the Higher Self without shifting back and forth from Spiritual Body to Physical Body alignment, you will truly experience what it means to *Consciously Embrace Your True Personality.*

- When Super-ego is still making its presence known, it simply means you are still living at some level of doubt, separation and Fear. This arrogance means you still believe you must let others know you are unique because of your gifts instead of simply continuing your Life Purpose mission to fulfill your Original Source Agreement.

- Anytime you question the guidance you receive from the Highest Self, you bring the Super-ego back into Physical Body alignment. When you are Spiritually aligned, asking questions is followed by immediate action based on the guidance provided to you by Source Energy. There are no follow-up questions to confirm that the guidance received is worthy of action. If you attempt to confirm the guidance, you are simply bringing Super-ego back into the forefront of your current life situation.

- By living life from a state of Being prepared to change direction at any given moment based upon guidance received, you will discover a realm of reality that brings you in Harmony with your Original Source Agreement and finally begin to fulfill your True Purpose in life.

- If you have not yet brought Knowing to the forefront of your daily life, you will have difficulty answering whether questions come from the mind or spirit. From a misaligned Mental Body perspective, the questions come from the mind based upon the illusion of problematic thinking. Yes, the misaligned mind believes in problems. All problems are a false reality based upon false beliefs that have either been drummed into your subconscious by outside influences or a limited thought process of scarcity and Fear.

- An answer to a question is that Source Energy is bringing you to the solution of a challenge you should take action on. The Higher Self focus on life is always in alignment with solution-based reality. When you understand that every life situation is merely an opportunity for Spiritual

Growth, you will consciously integrate the Original Source Agreement into your daily experiences. In other words, once the Light comes on – you will have the opportunity to stay grounded in the awareness of the reality of a Spiritual Being. Therefore, solutions present themselves miraculously without thought.

- A Higher Self question is another step up the vibrational truth of the Highest Self reality. When you consistently live your life from this perspective, bringing in your Divine energy, you break away from the form-based limited perspective of the mind.

By living centered in Being, you stop doing and begin to experience life as it has always meant to be in Harmony with your Original Source Agreement.

Chapter 5

Know What You Deserve

What Do I Deserve

You are a limitless Spiritual Being having a human experience sent here to heal the fragmented parts of your Soul. You are part of Source Energy and are, in fact, a formless, never-ending continuation of the creation of all life. Therefore, whatever form-based body you choose to use in the present moment is only being used to heal that fragmented part of you that questions the validity of who you truly are. You deserve unconditional Love, as it is the guiding Light within us that drives the physical body to take action from the perspective of Spiritual Oneness. It would be best to spiritually anchor this fundamental Spiritual Truth into your essence to understand your Divine destiny.

What you deserve is brought to you miraculously through the Divine power of Knowing - not doing! This chapter is devoted to keeping the Knowing awareness at the forefront of your daily reality.

It would help if you stopped thinking you are less than you are and started accepting that the formless part of you housed within the physical Being is guiding your life.

Therefore, the life situations you are experiencing are all part of the cleansing process of the Soul that drives your Original Source Agreement's purpose for being here.

The simple truth is that you, as a Spiritual Being, are the essence of Love, Peace and Light. Once you acknowledge this truth, you will see how your Life Purpose makes this vision real. As you shift your energy vibration toward your Highest Self reality, you begin to experience the rewards of living this current life situation from a perspective aligned with every other Soul. The Oneness felt when fully aligned with Source Energy is beyond the understanding of the typical mind. Therefore, you must continue to increase your energy vibration to experience all that is available through living at the Highest Self reality of life.

What would you take action if you knew that you could not fail? Would you continue to doubt, question, or analyze every possible aspect of the present moment? Would you continue to live your life based upon false beliefs anchored into your mind by outside influences that want to control you? Would you continue to bring the false beliefs of others with a negative outlook on life along with you on your journey? How you answer these questions is determined by your current energy vibration.

When you shift to a fully-integrated, Spiritually aligned Four Body System guiding your daily life situations, your life changes from mediocre to miraculous. The resultant aspects of your actions will begin to represent your new focus as a Spiritual Being, and you will experience guidance that resonates with you at this Highest Self reality. This shift means you will live as the God-realized Spiritual Being that you are instead of limiting yourself to the control dogma of a fear-based ego.

The egoistic mind still wants to convince you that you cannot possibly be a God-realized Spiritual Being. This ego-driven part of you is your Soul's fragmented part, which requires healing. The simple truth in the healing is discovering how to keep the Super-ego out of your life so that you can *Consciously Embrace Your True Personality* reality.

How Do I Define What I Deserve

The first part of defining what you deserve is understanding who is asking the questions that keep coming to your mind. There's a spiritual disconnect if the Super-ego is asking the questions, and, as you have already discovered, if you are still asking questions, it is the Super-ego speaking to you. This realization can be very confusing in your Spiritual Transformative Education process, mainly because there is a significant difference between what you want and what you need. By increasing your energy vibration, you will slowly but surely remove want from your life and focus on the needs of others.

When you are in service to others, the self-absorbed personality is released, and the Highest Self reveals itself fully. This shift from wanting for yourself to being of service to those in need is the complete opposite of what you have programmed to DO all your life to this point. It's not easy to remove this smokescreen from your life situation reality. The Super-ego will continue to tell you that you deserve this or that because you are helping other people. In truth, spiritual masters never help anyone for the benefit of their wants because they have released want from their lives.

When you stop the idle chatter of the Super-ego, you will hear the messages being sent to you directly from Source Energy. The spiritual guides will begin to fall away, and you will have Conscious Clarity of the reality available to you by communicating directly with the Divine Source. This direct communication is when you will experience the true definition of what you deserve. In truth, you deserve what you signed up for when manifesting your Original Source Agreement before you took on this human body's existence. All you could ever want falls away when communicating directly with Source Energy. Your wants turn into needing to serve others!

When you place other people before your own Super-ego wants, you discover the true meaning of God-realization. Through this understanding, you realize that by serving others, you are using the gifts you provide to benefit the world. When your Four Body System aligns with the Spiritual Body in the forefront of your daily life, you discover an inner peace that prevails over any Super-ego, mental wants. In truth, you are that which you came here to heal. You are the essence of Love, Peace and Light that has always been your True Personality. When you live life from this perspective, you bring your Original Source Agreement vision to your daily life situation and manifest a new reality.

When you discover the Divine power within you, you master the true meaning of *Consciously Embrace Your True Personality*.

Why Do I Challenge My Worthiness

Even in this advanced state of awareness you are currently experiencing, the Super-ego will continue to test you to see whether you are living a life of Knowing or Beliefs. This testing comes in the form of consistent challenges confronting your understanding of your worthiness of a life filled with Abundance.

Don't allow Fear or a false belief of unworthiness still anchored within your subconscious to upset your inner peace. You already know you are a Spiritual Being situated in a physical body. It is now time for you to dissolve any last Super-ego-based beliefs from your system that are causing a disconnect from your ultimate Spiritual Body alignment and Knowing.

From time to time, the old memory files will rise to the surface to test the strength of the Spiritual Knowing that is always present waiting for you to purge the remaining false beliefs from your Four Body System. The questions you ask now should be of a higher vibrational level, such that they are merely an inquiry into your final state of unrest.

The transition back to Spiritual Knowing is the last challenge you have programmed for yourself to ensure you are ready to move into the next level of reality.

There will be those in the spiritual community still living at the level of Super-ego that will continue to challenge your exact understanding of who you are. You will notice in the spiritual community that most spiritual teachers, although vibrating at a much higher frequency than those they are assisting back to Spiritual Body alignment, are still locked in a false belief system anchored in the duality of Fear.

If you are in any way fearful of any challenge that comes your way, you are still living at the Super-ego level of understanding, which is the Fourth Dimension of reality. This Fourth Dimension is even more complicated for the Super-ego to accept than it was for the old ego in the Third Dimension of reality. Once you believe you have transcended typical fear-based reality into the spiritual realm, you will think you have risen above that Fear. However, the testing will continue based on extreme challenges in your life situation. The closer you are to genuinely embracing your True Personality, the more complex the challenges will be.

However, once you are vibrating at the consistent frequency of Knowing, all fear-based beliefs will fall away as if by magic. This purging is because you will be vibrating at the Highest Self level of reality rather than the Higher Self level. At the Highest Self reality level, your remaining false beliefs are experienced as a slight nuisance rather than a problem.

The world will look much different to you once the illusionary idea of a problematic world is removed from your Four Body System. You will have risen above the false belief system and shifted into the True Spiritual Reality Dimension of life in the Fifth Dimension of reality.

Once you achieve the Fifth Dimension of reality in life, you will no longer need to be tested by challenges. This reality does not mean challenges will no longer arise from time to time. It simply means you will be vibrating at the level of Highest Self or God-realization, and challenges are viewed at a different level of vibrational reality, just as they were at the Super-ego level of understanding found in the Fourth Dimension. This sequential increase in energy vibration can be very confusing until you have experienced the "aha" moments, which clarifies each Spiritual dimension.

Please spend a few days sitting with this new reality of understanding to anchor it into your Conscious Clarity perspective of where you are now, shifting and living.

Does Life Hold Me Back or Does Ego

As your questions increase in energy vibration, you will experience a continued awareness of how every life situation is merely a choice to live by the power of Love or the limitation of Fear. Deep in the spiritual knowledge of Knowing is the catalyst to bring your life experiences to the level of God-realization or Highest Self awareness.

As you continue on your life journey, it will soon become apparent to you that you have all that you need within you to be Joyful each day, and the outside influences of a devious Super-ego will fall away more and more. As you live your life aligned with the Spiritual truth of your eternal existence, you will become immune to the stories people use in an attempt to influence you based on their limited perspective of what life is.

Your True Purpose is always rooted in the blessings of Love energy and will not be disrupted by the negative happenings around you if you stay Spiritually centered. When you are vibrating at the energy level of Love, it's not necessary to bring judgments to each life situation as the devious ego does. From this pure Love energy, all duality is slowly but surely dissolved, and the experience of True Purpose reveals itself at a higher level of understanding. You feel at peace, even during the challenges of old habits or beliefs bubbling up from some past story that locked you in as a prisoner of the old third and Fourth Dimension reality.

Nobody is better aware of what you need to take action on to bring about your next level of higher understanding than you. The Super-ego will continue its purpose of attempting to hold you back, but rest assured, you (the Spiritual Self) have the power to overcome any trickery brought forth by the control mechanisms of this lower vibrating Self. Keep moving forward by sitting silently to experience the guidance delicately calling out to you entirely. In the bliss of silence is where you will have your greatest epiphanies. You will feel the people that can only come from your Highest Self materializing into your reality as soon as you choose to live your LIFE rather than your life situation.

To bring about change in this world of duality, you must first "feel" the difference between the words "duality". This feeling means you must step out of the darkness and into the Light of the Highest Self and stay there. Only you can choose to do so!

Is Ego Tricking Me Again

Anytime, without exception, when you feel yourself slipping out of inner peace, it is your ego attempting to trick you again. This trickery is especially true concerning Super-ego and its never-ending attempt to anchor in a false belief that your connection with Source Energy is somehow of superior value because you are on a Spiritual path.

Never forget that even the lowest vibrating person is equal to you in the reality of Oneness. You can check in with your Highest Self at any time, and so can the rest of humanity. By bringing clarity to reality, you can realign your Mental Body in a way that changes your perception of who you and those around you are. When we Know that we are all connected in Oneness, we learn to treat everyone equally. It doesn't matter what position you hold in your life situation or career because that will dissolve when the physical body transitions back to the earth.

When you Know you are moving on the right path, your vision for yourself and others will be in Harmony. Knowing this means checking in through the meditative state of Being and consistently increasing your energy vibration. In the silence of this profound connection with Source Energy, you will experience the truth of your reality and how it relates to everyone surrounding you. Training the Mental Body to align with the Soul was part of the experience of the book *Consciously Live What You Feel.*

Now you are on the path to discovering how to "Consciously Embrace Your True Personality." Just know that the Super-ego will continue to trick you into believing you are better than someone else just because you vibrate at a higher frequency. This falsehood is an illusion of the mind because, in some manner, you continue to align with the Physical Body perspective of life.

We are always connected in Oneness as we journey through this life situation of challenges and false beliefs. Therefore, remember that you are only here to assist others in realizing their True Personality awareness. How you bring this vision to light will be determined by how humble you are when in the presence of your equals. The world can be a crazy, mixed-up place of confusion for many of us, but it is the deep Knowing that you are a Spiritual Being having a human experience that brings it into balance. By staying focused on the Original Source Agreement you are here to fulfill, you will understand that the duality of life is nothing more than an illusion or judgment of the mind.

Why Do I Feel Confused When Ego Comes Knocking

Remember, before Soul Merge, the ego's purpose is to confuse you. As the questions you ask rise in energy vibration, the confusion will begin to fall away, and you will experience the pure bliss of living with the Spiritual Body at the forefront of your daily life.

As your energy vibration level increases, there will be a transition point when ego falls away entirely, only to be replaced by Super-ego. This transition is when the Super-ego's confusion tactics make a last-ditch effort to control you. When the Super-ego feels a loss of control over you, it will begin to panic and do outlandish things to keep you in an unconscious state of confusion and wonder. It will start questioning every spiritual decision you make after you act on the guidance from Source Energy.

Once the Super-ego knows it is losing control over you, it will come knocking at your door with increasingly confusing thoughts meant to keep you prisoner of its manipulative patterns. When you start to experience this illusion, allow it to be what it is and identify the thoughts as Super-ego's Fear of losing control over you. Super-ego will test you in a variety of ways. At this point, your weakest areas of strength to the many manipulation challenges of Super-ego are in full force, and how you either react or accept what is happening will be your most significant test.

When you feel you are moving forward at an accelerated rate, your Super-ego may slam you with an outside interference that may seem overwhelming. However, you must stand tall and recognize the opposing force as the last-ditch effort to control you in stride. You are a Spiritual Being having a human experience and can overcome any illusion made of the mind. By staying true to your Highest Self reality, you will overcome the diversity and become even stronger spiritually.

The confusion you are still feeling is the final resting place for Super-ego. In many ways, being confused is a significant step towards rediscovering the Authentic Self. As you consciously dismiss the ramblings of Super-ego, you will discover the unquestionable reality of your true Spiritual worth.

If I Knew My Authentic Self, Would I Still Question My Worth

If you knew your Authentic Self, you would never question your worth. You are not who you think you are; you are the beautiful Spiritual Being representing a part of Source Energy. When you finally discover this unlimited truth about your Highest Self, you will shift your life situations to align with Knowing and the guidance that comes to you from Source Energy. You will no longer require thought to guide your path; you will have risen above that of mortal man.

The addiction people have to false power and control over others is nothing more than a smokescreen to hide the pain they are experiencing because of fear-based thoughts, holding them prisoner to a false sense of reality. The tactics used by this false, egotistic reality are many, but the one that stands out the most is bullying. In our capitalistic society, people learn to bully others, believing this false power over others will serve them well. They believe bullying places them in a position of authority over others. This delusional thinking is the reality of a third-dimensional reality of what life is.

Everyone can discover how to break away from this controlling false reality by simply removing the false belief that they are in some way superior to others. The egotistic mind will use the weakness of Fear against you and never allow you to discover who you are without a fight. This fear-based word "fight" is a delusional trick of the Super-ego that remains in you at the lower vibration level of the Physical Body. You will never be free of it unless you learn to keep your True Personality at the forefront of your daily life.

The True Personality does not need an ego. The True Personality uses Divine intervention in every moment and then takes action based upon the spiritual guidance of Source Energy. Thought does not precede spiritual action in actual spiritual life reality. Thought comes after spiritual guidance provides a spiritual solution to every challenge. When you align with the Spiritual Body at the forefront of your daily life situation experiences, everything becomes a lesson for yourself or someone else attempting to manipulate a life experience. As Jesus said, "Forgive them for they know not what they do" because Jesus knew they were not in their right minds. The people who crucified his body were fearful of the Divine Spiritual Power they were witnessing in the peaceful demeanor of Jesus.

By bringing your peaceful, natural nature to the negotiation table of life situations, you allow other people's egos to stand down without feeling threatened by a mirrored false reality. This experience will enable them to get in touch with their True Highest Self reality.

How Is Getting in Touch with Authentic Self Imperative for Happiness

The God-realized energy vibration level is where your natural state of Conscious Clarity harmonizes with Spiritual reality through your Authentic Self or Highest Self awareness. By being in this state of awareness daily, you release the fog or smokescreen of the mind and allow yourself to BE the Joyful state of reality only found within your Authentic Self. This Joyful state is not something the old ego or Super-ego understands because this reality is a Spiritual experience at a vibration level beyond the Fourth Dimension.

It would be best to increase your energy vibration to the Fifth Dimension of reality to experience this Joyful state. However, it is easy to experience happiness in the Fourth Dimension because it is unnecessary to vibrate that highly to live in a state of outward happiness. As you discovered in the Soul Merge level of the *Conscious Clarity Energy Process*™, and referenced in the book *Consciously Live What You Feel*, happiness is an outside false reality of the old ego that requires some outside influence to bring you to a state of happiness.

Therefore, when you ask "How is Getting in Touch with Authentic Self Imperative for Happiness?", it can be very confusing for the Super-ego to transform into the higher vibration of peaceful happiness because you still require some outside influence to bring happiness to your Mental Body. However, once you step into the Fifth Dimension of Joy, you are automatically happy because you have transcended the need for outside influences to achieve that state of awareness or spiritual enlightenment. Sit in silence with that realization for a while and digest its meaning.

Now that you are vibrating at the level of Joy, you will find it easier to understand what it means to "Consciously Embrace Your True Personality." If you have not yet chosen the path of Joy and living with the Spiritual Body at the forefront of your daily life situations, this would be an excellent time to review what you have discovered in Book 1 - *Consciously Live What You Feel.*

In this current chapter of *Conscious Embrace Your True Personality*, you are preparing to experience the beauty of Part II in this book. In Part II, Super-ego falls away, and you step into the reality of the Fifth Dimension where you do not need an old ego or Super-ego because you Know who you are - a God-realized, Spiritual Being. In spiritual truth, happiness is not a factor to even consider because it is outside your Authentic Self, formless reality and below the vibration of the path you are now on.

The most important part of the life journey is to stay focused on keeping the Spiritual Body in the forefront of your daily life situations and never allow other outside influences to distract you from your Divine Spiritual greatness!

How Do I Stay Focused

What you focus on mostly in your life is what grows exponentially! When you have a burning desire to stay focused on your Authentic Self and make a Conscious Clarity connection with Source Energy daily, the answers to all your questions will manifest as if by magic. It's staying connected with this Divine energy that will allow you to stay focused on what is truly important in your life experience.

When you connect with Source Energy, you not only hear the guidance coming directly from God, but you align yourself with your Original Source Agreement for being here on this planet. Most people don't believe they are Spiritual beings with human experiences. They think they are only the Physical Body and, therefore, are limited to what they can experience in this lifetime. This misconception or misalignment is known as living a false reality. Non-believers anchor themselves in Fear, low vibrational beliefs of Self, and the influences of other non-believers they continue to associate with.

When you ask about how to stay focused in Spiritual Body alignment, it's time for you to leave behind all the naysayer influences and "Consciously Embrace Your True Personality" once and for all without the disruption of fear-based dogma that typically drives all of society down a path of illusionary nonsense. The ego will continue to mock your spiritual guidance and will do whatever it can to control the experience you are having.

JUST STOP IT!

Get out of your head and follow the guidance that comes to you in every present moment.

When Does It Get Easier

Life becomes very easy when you step into the limitless possibilities of Conscious Clarity of heightened awareness. When you are in this state of Being, all you need to do when a challenge arises is close your eyes, allow acceptance of what is, and ask for clarity based on the knowledge that is always available to you. By acknowledging your Highest Self awareness, you can tap into the unlimited solutions that are just a few feelings away. You experience this knowledge when you are vibrating at a frequency that allows you the cosmic intent of your Original Source Agreement.

When you tap into this vast storage of knowledge found through the window of Conscious Clarity, you no longer experience problems known to the typical person. You step up your energy vibration to the level of Source Energy and experience life from the vibration level intended for you. Until you are vibrating at this level of understanding where solutions to every life situation challenge await, you will continue to be lost in the false reality that everything in life is a struggle. This struggle or conflict mentality is exactly where ego wants you to stay, lost in the seemingly never-ending story of the false beliefs perpetuating our society today. This struggle is a state of conflict within the unconscious self, whereas the control mechanisms of a misaligned Four Body System permeate.

Therefore, with the Spiritual Body at the forefront of your life, the answers are always found when aligned spiritually, not physically. The simplicity of this understanding is always there in front of you, just waiting for you to step out, embrace reality, and stay there.

You have been preparing for Conscious Clarity of spiritual awareness since you began reading this book and the one that precedes it, *Consciously Live What You Feel*. Until you stay connected with the reality that you are experiencing life as a witness to the life situation movie viewed at this very moment, you will remain lost in the seemingly never-ending lifetime of problematic thinking. This lower-energy vibration keeps you locked in a prison of self-doubt and victimization because the lower-energy vibrations do not know any better.

Looking at the scenario from a spiritual perspective, you will understand that you are acting out the reality of an infant who knows something but cannot put it into words because the language is not yet known. Therefore, if you know something but cannot articulate it in words, you can only feel the message coming to you. With this in mind, bring your Original Source Agreement intent to the surface by staying in a "meditative state of Being" throughout the day. If you are still having difficulty aligning with your Highest Self realities, then you are not spending enough time or effort in the silence of your Spiritual reality.

This limited perspective of reality is merely your ego continuing to play tricks on you to regain control of your life. But don't go there anymore; you are beyond that vibration.

Do I Need This Book

If you didn't need this book, you would have stopped engaging in its spiritual doctrine long ago. Every tool focused on preparing you to go deeper within the Authentic Self shows up at precisely the right time for you to manifest the synchronistic power of Oneness into your life. You can plan all you want for your future, but the ultimate guidance always comes from being in Harmony with the Highest Self awareness, which is your Authentic Self.

If you believe you are in Harmony with the Highest Self, your questions will disappear and shift to the Divine power of Knowing. When this shift occurs, you will intuitively take action on what is most important for your spiritual growth. The power of Oneness is what spiritual growth is all about. Oneness catalyzes a Joyful life filled with Love, Peace, and Light. It permeates your Highest Self awareness by Being the white Light Energy of your very essence.

Every book, movie, magazine, website and person that shows up in your life is part of the synchronicity of spiritual alignment with Source Energy; by staying connected to that Divine energy, the suitable media or person shows up to assist you in fulfilling your True Purpose for being here.

Keep your tools close to you, but realize that in actual reality, everything, both form-based and formless, shows up at precisely the right moment in time for you to experience your Original Source Agreement fully. Your potential for taking quantum leaps in spiritual growth is now becoming consciously clear to you. When you allow the guidance from Source Energy to permeate your very existence, it brings about changes that would never manifest if you were still living a life based upon Physical Body alignment.

All this realization or any other spiritual tools mean to accomplish is keeping you focused on the Highest Self awareness and preparing you for a life filled with the Love of Oneness!

Never allow anyone to tell you they have all the answers to your questions because only you know what is truly in alignment with your Original Source Agreement. All the solutions to your life's challenges manifest in the depth of your Authentic Self that goes beyond that of the Mental Body understanding. That is why it is so crucial for you to "recruit the mind to serve the Soul" by staying appropriately aligned with the Spiritual Body at the forefront of every action. By staying connected with the Oneness found in Source Energy guidance, you bring your visions to Light and understand more about your Highest Self in the process.

Your life is eternal, so why are you in such a hurry to have someone else other than Source Energy answer questions for you? Take your time and allow life's experience to be the Divine dance of Love it has always been meant to be. Enjoy its sweetness and allow your Spiritual Body to bring the Light of Source Energy guidance to all your daily activities. I assure you that you are on the right path to enlightenment of the Highest Self by simply allowing the Divine guidance to light your way.

If Everything Is In Proper Order, What's Taking So Long

Patience is the bedrock of all that is Divine in the Universe. When you genuinely understand the limitless possibilities available to you each day by simply viewing life with a conscious awareness of the Authentic Self, you will no longer question the Conscious Clarity of Knowing.

Time is only relevant to the ego because it needs to have control of what is. This false relevance is why the ego needs a timeframe for every*thing* it manifests in this life situation, which is only the fragmented part of your True Life. When you stop thinking and spend more Earth time Being that which you are, you will begin to see the limitless possibilities as they unfold before you. The idea that you must live by a clock based on what is essential only to the ego is the basis for all misunderstandings of the Highest Self reality.

The ego will have you believe that you must set appointments for everything you think you need in this life situation; in fact, all you truly need is to follow the Source Energy guidance that constantly flows through you. This guidance is the only necessary energy level that truly matters. Yes, it is important to keep appointments on the surface of life because it is your responsibility to follow through on what you agree to. However, ask yourself how often something you planned suddenly changed by an event totally out of your control. When you begin to view life from the perspective of a greater Divine power of intervention in your life, you will start to see that all planning based upon some timeframe that you believe is important will change if it leads you away from your True Purpose for being here. That's not to say you will lose control of your free will; it simply means there will be an intervention that guides you closer to your True Purpose.

Most people believe that when their plans change because of some unexpected event, it has to do with bad luck or that the alteration victimizes them, when in fact, any ego-based plan altered by a Divine intervention always leads to some form of healing. The healing may not be for oneself; it may be for the benefit of someone else who is part of your life situation. There is always a lighter side to any alteration of your plans; be alert and pay close attention to what is happening around you during these periods of change. There will be a Divine reason operating in your life situation's reality. If you are vibrating at a high enough energy, you will see the resultant factor of the plan change with Conscious Clarity in the present moment.

However, if you are in victim mode, you will completely miss the reality of Divine intervention. Everyone has had an experience where some intervention made something better. Ask yourself when the last time was that you said, "As it turned out, if this would not have happened, I would have missed an opportunity." No matter who you are or how long you have been on this planet, this scenario has or will play out for you at some point in your life situation to modify your ego-based reality.

Be patient with yourself and allow the Divine interventions to flow into your life as Source Energy plans them out because they will be in Harmony with your Original Source Agreement.

Will Spirit Always Guide Me

Source Energy will always guide you through feelings directly related to your Chakra Energy System flowing through you. If you feel easy, relaxed and in a state of meditative bliss, you will know this is the Spirit of God flowing and instructing you to follow the path laid out for you in this state of Highest Self consciousness. All action taken from this energy vibration level will align with Love because it does not understand the false reality of Fear or conflict.

Feel your energy flowing through your body as you take each breath, and know without doubt that you are in the hands of Source Energy reality. By staying aligned with the Spiritual Body at the forefront of your every action, you will experience a life of pure Joy. This joyous dance with Spirit is an incredible journey because it never questions the guidance which flows from this Highest Self level of reality. When you stay in this state of awareness, you vibrate at a frequency that few ever experience.

Being in the flow of Spirit is like no other feeling you will ever experience. It is your natural state to BE! This Divine energy source feeling is part of the totality of Oneness, which everyone feels. Still, it is confusing because the false reality of the ego's control blocks its messages. When the Mental Body is misaligned, it takes direction based on Fear rather than Love, which is the natural state of Being.

By staying connected to the Spiritual Body at the forefront of your Four Body System, you experience a reality that is otherwise lost completely if you follow Physical Body misalignment. You have been brainwashed for so long that the false reality of the human experience is anchored deeply into your subconscious mind. Through dedicated spiritual work, you can break free from this control tactic that has been anchored into you so deeply. Spiritual Transformative Education breaks through this barrier of Fear and brings out the actions of a person who is aligned Spiritually in Love.

Listen to the subtle guidance flowing through your body; Source Energy is bringing you the vibrational energy you need to act in a Loving way. It permeates your existence every moment, but you must re-learn silence to listen with feelings rather than false beliefs anchored in your physical brain. When you feel the silence between the thoughts, your life evolves in a manner impossible for the ego to understand. So, if you are still confused, ask yourself how you are aligned.

How Do I Know It's My Highest Self Communicating

You know your Highest Self communicates with you when you begin living your life from a perspective of Love rather than Fear. All fear-based communication comes from the false illusion or ego. All Love-based communication comes from a Divine Source of Energy. Observe your feelings and check in with your Spiritual Highest Self energy vibration to ensure that the clever control of the Super-ego is not tricking you.

Until you have fully anchored the reality of Spiritual Body alignment into your everyday experiences, you will keep asking the same questions and never truly understand that the answer is always the same – LOVE UNCONDITIONALLY!

You will continue to lapse into a state of ego-based reality until you have shifted from "Thinking" to "Knowing". The most challenging part of this journey is surrendering fully to the power of Love energy bottled up in your Spiritual Body reality. The Authentic Self fully understands what is going on with you. The Authentic Self understands how challenging it is to merge the Super-ego and Higher Self fully. You are brainwashed into the false reality for years as you are growing up. This brainwashing is ego-manipulating fear-driven thoughts to accomplish acceptance of the superficial side of life. You will continue this roller coaster ride of egotistic doubt until you shift your vibrational energy level to the limitless possibilities found deep within yourself.

You have come a long way in your life situation experience, but you still have a long way to go to anchor your Highest Self reality fully into your life. If you are not ready to fully integrate your Highest Self into your everyday journey, you will continue to learn the lessons of the *Conscious Clarity Energy Process*™ the hard way. The hard way is through the random shift back and forth from third-dimensional thinking and fourth-dimensional Being without the reality of the Spiritual fifth-dimensional understanding in alignment with your Original Source Agreement.

You must bring your True Purpose vision to light by moving past the false assemblage point of the ego into the limitless reality of the Highest Self realization. Right now, you are at a fork in the road of reality, and until you have learned everything the hard way to its fullest extent, you will continue with the conflict of shifting back and forth. Why would you want to continue this disparaging path?

If Fear keeps popping in and out of your reality, you are experiencing what is known as a "Conflict of Thought." You unconsciously manifest this false illusionary point of reference by alternating in and out of Love and Fear-based emotions still anchored into your subconscious mind.

Spend more time in silence and pay close attention to your emotions because they are the monitoring point or reference between Love and Fear.

What Is the Purpose for This Conflict of Thought

The conflict of thought is nothing more than Super-ego being clever in an attempt to continue to test the Conscious Clarity of who you are. By understanding the unconscious thoughts still anchored in your mind by physical body alignment, you can learn to eliminate these false beliefs permanently. This elimination process is accomplished through the Divine power of deep silence in a meditative state.

Spend more time in silence, and your energy vibration assemblage point will shift to the next level of Conscious Clarity. It's challenging to purge what has been deeply anchored into your subconscious mind because the subconscious mind does not know the difference between truth and fiction. It believes whatever you focus on, mainly the

Super-ego, will take advantage of this last-ditch effort to control you. Acknowledge what is happening and move forward by purging the negativity with the power of knowing who you are; when fear-based thoughts pop in, breathe and allow them to pass through you.

When you are Spiritually aligned, you can quickly increase your assemblage point to the next level of reality. Bring your spiritual vision to light by connecting with Source Energy from a higher reality found only by silencing the Mental Body. You can do this by spending more time in silence or non-thought reality. The more you go to silence to receive the solutions to the final questions that still hold you back from experiencing a life of pure Joy – the better off you will be!

There are two ways of thinking: first, through the perceived usual way dictated by society with the Physical Body alignment at the forefront of your life situation, or second, with the Spiritual Body at the forefront of your life experiences. The choice is always yours and yours alone, which means you can shift your reality at any given moment to a life filled with Love, Peace and Light. Through Conscious Clarity of thought, you can align yourself in a manner that brings clarity and embraces your Original Source Agreement.

Conscious Clarity of Thought is only possible if you listen to the Source Energy messages found in silence. This listening is complicated for Super-ego to understand because it is so invested in years of false programming that seems so natural on the surface of your life situation. Even today, societal reality bombards you with the influences of the Third Dimension, which is to keep you prisoner in its low-vibration reality.

Try spending less time watching TV and more time reading books that inspire you. If you go to the movie theater, only go to movies vibrating in Harmony with your Highest Self reality of life. Bring change to the surface of your life situations by being a conscious observer of what you are thinking and who you are still spending time with. If you are experiencing negative thoughts based upon the influences surrounding you, change your surroundings or take a few moments to purge the destructive thoughts from your Mental Body. Don't waste another minute of your life giving away your Divine power to the whims of a Super-ego.

In the next section of this book, you will begin to experience life with Super-ego fully merged into Spiritual Body alignment and understand the meaning of *Consciously Embrace Your True Personality*.

Chapter 5 Suggestions - Know What You Deserve

What you deserve is brought to you miraculously through the Divine power of Knowing – not doing! This chapter is devoted to keeping the Knowing awareness at the forefront of your daily reality.

- The simple truth is that you, as a Spiritual Being, are the essence of Love, Peace and Light. Once you acknowledge this truth, you will see how your Life Purpose makes this vision real. As you shift your energy vibration toward your Highest Self reality, you begin to experience the rewards of living this current life situation from a perspective aligned with every other Soul. The Oneness felt when fully aligned with Source Energy is beyond the understanding of the typical mind. Therefore, you must continue to increase your energy vibration to experience all that is available through living at the Highest Self reality of life.

- When you stop the idle chatter of the Super-ego, you will hear the messages being sent to you directly from Source Energy. The spiritual guides will begin to fall away, and you will have Conscious Clarity of the reality available to you by communicating directly with the Divine Source. This direct communication is when you will experience the true definition of what you deserve. In truth, you deserve what you signed up for when manifesting your Original Source Agreement before you took on this human body's existence. All you could ever want falls away when communicating directly with Source Energy. Your wants turn into needing to serve others!

- From time to time, the old memory files will rise to the surface to test the strength of the Spiritual Knowing that is always present waiting for you to purge the remaining false beliefs from your Four Body System. The questions you ask now should be of a higher vibrational level, such that they are merely an inquiry into your final state of unrest. The transition back to Spiritual Knowing is the last challenge you have programmed for yourself to ensure you are ready to move into the next level of reality.

- Once you achieve the Fifth Dimension of reality in life, you will no longer need to be tested by challenges. This reality does not mean challenges will no longer arise from time to time. It simply means you will be vibrating at the level of Highest Self or God-realization, and challenges are viewed at a different level of vibrational reality, just as they were at the Super-ego level of understanding found in the Fourth Dimension. This sequential increase in energy vibration can be very confusing until you have experienced the "aha" moments, which clarifies each Spiritual dimension.

- To bring about change in this world of duality, you must first "feel" the difference between the words "duality". This feeling means you must step out of the darkness and into the Light of the Highest Self and stay there. Only you can choose to do so!

- Once the Super-ego knows it is losing control over you, it will come knocking at your door with increasingly confusing thoughts meant to keep you prisoner of its manipulative patterns. When you start to experience this illusion, allow it to be what it is and identify the thoughts as Super-ego's Fear of losing control over you. Super-ego will test you in a variety of ways. At this point, your weakest areas of strength to the many manipulation challenges of Super-ego are in full force, and how you either react or accept what is happening will be your most significant test.

- The confusion you are still feeling is the final resting place for Super-ego. In many ways, being confused is a significant step towards rediscovering the Authentic Self. As you consciously dismiss the ramblings of Super-ego, you will discover the unquestionable reality of your true Spiritual worth.

- The God-realized energy vibration level is where your natural state of Conscious Clarity harmonizes with

Spiritual reality through your Authentic Self or Highest Self awareness. By being in this state of awareness daily, you release the fog or smokescreen of the mind and allow yourself to BE the Joyful state of reality only found within your Authentic Self. This Joyful state is not something the old ego or Super-ego understands because this reality is a Spiritual experience at a vibration level beyond the Fourth Dimension.

- The most important part of the life journey is to stay focused on keeping the Spiritual Body in the forefront of your daily life situations and never allow other outside influences to distract you from your Divine Spiritual greatness!

- What you focus on mostly in your life is what grows exponentially! When you have a burning desire to stay focused on your Authentic Self and make a Conscious Clarity connection with Source Energy daily, the answers to all your questions will manifest as if by magic. It's staying connected with this Divine energy that will allow you to stay focused on what is truly important in your life experience.

In the next section of this book, you will begin to experience life with Super-ego fully merged into Spiritual

Body alignment and understand the meaning of *Consciously Embrace Your True Personality*.

Part Two

Super-ego Falls Away

Chapter 6

Understanding the Voice Inside

What Is My First Step to Understanding the Voice Within

The first step to *Consciously Embrace Your True Personality* is to understand the voice within you, which is the Source of Energy guiding you at every moment of your Life. By listening to this inner guidance, you will understand (for some of you for the first time) who you are and the unlimited potential you have to share with the world.

You are not here to serve only the false reality of an egotistic, third-dimensional life situation anchored in Physical Body alignment. You are here to serve the entire world, including those who may not be in your general geographic area or circle of current friends. Once you genuinely focus on aligning fully with the Spiritual Body experience of Life, your Original Source Agreement, you will transform from the mediocre lifestyle you currently live to the total Abundance of Life you are responsible for sharing with others.

Make no mistake; there is an unlimited Divine power within you that is your God-realized Self. This Divine power is the Highest Self, the Creator of all that was or ever will be. You are the Spirit (spark) within the Physical Body that can transform the world into a deep understanding of Love, Peace and Light. It is time for you to stop playing small and step up to the Original Source Agreement you made with Source Energy before taking residence in the Physical Body you now reside in.

Release your Super-ego and step into the True Personality blissful Life you are pre-programmed to experience. Stop the Third Dimension "doing" and bring your energy vibration up to the level of the Fourth Dimension, Being. Drop the false identity of the different roles you have been playing and change the lives of others by simply Being yourself for the rest of your Life. Remove all identifiers of egotistic society from your daily actions and focus all your energy on the Abundance that awaits you.

Your actions up to this point have been self-centered in the false reality that you, in some way, are only this Physical Body that you are currently occupying. You are simply using the Physical Body, so bring this reality transition to the forefront of your current life situation's attention. I guarantee your life situation will shift to a higher assemblage point or energy vibration.

Spiritual Transformative Education is about shifting to Spiritual Body alignment, the natural way to experience your Eternal Life. Therefore, the life situation or lifetime you are currently using to grow spiritually in the image of the Source Energy is nothing more than a stepping point to move forward in Conscious Clarity of who you indeed are.

Stay connected in every moment with this incredible Source Energy guidance constantly reaching out to you. You already know how to sit in silence, but are you truly listening to the guidance given in these moments of inspiration?

How Do I Keep Inner Voice Active in Daily Life

Daily Life or life situations are all part of the human illusion of one's Self, based upon Mental Body thought patterns and beliefs. Eternal Life or Spiritual Life is Knowing that you are a Spiritual Being having a human experience and Conscious Clarity of the Highest Self.

When you experience Life through the power of Conscious Clarity of the Highest Self, you become immune to the low-level vibration of day-to-day thought. This awareness means you no longer have false beliefs about what is real. You understand that listening to the inner voice or Source Energy guidance is necessary for you to thrive in this life situation. By accepting what IS and regarding your feelings as sacred observation points on your journey, you can easily stay connected to Source Energy's guidance.

Listen to the guidance constantly flowing through you by observing your feelings with Conscious Clarity. When you feel that something is taking you away from your natural Spiritual state of Being internally peaceful, you will know that you have unconsciously shifted back to Physical Body alignment. Remember, your feelings are the stepping stones for staying connected with Source Energy. You can change your life situation by always staying in direct contact with your feelings. By actively observing your life situation, your Spiritual Life will continue to evolve.

Staying connected consciously is not always easy because of the outside influences that bombard you daily. However, suppose you dedicate yourself to bringing Spiritual Body alignment to the forefront of your daily life experiences. In that case, you will find it easier to adjust your day-to-day thinking to align with your Original Source Agreement. Do the work upfront; the rewards will multiply for you before your eyes like magic. The mind doesn't understand the natural flow of intent because it is too busy explaining what is happening around you logically or based on day-to-day thinking dynamics.

When you shift your perception of Life from day-to-day, limited thought to the higher vibration of Conscious Clarity, you will see how your Life unfolds abundantly because all Clarity resides in the silence of non-thought reality. By simply shifting your assemblage point or energy vibration to the higher levels of reality found in Spiritual Body alignment, you begin to see clearly. When you focus on the intention of Spiritual-based reality, day-to-day thought dissolves, and the higher-energy vibration of Conscious Clarity understanding evolves to the next level of reality.

This level of understanding is very confusing for the typical misaligned person, which is most of the population now. The mass consciousness is increasing in energy vibration, but it has a long way to go before it reaches the higher realms of understanding what Life is truly all about. Once your eyes are open to Spiritual reality, you won't want to return to day-to-day thinking dynamics.

You are more likely than not to find yourself shifting back and forth from Spiritual Body to Physical Body alignment, but the good news is that this shifting back and forth will become less and less controlling as time goes on. You will find yourself at a tipping point of awareness soon and finally bring your vision or Original Source Agreement to the Light of your Highest Self reality.

Is It Important To Always Listen To Inner Voice

Nothing in your Life is more important than listening to the inner voice of Source Energy, which permeates every moment of your existence. The challenge for most people is that they continue to reason with their Mental Body reality when they momentarily slip back to Physical Body alignment during challenging times.

When Super-ego believes it has control of your thoughts, it will create a planned-out story to make you think that you have risen to an energy vibration that no longer requires you to sit in silence to communicate in a one-on-one conversation with Source Energy. Super-ego has its own set of stories that it creates to control the thoughts that are still anchored in you by over-thinking your Life. When you are Spiritually aligned, you will take immediate action based on Spiritual Guidance rather than thought.

The Spiritual Body Alignment Path of Life is not just another rule-based, sequential illusion. A Spiritually aligned person harmonizes with pure Love and can overcome any obstacle. However, it must be an absolute path to have the resultant factor that Source Energy promised you in your Original Source Agreement. You must stay on the Spiritual path daily to fully align with the Original Source Agreement you created with Source Energy. Daily Spiritual alignment requires continuous practice on your behalf.

As you continue to dismiss the clever actions of the Super-ego, you will understand that it will always be there in the background, attempting to convert you back to Physical Body alignment. This constant presence of Super-ego is why you must continue your Spiritual Practice of sitting in a meditative state daily and consciously focus on the intention of communicating in a two-way conversation with Source Energy.

The inner voice of Source Energy will eventually overcome your typical day-to-day thinking. It will transcend any clever actions of the Super-ego and immediately alter any misalignment when the Super-ego interferes. This adjustment is when your Authentic Self Power will show you the path of an enlightened Being. However, until that time comes, you should be on constant alert, watching the manipulations of Super-ego.

The Spiritual Being that you are will bring Conscious Clarity to you in every moment of your Life when you are correctly aligned. Never doubt this fact, as it is the stepping stone for all happiness and Abundance in your Life.

Has Inner Voice Ever Let You Down

The inner voice or inner guidance has never let you down. If you were to take the time to review your Life as suggested in *Consciously Live What You Feel,* you would determine that the results of your lifetime are all based upon either ego choices or spiritual choices. The guidance within presents Conscious Clarity in moments of silence, not necessarily complete physical silence, but the silence of the mind. You could be in the middle of an extreme physical body activity where outside interferences are at their peak, and you can still hear (feel) the inner voice guidance flowing from within you. You should pay close attention to the guidance presented to you during these moments.

When the Mental Body aligns with the Spirit, all that is required for you to hear the messages coming directly from the Source Energy is to feel the vibration of each moment of your Life. Your feelings will bring you the solutions to all challenges in your Life, and your actions will guide your earthly endeavors. All action from the Inner voice (Source Energy) will bring you to the full potential of each situation or learning experience. So, stop fighting and bring peace to each moment!

Spiritual Body alignment will always guide you to the path of least resistance, providing the guidance you need each moment. It matters not how small or large the challenge is; accepting spiritual guidance will always result in a much better outcome than what a misaligned Mental Body can manifest. You must constantly prove this to the ego by using the tools made available to you in Book 1 of this series to understand why the ego does what it does.

Mentioning alignment of the Four Body System again is to clarify any remnants of ego left unaligned (and there may be many) within the Four Body System. You will have yet another opportunity to bring this awareness to the forefront of your reality. Connecting with Source Energy through Conscious Clarity of thought is the key to all Abundance in Life. It is the key to bringing about change in the world and the catalyst for all Love, Peace and Light in your daily Life.

Use your mind to recollect when you completely surrendered to Source Energy guidance. Then, remember when you were at the end of your human capabilities and asked for help from Source Energy. You know deep within you that each of these moments aligned in a manner that was in direct proportion to the limitless possibilities available to you. "Aha" moments of connection with Source Energy stand out in our lives. The Super-ego wants you to forget these moments in a last-ditch effort to retain control over your physical existence. However, if you maintain proper Spiritual

Body alignment, you can discern the alignment differences with Conscious Clarity.

Conscious Clarity is a process for staying connected with Source Energy so that you can experience Life the way you intended it, which is in Harmony with your Original Source Agreement.

Why Do Most People Live in Ego

You have grown significantly spiritually if you now understand that you have been programmed since the birth of the body to follow a "group think" mentality. This low-vibration state of Being follows a limited belief structure meant to keep you enslaved in a Physical Body alignment scenario. It is easy to keep you under the control of an egoist society by keeping you in the fog of a low-vibration reality. Our society is run by those in power who are strictly "money-driven", so you are manipulated into following the rules and regulations established by a few individuals with the most "money." This control mechanism may sound like a conspiracy theory on the surface; however, as we dig deeper into the control dynamics, we see it is a sad, but true, reality.

This reality is accurate for each Category of Life, diagrammed in *Illustration D* at the back of this book. Other than Spiritual Life and Soul Merge, each category is designed for egos and government rules to keep you locked in a belief system that is a low-energy vibration control mechanism. If you still have difficulty seeing this control system for what it truly is, examine each category thoroughly.

Begin your research with the Financial Freedom area of the eight categories as an example. In the United States, everyone is assigned a social security number shortly after birth. This number then tracks everything you do based on how you spend your money or the credit allowed you. This money control system follows your every move regarding what you own and how you utilize the credit system established by the lawmakers you voted into power. Suppose you closely monitor your "Credit Score", which is nothing less than a control mechanism of judgment. In that case, you will quickly see your movements follow different categories based on this rule-based measuring control tool. Credit Score dictates your monthly monetary self-worth. Creditors report to three dedicated agencies that track your financial actions. Credit agencies provide nothing more than a snapshot of how credit to the masses is distributed based on how you use your money and the credit allowed you. However, this control mechanism differs for the ultra-wealthy who shelter their actions.

Suppose you watch your spending patterns closely and experiment with this purchasing power. In that case, you will notice that your Credit Score will vary monthly depending on how you function in this societal control arena. It's pretty disturbing that we have allowed manipulation by others based on a credit number we have little control over. The whole financial system benefits those having the most money and credit who get the best rates. The system always provides the lowest rates for borrowing to those who understand the system. However, this financial system detail is not part of our general education system doctrine. To learn about it, you must seek higher education courses to extrapolate the system's inner workings.

All of this was created by those holding most of the country's assets and through lobbyists and a corrupt banking system that has proven over and over to be less than honest. The control continues and most society follows this "group think" mentality without questioning it.

When those in governmental power vibrate at a third-dimension, low energy frequency, the masses suffer predominantly. That's because the system design basis is egoistic separation and a philosophy of "what's in it for me" or the "state" I represent rather than Oneness and sharing.

What Can Happen If I Only Listen to Inner Voice

Your potential is limitless if you always listen only to the inner voice that guides you naturally rather than participate in the "group think" mentality. A blissful life is possible if you open your heart to the energy vibration of Source Energy available to you each moment. Through alignment with this Divine power, you have the capacity for greatness and Abundance in your Life.

Happiness is possible, even for those who have chosen a life of victimization. When you bring the natural Joy within you to the surface of your actions, all the categories of Life are balanced. With balance, you learn to appreciate each area of your Life for its true potential, and you take action only on what is best for the Oneness of the world. You know deep within you that you have the Divine spark to change anything outside of you, but it takes work.

How often have you heard the inner voice guide you in a specific direction and you dismissed it? We all go through this mental uncertainty at one time or another. You hear the inner voice's guidance and dismiss the guidance, and then when something negative happens, we say to ourselves – I should have listened to the guidance!

Spiritual guidance is a tiny whisper that may seem insignificant at the moment, but it can be the stepping stone to greatness. Therefore, when you feel that you should take action in a different direction than what the misaligned Mental Body is telling you – DO IT!

The inner voice will never fail you. Just take action on the guidance you receive and watch the results of that action. Nobody but you can realign your Four Body System to harmonize with what Source Energy has in store for you. By taking action on each feeling you have, you will experience the Life you Know deep within you that you deserve.

Many of you are still uncertain – it's okay; it's all part of the *Conscious Clarity Energy Process*™. If you still have that Physical Body alignment nagging at you, let the process of Conscious Clarity move you to new heights by simply laughing at the ego's continued manipulation. Don't allow yourself to be one of those who accept what you "think" is correct. Release the Mental Body control mechanism once and for all and bring greatness to Life's surface.

You know it takes work to change anything deeply anchored in your subconscious. Commit yourself to being patient and kind as you build your energy vibration to align with your Original Source Agreement.

Listening to the inner voice will never disappoint you but surely enlighten you.

Why Is Inner Voice Quiet at Times

The truth is the inner voice of Source Energy is never quiet. It guides you every moment, but you must "be still" to hear the messages. If you believe that God has deserted you, you are not listening through feelings. You are still thinking and participating in the world of Physical Body alignment. Remember how clever the ego can be when it uses outside influences to anchor in a false belief, holding you prisoner to its manipulation.

Stop following beliefs and realign your Life with the Spiritual Body at the forefront of every action you take. Your Life is a joyous dance of wonder, realized if you get out of your head. Bring about Love, Peace and Light in your daily activities by paying close attention to your feelings; they will guide you in the best direction. If you are out of alignment, the feelings you experience will be of a low-energy vibration, which blocks your Kundalini Energy. If your Kundalini Energy is blocked, you will experience an uncomfortable feeling or tightening of the body.

You do not need to understand everything based on scientific studies or the majority acceptance of what is. Just go with the flow of your energy vibration and monitor your Chakras. Let your inner voice control your Life and you will always be in Harmony with your Original Source Agreement. Your situation will improve by bringing your Spiritual Body to the forefront of your Life. You know this is true because you have already experienced the different outcomes. You can stay a prisoner of society's manipulations or move past that "group think" mentality and step into the Light of the actual reality of Source Energy.

Once you fully embed the philosophy of Spiritual Body alignment in your Life, changes will show up as if by magic. Remember, the mind cannot "think" you into a life of Abundance. Only the Spirit can move your assemblage point to a new limitless reality. If you "think" the inner voice is quiet – STOP THINKING – because you are simply blocking the guidance sent to you.

Sit in silence more often and allow yourself to bring the recollection of your Original Source Agreement to the forefront of your Life so that you can move forward while using this human form. In silence, you can truly understand what is conveyed and what is ultimately in store for you. By consciously aligning yourself with the Spiritual Body at the forefront of your Life, you will hear the inner voice of Source Energy with Conscious Clarity.

When you feel the silence is deafening, you will be fully aligned with the inner voice of Source Energy and recollect your Original Source Agreement.

What Happens When Thought Takes Over

Suppose your Life is overflowing with the problems of low-vibration energy, found with Physical Body alignment at the forefront of your daily Life. In that case, you are experiencing confusion about your True Self. The Super-ego is still using you and, therefore, is holding you back from the true potential of the Highest Self reality.

When your thoughts take over control of your Life, you are constantly "thinking" and "analyzing" every challenge that may come before you. You are turning challenges into problems of the Mental Body and are causing yourself to live a life of doubt and problematic reactions to what is happening around you.

The Super-ego wants you to doubt whether or not you are genuinely hearing Source Energy. Super-ego will manipulate your thinking into a frenzy of confusion and uncertainty if you attempt to "physically" increase your energy vibration. This situation is a perplexing illusion because the Mental Body has little to do with reality. The Mental Body can only follow directions because it is part of form-based reality.

The confusion comes in when the Mental Body misinterprets the outcome of an action as something less or more than it is.

Therefore, if you are mentally trying to increase your energy vibration through doing some "thing" that has been influenced by outside interference; you are locked into Physical Body alignment without even knowing it! How's that for manipulation? – Wow!

You can only move your energy vibration assemblage point forward by "recruiting the mind to serve the Soul." Then, you can allow your energy vibration to shift Spiritually by accepting what is. Conscious Clarity of what IS will bring you an awareness you have not felt before. Conscious Clarity will bring you to the reality of True Self. Then, you use the mental body for the purpose you created it for – to serve the Soul.

Can True Essence Be Explained in a Way Everyone Will Understand

When you "recruit the mind to serve the Soul", your Four Body System is aligned with your Authentic Self/Highest Self reality or True Essence. Then, you find yourself following the guidance from the inner voice of Source Energy without question, and your Life becomes a beautiful dance of inspired consciousness and Clarity about what's important. Everyone can understand this level of Conscious Clarity awareness. However, the choice to do the necessary work to shift to this level of understanding can only harmonize with the value of Oneness.

When you realize that you have been sent to this Earth school to *Consciously Embrace Your True Personality*, you will understand that your True Essence is always Spiritually explained. When you genuinely realize or recollect your Original Source Agreement purpose, your level of understanding will be from a different perspective. What a low vibrating society falsely taught you will have little or no value.

Your Life is a fantastic dance of Spiritual action permeating every moment. Deep within you, you know this is true, and you also know that this True Essence radiates through the Spiritual, Meditative State of Being. When you follow your True Purpose for being here, you automatically become a teacher of Spiritual reality and transcend the Mental Body misalignment found in a Physical Body alignment reality. By walking your path with Spiritual Body alignment at the forefront of every action, you elevate your energy vibration to the level of Oneness, which is your true calling.

Don't ever doubt that you can convey this message of Conscious Clarity to others in your Life. We are all teachers and students of Life itself, and only you can choose to live your Life from a Spiritual perspective. Once you finally commit to changing your Life from one based upon Beliefs to one of Knowing instead, you will move forward at an accelerated energy vibration rate. You will never look back to those false beliefs that have held you a prisoner by the manipulations of others attempting to control you. Your Life will focus on Oneness and how you can serve others before your self-centeredness.

Why Do the Number of Questions Seem Too Much to Tolerate at Times

Once the shift to Spiritual Body awareness is complete, recurring questions that have been bothering you all your Life will resurface. Furthermore, when you seek spiritual truth, the ego's confusion slowly shifts from low-energy to high-energy questions. Higher-energy questions generate a way of Knowing what is best for you and asking Source Energy for guidance. You Know you are a Spiritual Being having a human experience; therefore, how your Life evolves is directly proportional to the level of understanding or Spiritual Growth you project into the human experience.

Now that you are experiencing Life from a Fourth Dimension perspective, you will allow all the false beliefs you had in the past to fall away from your Life. When the shift happens, the questions will be more vibrant. You will ask questions about serving others rather than the typical self-centered questions of an ego-controlled Mental Body. At first, the questions will align with understanding how - "How could I have been Spiritually blind" for so long? This aha moment is uncomfortable because you have been brainwashed or pre-programmed for years. The ego will still attempt to keep you trapped under its control. Therefore, breaking the self-centered pattern of victimization will take a while for you to purge it thoroughly. Be gentle with yourself, and know you will eventually see the Cosmic Light. Remember, you are the only one who can permit others to control you, and it is time for you to step into your greatness.

So, when the questions seem too much to tolerate, stop thinking and bring your Spiritual Body awareness to the forefront of your reality. Conscious Clarity of thought from a Spiritual feeling perspective will overcome any false beliefs of the past. Therefore, if it feels good, go for it. If not, dismiss it and move on to the next level that feels comfortable from a Spiritual perspective. And remember, the ego will still attempt to use its trickery to hold you a prisoner to the Physical Body alignment patterns of a dysfunctional human being.

Keep your Mental Body focused on following Source Energy guidance and increasing energy vibration. It's all part of the *Conscious Clarity Energy Process*™ and is a blessing to experience. As you slowly allow that which does not serve the greater good or Oneness to fall away from your Life, you will see that you have the Divine power within you to achieve true greatness.

If Inner Voice Is Unlimited - Am I

The inner voice is the Source Energy speaking through you. You are part of this energy because you were made in its image. Therefore, you embody the "I AM", meaning you are part of the Oneness itself. As part of this Divine limitless force of energy, you are the essence of Source Energy and can achieve all that is beyond the level of mental understanding. In other words, you are the "I-AM-Ness" of all Spiritual Life!

When you begin living this God-realized understanding of the Highest Self reality, your Life will harmonize with Oneness and your Original Source Agreement will become clearly defined. You will stop doubting yourself and bring about change to the world as you never thought possible. The outcome of your actions will always be rewarded with a balanced life when you step up to the greatness of a Spiritual Being perspective. All that aligns with your Original Source Agreement will begin to appear, and you will have a completely different outlook on each life situation that presents itself to you.

In truth, you are a solution-based Spiritual Being that can overcome any challenge created by those wishing to control you, including your human ego. Never underestimate your level of Divine power; always do what you agreed to do here. During your Original Source Agreement planning with Source Energy, you agreed to experience Life at the God-realized level of understanding. However, somewhere along the path of humanness, you got side-tracked and began living your Life at a lower energy vibration level. Playing the life experience small rather than stepping up to your full potential because you lost touch with who you are.

The most challenging part of living a life at the level of Physical Body alignment is accepting who you are at the Highest Self level of understanding. You are programmed to believe you are less than a Spiritual Being having a human experience. Your teachers have held you back at the academic level of understanding, and that is why it is so crucial for you to stop thinking and over-analyzing every moment of your current life situation.

Always stay present in the reality that you are not the Physical Body you are currently using. You are the Divine spark of the Highest Self energy housed within the Physical Body. Therefore, you are capable of all possibilities in the realm of Oneness and eternal Life. It's time for you to get out of your head and open your heart to God-realization.

Stop playing Life Small - Shift your awareness to *Consciously Embrace Your True Personality*!

How Do I Thrive with Conflict All Around Me

The key to thriving with conflict surrounding you is - understanding fully that nothing ever happens to you; life situations are simply happening around you. You are the Highest Self energy within the body, and that which is within is eternal. You are not the Physical Body; you are the Spiritual Body, which should never surrender to the conflict of the form-based world.

The Super-ego will attempt to corrupt your Highest Self's reality thinking. Super-ego fears you are acting upon what guidance presented during Source Energy conversations. Monitor your feelings and pay close attention to your Kundalini Energy flow. If your Chakras become blocked, it is a sign that you have reverted to Physical Body alignment. When that happens, you surrender your Divine power to the ego's will.

Your Life should naturally flourish and thrive in the joyous Abundance of Spiritual Body alignment. By questioning how you will thrive with conflict surrounding you, you are falling short of the Highest Self reality of your Life. This lifetime is merely your life situation, not your eternal Life. When the

Spiritual perspective of Life is fully understood, you will no longer question what is happening around you. You will accept it for what it is and move forward with your Life Purpose.

Until the mass consciousness of the world expands to the level of Spiritual Body alignment understanding, there will always be conflict surrounding you. Allow it to be what it is, and follow the guidance within you. Source Energy guidance will let you know if you need to bring Light to the conflict. This is beyond the ego's level of understanding. It is beyond the level of third-dimensional reality. You have no appreciation of Life until you understand the bigger picture of why you are here.

Life is truly a blessing. To be here now in this human form is a gift, an opportunity to fulfill your Original Source Agreement from the Highest Self reality of Life. Living your Life from the Spiritual Body alignment perspective is more accessible than your ego wants you to believe.

Feel the Kundalini Energy flowing through you; then, the God-realized Being that you are will awaken to the level of Oneness, and you will understand your True Purpose for Being here now.

Why Does the Spiritual Realm Seem So Natural

Your natural existence is in Harmony with Life's Spiritual Body alignment perspective. It is in Harmony with your Life Plan (Original Source Agreement) and the gifts you brought with you. If used to their most significant potential, these gifts will bring you an Abundance of anything you need to have a balanced lifetime in this incarnation. When you finally accept the truth of who you are and how much you have to share with the world, Life becomes a joyous dance of endless possibilities.

Imagine how you would feel every day if you just released the false beliefs from your mind. Picture yourself living Life beyond the constraints of the misaligned Mental Body. How would you feel without the constant distractions of the mind? The false stories of the ego are not you. You are the Spiritual Being within a physical form. You have the Divine Source Energy within you to bring about the changes that seem mentally beyond your grasp.

As you grow more aware of your spiritual strengths, which can overpower any false reality of the misaligned Mental Body, you stop fighting everything in your situations and flow with Life. An adequately aligned mind is a powerful tool that can be used to its full potential by simply listening to the inner voice of Source Energy. You can and will experience a life of bliss and Abundance once you finally give up the egoistic patterns deeply embedded into your subconscious mind.

As you slowly (but surely) stop thinking when challenges arrive in your life situation, your perception will shift. You will embrace the feelings that guide you from within and understand what it truly means to be free. To be free of the misaligned Mental Body, false stories and referenced reality or false truths of outside interferences is your natural state of Being.

So ask yourself, how can anything outside of me bring a lower-energy vibration without my permission? The answer is quite simple – it's not possible! You must provide authorization for your ego to control you – SO STOP IT – SAY NO!

If you do not feel at peace in any given life situation, you are out of alignment and need to shift your perspective immediately. You have no reason to live a life of constant doing, planning and worrying!

Your natural state of "Being" requires nothing from you or anyone else to bring about change in this energy process that you are reconnecting with now. You have come a long way from where you were just a few months ago. Therefore, bring your true vision to light now, and you will experience the Life you came here to experience. Stop making it so hard on yourself, and enjoy the process.

Is "Being" Part of the Process

As you grow in Spiritual Enlightenment, you soon discover that Life is a process. You begin to *Consciously Embrace Your True Personality* and find that sharing your life experiences with others is not just for you, but more importantly to be the teacher for others. We are all teachers and students, but our roles change as we grow in Spiritual fulfillment of the Highest Self.

My most outstanding teachers were those more concerned with how I feel rather than what I think. At the time of my many lessons, I didn't realize how vital those fantastic people were to my overall well-being. The teachers who would answer the many, many questions I would ask of them were the ones who were the most advanced in energy vibration.

As a small child, I always enjoyed older people more than those of my age group. I found that those who were ten to twenty years my senior were the ones who had the most stories to share. I quickly learned how to bring out the deepest secrets of my loving teachers. They knew they could share their life stories with me without fear of rejection or judgment. They knew I would keep their secrets and not be critical of them. It's incredible what people will share with you honestly if they feel safe.

Living a non-judgmental life is not always easy; however, it is truly the only way to someone's heart and Soul. Discovering how to BE in this world rather than DO in this world is one of the greatest gifts you can experience. When you allow those around you to Be who they are without any fear of judgment, the level of communication opens up to a new level of energy vibration.

When you consider all of the egoistic dysfunction in this world, it's a wonder we as a humanity haven't wholly obliterated our world. What holds us together is a familiar inner voice of moral understanding. The art of Being is becoming more prominent in our society today as more and more people open up to the idea of living from a moral and Spiritual level of energy vibration.

Our world is filled with optimists and pessimists as well. However, we can choose which energy vibration level we bring to the dance of Life!

Where do you stand today concerning your Spiritual Enlightenment? Are you still living in the Third Dimension of ego, or are you growing spiritually and stepping up to your true potential of Knowing you are a Spiritual Being living the experience of humanity? Do you acknowledge that you are part of a bigger plan, or are you locked into a lifetime of following the pack?

Is the Process All Part of the Bigger Plan

The Conscious Clarity Energy Process™ is part of the experience of living a bigger plan than what you may see on the surface of humanity. You are the messenger of the world, and until you decide to speak up and share your gifts with this world, you will remain a prisoner of the ego. There is an overlap of understanding at each junction of Spiritual Enlightenment. We shift our awareness from not knowing to Knowing when we raise our energy vibration to the level of God-realization understanding. At this juncture, we stop the limited beliefs of a Physical Body alignment and live a focused life outcome of pure Joy.

If you do not believe you are part of a bigger plan than the surface of life situations, you are cutting yourself short. You are allowing the limitless plan of Source Energy to slip past your grasp because you have allowed yourself to be held prisoner by those outside yourself. By living the follower path rather than the leader, you accept a lifetime ruled by outside influences instead of listening and following the guidance of Source Energy vibration.

Now would be a good time to step into your greatness by simply "Being" who you are. Stop the endless cycle of third-dimensional nonsense and jump onboard the fast train to Spiritual Enlightenment. We all can take a quantum leap of faith by simply Being part of the bigger plan. You can bring your Original Source Agreement to the forefront of your daily existence anytime. When you focus on the more significant outcome based on Love, Peace and Light, your experiences in life change. You are on the path of Spiritual Enlightenment and understand what living a God-realized acceptance of Life means.

Every level of Spiritual Growth comes with a fantastic resultant factor: KNOWING!

By now, you should be experiencing many overlaps in your life situation from Third Dimension to Fourth Dimension reality. The Super-ego stands out for what it is, and accepting who you are should permeate your new reality. The false Self is now released and the Highest Self is guiding your path. Fear is now a thing of the past, and your Life is evolving from a Spiritual perspective of Life.

You are now at a level of energy vibration where you can understand the differences between beliefs and Knowing. The guidance from the Divine inner voice should be your daily guiding Light. The results you intend to experience in this lifetime should be realigning with Abundance and living a life based upon understanding Love, Peace, and Light.

Cherish your Love for the world and bring your Original Source Agreement into reality daily!

Chapter 6 Suggestions - Understanding the Inner Voice

The first step to *Consciously Embrace Your True Personality* is to understand the voice within you, which is the Source of Energy guiding you at every moment of your Life. By listening to this inner guidance, you will understand (for some of you for the first time) who you are and the unlimited potential you have to share with the world.

- Nothing in your Life is more important than listening to the inner voice of Source Energy, which permeates every moment of your existence. The challenge for most people is that they continue to reason with their Mental Body reality when they momentarily slip back to Physical Body alignment during challenging times.

- The inner voice or inner guidance has never let you down. If you were to take the time to review your Life as suggested in *Consciously Live What You Feel,* you would determine that the results of your lifetime are all based upon either ego choices or spiritual choices. The guidance within presents Conscious Clarity in moments of silence, not necessarily complete physical silence, but the silence of the mind.

- Your potential is limitless if you always listen only to the inner voice that guides you naturally rather than participate in the "group think" mentality. A blissful life is possible if you open your heart to the energy vibration of Source Energy available to you each moment. Through alignment with this Divine power, you have the capacity for greatness and Abundance in your Life.

- The truth is the inner voice of Source Energy is never quiet. It guides you every moment, but you must "be still" to hear the messages. If you believe that God has deserted you, you are not listening through feelings. You are still thinking and participating in the world of Physical Body alignment. Remember how clever the ego can be when it uses outside influences to anchor in a false belief, holding you prisoner to its manipulation.

- Your natural existence is in Harmony with Life's Spiritual Body alignment perspective. It is in Harmony with your Life Plan (Original Source Agreement) and the gifts you brought with you. If used to their most significant potential, these gifts will bring you an Abundance of anything you need to have a balanced lifetime in this incarnation. When you finally accept the truth of who you are and how much you have to share with the world, Life becomes a joyous dance of endless possibilities.

- As you grow more aware of your spiritual strengths, which can overpower any false reality of the misaligned Mental Body, you stop fighting everything in your situations and flow with Life. An adequately aligned mind is a powerful tool that can be used to its full potential by simply listening to the inner voice of Source Energy. You can and will experience a life of bliss and Abundance once you finally give up the egoistic patterns deeply embedded into your subconscious mind.

- As you grow in Spiritual Enlightenment, you soon discover that Life is a process. You begin to *Consciously Embrace Your True Personality* and find that sharing your life experiences with others is not just for you, but more importantly to be the teacher for others. We are all teachers and students, but our roles change as we grow in Spiritual fulfillment of the Highest Self.

- Where do you stand today concerning your Spiritual Enlightenment? Are you still living in the Third Dimension of ego, or are you growing spiritually and stepping up to your true potential of Knowing you are a Spiritual Being living the experience of humanity? Do you acknowledge that you are part of a bigger plan, or are you locked into a lifetime of following the pack?

The Conscious Clarity Energy Process™ is part of the experience of living a bigger plan than what you may see on the surface of humanity. You are the messenger of the world, and until you decide to speak up and share your gifts with this world, you will remain a prisoner of the ego. There is an overlap of understanding at each junction of Spiritual Enlightenment. We shift our awareness from not knowing to Knowing when we raise our energy vibration to the level of God-realization understanding. At this juncture, we stop the limited beliefs of a Physical Body alignment and live a focused life outcome of pure Joy.

Chapter 7
Aligning Through Love

How Does Love Fit with All This Spiritual Learning

Love is the basis for all Spiritual learning. Love is the Divine spark of Source Energy within you and the most dominant source of energy vibration you will experience at the Highest Self level of understanding. Love is your natural state of Being and is constantly with you in every moment. Love will never fail you. Love is the Light of a God-realized Being.

When you align yourself with the power of Love, you instantly eliminate all Fear in your life. Because Love has no boundaries, it is the only way to experience life to its full potential. Love is the key to a life based upon positive outcomes, Spiritual Enlightenment and Abundance. When walking the path of Love, you find yourself entirely open for acceptance of what IS and naturally radiate the vibrational energy field of Love in every present moment.

We all can keep Love at the forefront of our existence. The challenge is to dismiss all that is non-loving or fearful based on the influences of a fear-based society. We can all bring the Divine energy vibration of Love to our everyday journey. However, when we live in a society based on Fear, it becomes a constant challenge to dismiss all the control mechanisms of the fear-based programming that permeates our daily environment.

If you pay close attention, you will discover that society is programmed to be fearful. This fear-based programming is the false negative reality that we must fight for everything we want to achieve in this lifetime. As an example, focus on politicians. You will notice that everything is a "fight" for them. Most politicians live a life based on separation rather than unity. They constantly argue their positions rather than simply discussing what they can achieve for the greater good of all lovingly. They live based upon the Fear of losing their political position rather than genuinely taking action on what is best for the world.

Then, to add to the "fight", most media programming is based upon positioning negative or fear-based emotions into the subconscious mind, leaving the viewer fearful of what is happening in the world. Most media programming is yet another "fight" to outdo one another's story to influence your opinion. Their motto is "Breaking News" to keep you on the edge of your seat and to mentally program you to accept their "story" as fact. In most cases, they do not know better because equally damaging others have trained them.

There is a better way! To truly understand how to experience life from a Higher Self reality, align yourself with the power of Love!

The Power of Love Will Always Overcome Any Negativity

You have a choice; you can live based on the root emotion of Love or Fear – it's really that simple. Through Love, we excite the higher energies of compassion, guidance, awareness, Peace and Light. You can overcome negative thought patterns and experience life by aligning with Love energy.

Yes, you can now decide to align with Love and never again allow the control methodology of a fear-based society to influence your reality. Take a few moments to review the resultant differences between the various levels of dimensional consciousness described in Illustration E, *Energy Vibration – Life Fuel Source,* at the back of the book. The results of your life are clearly outlined and will bring awareness to your energy vibration level in the present moment.

The most important thing you can do for yourself right now is to move your vibrational assemblage point to a higher level of understanding. As stated many times throughout the *Conscious Clarity Energy Process*™, your reality will be blessed with Conscious Clarity when it aligns with the Spiritual Body in the forefront of your life. By doing so, you will experience pure Bliss centered on the Cosmic Intelligence of Love, Peace and Light.

When you are aligned Spiritually, you see your lifetime in a way few can understand. We live in a Fourth Dimension world, and the mass consciousness is evolving beyond the negativity of the Third Dimension control paradigm. Love will always overcome negativity because it is the highest source of all forgiveness and acceptance of what IS. When you live through the power of Love, your reality is in Harmony with Source Energy and the Original Source Agreement you created.

If you live with compassion, listen to the guidance from within, and bring awareness to the Light of Love that is your natural state of Being, your lifetime will be Joyful in each present moment. You bring all the secrets of Cosmic Intelligence and partake in life as planned initially. Yes, live life based upon Love, and all your challenges in this lifetime will be a blessing just waiting to be recollected and aligned with Source Energy.

Always remember, you are not the body that houses you! You are the Spiritual Being within the core of the form-based structure known as human form. Keep this at the forefront of your reality, and you will experience a lifetime filled with Abundance. The Love for all Human Beings will keep you centered through the Conscious Clarity of True Self.

When your experience anchors in Love, your True Self shines through and dissolves any negativity that arises from the lower levels of understanding – you experience life from an Authentic Self perspective.

Why Is It That When We Love, We Are Living Our True Self

Source Energy only knows Light; since Love is Light, your experience of True Self awareness is always pure Light. The Joy from within you comes to the surface of your reality, and those around you experience the resultant effects of an Enlightened Being before them. Did you know the Light of Love is your normal state of Being?

When you finally accept that you are part of Source Energy, you will understand that you have the creative power of this Cosmic Intelligence guiding your life. You will listen to the guidance from within and never get lost in the lower energy vibration of Fear and negativity. Wear your rose-colored glasses well, as they will keep your perspective of life anchored in the Divine power of Love. Be proud of your natural Being and let others know you have discovered the secret to an abundant and balanced life.

Bring your discoveries to others and allow them to ask questions because when anchored in Love, you are the most compelling influence they could ever ask for in this lifetime. You will be viewed as an anomaly until those around you awaken to the Cosmic Intelligence of Love. Let it be what it is, and go about your daily life with your True Self shining through. Those around you will take notice and wonder what it is that is different about you. They will feel the Love you have to share with them and the rise in their energy vibration when they are around you.

Create a reality based on the Divine power of Love, and you will never feel alone because you can never escape the Divine power of Oneness anchored in Love. Love has no boundaries, rules or human-based reality; Love always conquers the lower energy vibrations of Fear. And always remember, your experiences in this lifetime align with the energy you bring to each life situation. The energy vibration of your actions will clearly define your resultant factor.

When you look back on your lifetime experiences, it will be evident when you were Spiritual Body aligned and when you were Physical Body aligned. You are the only one who understands why you did what you did throughout your lifetime. And, the truth is, when you are completely honest with yourself, you will admit that you are the creator of all the circumstances of your lifetime. You have agreed to every life situation and are the only one responsible for your current life outcome.

By bringing the power of Love to the surface of your daily life situations, you can genuinely understand how Love has affected your life situation in the present moment.

How Has Love Influenced Your Life

When we align Love with our purpose for Being here, life becomes a magical journey of Abundance and deeply embedded Spiritual reality. With Love at the forefront of every action, we set examples for everyone around us, blessed with pure Love, Peace, and Light. We progress in this dance called life as Spiritual Beings rather than the characteristics of a limited human being.

When we anchor in the fact that we are Spiritual Beings within a human experience, how we look at life's situations and challenges becomes different from what most humanity calls reality. When we KNOW who we are and couple that Knowing with the gifts we brought to share with the world, we begin to understand how much Divine Love Energy we have to share with others. We realize that we are here to be of service to others around us and discover within ourselves the incredible way that Love influences our lives and those on our path.

If you take the time to recall how Love has influenced your own life, you will understand that this Divine force for good has exponential effects when you are feeling unconditional Love for yourself. Furthermore, when you recall your Original Source Agreement, it enhances your understanding immeasurably. You discover there are no limits to what you can achieve in your lifetime if you follow the guidance from Source Energy because Source Energy is pure Love. Listening to the silence between the words when Source Energy speaks to you will bring different results to your life journey.

By focusing on Love, you will truly understand life and take action only for the benefit of all. You will bring a perspective of reality based on Love to the world. Therefore, all Fear will purge from your egoistic mind. This alignment with Love is an entirely different way of thinking for most. It will be tested by others over and over again until they finally understand for themselves how powerful Love is. Allow others to do what they may. However, bring up their energy vibration by sending out Love to every life situation you share with others, whether or not you agree with them.

When people in your daily life observe your actions and see the results of your loving reality, they will begin to see that Love conquers all life challenges. People will start to say things to you that they were only keeping to themselves before, and they will understand what it means to be in Spiritual Harmony.

How you approach each life situation can be a blessing or less based on how your Four Body System is aligned. Therefore, always remember where you are currently vibrating and be ready to view life situations from a Conscious Clarity perspective.

This perspective means paying attention to your feelings like never before to keep your Kundalini Energy flowing by placing Love at the top of your action list.

When You Are in a State of Loving Energy, How Do You Feel

When you are in a State of Loving Energy, you will feel blissful because your energy vibration harmonizes with the Source Energy and your Highest Self. As you already know, Source Energy is pure Love; therefore, you are integral to that Love energy.

The easiest way to understand this is to keep yourself properly Spiritual Body aligned, and you will "naturally" be in a state of pure Love. Some professionals (especially in the psychology industry) will tell you that you cannot always be in Bliss because "that's not how human beings' minds transmit to reality understanding." They believe this absurdity because they equate Bliss with happiness rather than inner Joy, which is your natural state of Being. The psychology industry is focused on Mental Body awareness, typically out of Spiritual alignment or rooted in Physical Body alignment. And, you know, Physical Body alignment is rooted in the emotion of Fear.

Therefore, it can be very confusing if these experts constantly tell you that it is natural not to be in a constant state of Bliss. The confusion comes into play only if you are still anchored in a misaligned Four Body System with the Physical Body at the forefront of life. By believing it is unnatural to be in a state of Bliss, you once again become a prisoner of the Mental Body programming forced upon you by the false teachings of an outdated psychology industry. Most of the psychology industry adheres to the old, third-dimensional reality, not fourth-dimensional Spiritual Knowing.

If you still believe you are only the Physical Body, you are continuing to hold yourself prisoner to the egoist beliefs of a low-vibrating society. This low vibration is why staying aligned with the Spiritual Body at the forefront of your life is vital. The Joyous Spiritual Entity, which you indeed are, is naturally in a state of Bliss, but the outside influences may still confuse you.

When you stop thinking from a misaligned perception, your whole life changes. You no longer listen to so-called mental experts, and you acknowledge the truth about how only you can permit anyone to misdirect your understanding of who you indeed are. The Mental Body must serve the Spiritual Body if your perception of life is to evolve. Your progression is why Spiritual Growth should always be your focused intention, not egoistic or self-centered aspiration.

Remember, many beliefs anchor in half-truths and misconceptions of your Highest Self power over any given life situation. So stay aligned with the Spiritual Body at the forefront of your daily life and "recruit the mind to serve the soul." You are not the Physical Body in which you currently reside; you are simply using the Physical Body temporarily to transport your Spirit from one physical place to another.

As you consciously remain in a state of Bliss, you will find that all your false beliefs will disappear, and your loving experiences always come from the Spiritual Joy within your Physical Body. Nothing outside you can ever bring you to the natural state of Joy you genuinely are. Happiness is nothing more than a form-based resultant factor of that which surrounds you. This difference in perception is the Spiritual Key to understanding how you can be blissful in each moment, sharing Love with everyone.

If you believe what society as a whole is still telling you, you are placing yourself in a life situation that is far less than what you were pre-programmed to achieve when you first arrived for the birth of the Physical Body.

If You Feel So Good in Love - Why Choose Differently

It's important to remember that most of the world is still living in a state of Third Dimension, false reality, where a clever ego drives their choices through the manipulation of Fear. However, in the Fourth Dimension or Spiritual Body alignment reality, the natural focus is always on Love. Spiritual alignment is where free will results in actions taken from a loving perspective. The Highest Self awareness action is centered far beyond the limitations of the Third Dimension.

People get confused because they are programmed daily by society to feel that they do not deserve to Love or be Loved. The sad part of this whole illusion is those attempting to program you are, in most cases, not even aware they are doing so. When most of humanity believes in an old paradigm or Third Dimension society, it isn't easy to shift back to an alignment based upon Love. Love has always been the solution to all unrest in the world. However, the politics of Fear have been so deeply anchored into the subconscious mind that it takes work to escape its grasp, and most people are not willing to leave their comfort zones to purge this false reality.

I promise everything will change once you finally break through to the Light of a Spiritual reality. Through Spiritual reality, your perception changes and your energy vibration shifts in a quantum leap into the reality of genuinely recollecting your Original Source Agreement. You do indeed have free will to choose in each present moment to do so, but your energy vibration will be the determining factor in the Spiritual Growth achieved.

If you continue to shift back and forth from Spiritual Body to Physical Body alignment, you will remain confused and under the manipulative control of a cleaver ego. Therefore, always *Consciously Embrace Your True Personality* and follow the loving guidance from within. You can stay connected with the Highest Self reality of life more straightforwardly than you may believe. However, it can be very challenging for a deeply programmed ego to accept this new reality. Therefore, as usual – be gentle with yourself. You are purging a lifetime of false truths, and it will take you some time to anchor in the practice of shifting to a new awareness of truth.

Most of humanity shifts back and forth from Spiritual Body to Physical Body alignment because it takes a lot of Kundalini Energy to burn off years of manipulation. However, once you start to "feel" the results of shifting to the Highest

Self reality of Spiritual Body alignment, you will discover the work is worth it.

When the clever ego comes into play and states, "This is too hard", just smile and understand the shift becomes easier the more you practice releasing the manipulation of the past.

Stay focused in the present moment by bringing awareness to the truth - You are on a Spiritual journey, not only a physical one.

Does Drama Have an Effect on Love

Drama is nothing more than another clever manipulation of the mind. It produces a false reality or fog around your conscious awareness of the truth and confuses you. It can never affect your natural loving Spirit unless you permit it to do so. Remember, in your Original Source Agreement, you pre-destined every possible scenario in your life. Your free will choice and current energy vibration assemblage point will determine your actions. Therefore, stay Spiritual Body aligned and dismiss any false drama in your life.

It takes much more energy to live a life based upon the false illusion of Fear than LOVE. The drama you bring to any life situation is always created by you, even though life situations outside you influence it. Whenever you feel your

Chakras blocked, it's a good bet that you have given control of your life situation back to the clever ego. Please don't allow this false illusion to manipulate you into believing you have no control over it; you are the only one who can change your life situation in a heartbeat. By staying consciously aware of what is happening, you can escape the ego's continued attempts to trick you.

If you feel a drop in your energy vibration, close your eyes, sit silently, and ask for guidance to release the blockage. All drama is nothing more than a script written by egos – don't fall victim to the manipulation. Remember, you cannot experience the emotions of Love and Fear at the same time. So, if you feel out of sorts and are experiencing an energy drop, your ego has regained control over you again.

Drama is your creation, so bring your vision of a Love-based reality to Light, and the drama will disappear as if by magic. You can release all fear-based thoughts and negativity from your life. You are the one who is in total control of the life path you are taking at each moment. If you feel like you are working too hard at purging the drama and nothing is changing, it's because you haven't honestly released the negative thoughts from your Mental Body.

Silence is the key to purging unnecessary thoughts from your Mental Body. The space between the thoughts is where all healing manifests and only you can choose Love over a Fear-based reality to implement the changes.

Why Is Love So Easy

Love is easy because it is your natural state of Being and can only bring about the Highest Self reality into your life. The experience of fulfilling your Original Source Agreement or Life Purpose Plan is only possible by Spiritual action focused on Love. This natural state is void of Fear and only understands the greater purpose in store for you. By keeping the higher vibration of Love in the forefront of each action, you naturally accept what is rather than fight each moment.

A life focused on love energy is a powerful existence. It is a continual vortex of Kundalini Energy flowing through you. Love energy never diminishes. The truth of this reality is complicated for a misaligned person to understand as it is beyond the scope of their Mental Body reality. When Kundalini Energy flows through your Chakras unrestricted, the flow of Love is always the dominant factor.

As children, we experience Love through how we are cared for. We understand this to be our natural state, even if we don't know what it means from a Mental Body perspective. Because we are pure and not yet inundated with the Fear-based reality of society, we share the Love we feel for everyone. We don't understand the false conception that we must "be fearful of strangers." Being fearful of strangers is something taught early in life. We are naive from a societal false understanding perspective and radiate Love. Then, as we become older, we become more guarded due to the fear-based programming of well-meaning people around us.

Imagine what your life would be like today if you never listened to the fear-based people. What would you be doing that is different? Would you still be the same person you are right now? Or would you be a more loving, caring and sharing individual? You are unknowingly programmed to keep guard by listening to most of society and not fully trusting. This programming is even more prevalent in regions where dictators and low-energy civilizations rule.

When we live a life based upon the Cosmic Intelligence of Universal Oneness, we return to Love and our natural state of Being. Spiritual Transformative Education is all about this unity. Love is the core or root of all Spiritual teachings. That's because the return to Love brings us back to the beautiful Peace and Light of our Spiritual Highest Self reality. When we fully anchor in this natural state of Being, we stop listening to the fearful outside influences of negativity. We open our hearts fully and experience life as intended. We continually strive to increase our energy vibration to the Highest Self reality and dismiss all that separates us from Oneness.

Love conquers all unrest in the world, and Love brings about the Highest Self reality of Oneness into our daily lives. When we feel connected in the Oneness of the Universe, we transmit loving energy to everyone around us. This awakening is walking the path of Spiritual Enlightenment. A Spiritually Enlightened person does not subscribe to the absurdity of Fear, because they know all Fear is nothing more than the illusion of a misaligned Four Body System.

A Spiritually Enlightened person brings back the natural flow of Love energy to the forefront of life. The Spiritual Body is at the forefront of daily life experiences, and Kundalini Energy flows unrestricted. Love remains the new constant, and Fear is dissolved once and for all.

How Do We Keep Love the Constant in Our Daily Life

When you decide to allow Love to be your guiding Light in your life, all that ever was currently is and ever will be is in alignment with the Highest Self energy. Therefore, if you know you are a God-realized Spiritual Being, all you need to do is keep Fear out of your Mental Body awareness, and you will naturally "be loving". Love is your true destiny!

Considering the amazing energy that you are, which is the Divine part of the totality of life itself, you have nothing to lose when you align yourself with Love as your natural state of Being. It's time to stop playing small and fully immerse yourself in the beautiful dance of a loving, Peaceful, God-realized Spiritual Being.

Until now, you have been questioning all the tools necessary to keep your Spiritual Body aligned in every life situation. Have you used your tools daily or played small and kept them hidden from the world? Have you used the gifts you brought in this incarnation to their fullest potential? Have you continually focused your attention on the intention of increasing your energy vibration daily? Do you consistently "feel" the guidance of Source Energy flowing through you? Are you in alignment with your Original Source Agreement, and do you genuinely recall the essence of that agreement?

Now is the time to stop asking yourself questions that typically arise from this book's root questions. It's time for you to implement the solutions given to you in each chapter and each section. The Super-ego is more clever than you could ever understand from a Physical Body perspective. If you were to eliminate all negativity and darkness from your life, you would then understand the low-energy vibration of the Super-ego. It is no different in a physically aligned person than the even lower-vibrating ego you became aware of in Book 1, *Consciously Live What You Feel*, at the low energy fields.

You have been looking outside yourself for far too long for solutions to achieving an abundant life. You are the only entity that can bring your life to a heightened state of Spiritual Enlightenment. You need to finalize the purging of false beliefs and stay focused on your Spiritual Growth every moment of your life if you are to truly understand the blessings found in Love or the Highest Self energies.

Sit with this awareness and feel the energy of the Love within you. Bring that Joy to the surface of your life, and you will be aligned with Source Energy and truly understand the magnitude of it all.

Do You Believe Love Conquers All

Only Love can cure all the unrest in the world. Through the high energy of Love, we become our True Self and live at the Highest Self abundant level of its power. Unfortunately, the Fear the ego uses to manipulate the world is anchored so deeply in the subconscious that the Light of Love Energy continues to take a backseat to most of humanity's understanding.

No other emotion other than Love can bring the inner Joy of life to the forefront of the mass consciousness of the world. When deeply clouded in Fear, this false reality dims or truncates the Divine power of Love. The fear-based smokescreen of the manipulative ego holds the mass consciousness at the lowest-energy level of a false reality. However, those who genuinely understand that Love conquers all, meaning it eradicates all lower energy found in fearful thinking, see life differently than most humanity.

All this means is that the vibrational energy of a Spiritually Enlightened person living at the vibrational level of Love Energy is vibrating at the level of the Highest Self reality. Most of society would have you believe you are not worthy of living at this energy vibration level. However, what others believe is not your concern. You are the only one who can step up your energy vibration so that you can feel this Divine reality.

Never allow others to block the flow of Joy within you from moving to the forefront of your life. It's not your responsibility to even care what others think. That statement may sound arrogant based on what the psychology industry would have you believe. Still, it is part of the Spiritual Intelligence level of understanding that most psychologists do not understand.

Only Love can bring your Divine feelings to Light; living Love Energy means living life at the level of God-realization. The Light of this Divine, the Highest Self reality of life, is so bright that it makes egos fearful of its power. Yes, ego always attempts to block this Divine Light from guiding your journey. The ego is very clever and will use society's limited beliefs to hold you prisoner. Therefore, your false beliefs deeply embedded in your subconscious mind require purging to experience the true power of Love Energy.

The challenge is consistently placing Love at the forefront of your life situations. When most of the world is vibrating at the programmed level of Fear, at first, it's a lot of work to overcome this constant bombardment of negative or low-energy, delusional thinking. You are much more than the programmed mind, so step up to believe who you are. When Jesus said, "You shall do far greater works than I have done," it wasn't to be taken lightly. Jesus understood the full potential of Love Energy and asked everyone to follow its Divine power.

Is Love the Focus of Your Life

Living in a state of Love is simply a choice and can be your focused attention in a heartbeat. The Higher Self knows this and is always waiting to bring your energy vibration to the point of Harmony with the Highest Self. However, the Super-ego may be holding you back from achieving this energy vibration level. The path to Spiritual Enlightenment is complicated if you are still shifting back and forth from Spiritual Body to Physical Body alignment.

Returning to one of the previous lessons found in Book 1 – *Consciously Live What You Feel*, you will recall that the difference between Higher Self and the Highest Self reality is a slight shift in energy vibration. The Higher Self is the Soul or Spiritual Seeker within you, the Spiritual Being you are when first incarnated within the Physical Body. At the Higher Self energy vibration level, you know you are a Spiritual Being and have a purpose for Being here. However, you may not fully understand your purpose for Being here or the alignment with your Original Source Agreement. You may not be able to clearly "feel" the power of the Divine Highest Self reality yet.

When you finally change your energy vibration to Highest Self reality (yes, it is a choice), you will understand that you are an intricate part of the Oneness or I-Am-Ness of the Universe. At this energy vibration level, you deeply anchor into the reality of a God-realized Being in the Fifth Dimension. You Know you are walking the path of a Spiritually Enlightened Being by bringing Love to the forefront of every moment. You consciously shift to this new higher energy understanding and use the Cosmic Intelligence of the Universe to guide your journey.

At the energy level of Love, you bring your full potential to the surface of each life situation and accept everything surrounding you in every moment. Still, you do not allow it to influence you from a Super-ego perspective. Love eliminates all the fear-based thoughts that may still cloud your Conscious Clarity of your Highest Self reality. There is no going back when you make that final shift to Highest Self reality. Once you "feel" the power of this Divine intervention in your lifetime, your life evolves to the next level of energy or dimensional reality.

Love is your Highest Self reality found in the Fifth Dimension of life. When you step up your energy vibration to this level of understanding, you radiate Love every moment. When you finally do shift, you will see the blueprint of your Original Source Agreement. You will fully connect with the Conscious Clarity within the Cosmic Intelligence of the Universe.

When you recollect your Original Source Agreement, you will have achieved the level of understanding found in the Fifth Dimension. All you need to do is follow the guidance presented to you from within and allow the last remnants of Fear to fall away from your consciousness.

Why Isn't Love the Focus of Your Life

At this point in your lessons or rediscovery of the Highest Self, you are vibrating at an energy level that should be nurturing your life. You should be anchored deeply in Love, and your experiences should be making a shift towards outcomes that are genuinely only experienced when you are living a Joyous life filled with Love, Peace and Light.

If your life is not changing and revealing your True Purpose for Being here, you still live in Fear at some level. Some of you may become frustrated with your Spiritual Growth process because you still do not fully understand the Divine power within you. If you still believe you are just the Physical Body, somewhere along the path of seeking the answers to your questions, you have still been experiencing Fear.

Remember, Fear is nothing more than the illusion of doubt programmed into your subconscious mind. Doubt controls you. It brings you to question what you already know as truth. Then, the misaligned Mental Body produces a story that aligns with the doubt. You start to slide back down the energy ladder and manifest fearful outcomes in a circle of confusion.

It only takes an instant to slip, but the deeper you slip back into the emotion of Fear, the more challenging it becomes to realign yourself with Spirit. The Super-ego will take this fearful attitude and build a wall or smokescreen around your Spirit. If the outcome in your life situation has not yet brought you the rewards you are moving towards, the Super-ego could be stagnating your Spiritual Growth. Don't fall for this clever trick of the Super-ego. Just because your energy vibration has increased does not mean your resultant life situation will change instantaneously. BE PATIENT!

Today's world is programmed for "instant gratification" and still believes that action must have an immediate energy shift for the better. If you truly understand the power of Love, you will smile when the Super-ego attempts to regain control over you in this manner. Remember, it took you your lifetime up until this moment to get as far as you are now. Why would you believe the change would come in an instant? Yes, you have been focused on Love for a while now, but you still need to accept what IS. Because what IS mirrors your past beliefs and your actions before increasing your energy vibration. If you keep shifting back and forth from Love to Fear, your results become conflicted. Being centered in the Conscious Clarity of the Highest Self should be your goal.

Here enters the dilemma: if you genuinely Know who you are and have placed Love at the forefront of your actions, change will surely come. However, on the other hand, if you still allow yourself to fall back into Physical Body alignment where you are playing the victim of an unfulfilled lifetime, the Super-ego has won back control over you.

Pay close attention to the intentions you are placing on the current path of your journey – now more than ever! Your choices will have an immense ripple effect on your results because you have almost reached the top of the mountain – Spiritual Enlightenment. Now is the time to anchor your Highest Self into the Cosmic Intelligence or Source Energy guiding you. So, make inspiring, Spiritually Enlightened choices that ensure rewards will manifest naturally.

Why Do We Have Free Will

Source Energy has provided us with free will to make choices to teach us how to experience life at the level of Love. Remember, Source Energy (God) created us in its image; since you are an intricate part of Source Energy, you are Love.

Humans created Fear based upon the false reality of the ego, which they created to portray life as only the Physical Body falsely. There is no other explanation necessary to understand this Spiritual Truth. The truth is what it IS; nothing more or less needs clarity. Therefore, by merging the ego with the Soul (which you discovered in *Consciously Live What You Feel*) and allowing the Spiritual Body to be at the forefront of all your decisions, you can quickly purge the false reality of life. Make all your choices based on the energy of Love, and you will eventually experience the results you know you deserve. Remember, there is a difference between Knowing and "kind of believing most of the time." The resultant energies are entirely different when Knowing is in Harmony with Source Energy.

Yes, the outcome of your choices becomes much more noticeable at the higher levels of energy vibration. This resultant factor is because your assemblage point (at the higher vibrations) harmonizes with the Conscious Clarity of Spiritual Knowledge. The higher levels of energy vibration allow us to experience life from the perspective of Cosmic Intelligence rather than ego-based thinking. At the Highest Self-understanding level, you experience the true reality of who you are and anchor in Love Energy. Once you shift to the Highest Self reality of understanding, you are no longer attempting to remove barriers or the smokescreen of the ego.

Therefore, the outcome is in Harmony with the level of a God-realized Being or Love.

The truth is your free will choices will vary depending on the alignment of your Four Body System. If you stay locked in the control of the Super-ego, your assemblage point will not shift to the Cosmic Intelligence level of life, and you will remain ignorant of the Divine power of Love. Therefore, your life is limited, and you cannot experience life from the level of the Highest Self reality.

As you already know, when you truly understand that you are a limitless Spiritual Being having a human experience, your perception of life is different. When you discovered how to eliminate Fear from your life (back in Book 1 - *Consciously Live What You Feel*), you permitted yourself to live life to its fullest potential. Therefore, anchor in what you discovered about yourself and bring Love to the forefront of every decision you make from this moment forward.

In other words, again, stop playing small – you are more than you believe/think you are!

Can You Remember Times When Love Helped You

The mind is a powerful tool to bring Peace to an otherwise conflicted Mental Body. It's not that we don't have gifts to share with the world so much that hold us back from Spiritual Growth; it's a dysfunctional mind that holds us back. Misalignment of the Four Body System produces chaos. Conversely, a Spiritually aligned system harmonizes with Source Energy. You can prove this to yourself by remembering times when you felt empowered by compassion for others and bringing Light to someone who may be emotionally down. This empowerment is called Love and is the only true emotion in your life that matters.

Journaling a few moments daily is one of the best ways to remember how Love serves you and others. Journaling is indispensable for someone constantly shifting back and forth from Spiritual Body to Physical Body alignment. By journaling how your day went, you can reflect on when you fully aligned with Love at the forefront of your reality.

You can start journaling today. Just spend a few moments in the morning to write a few sentences of your intent for the day. Then, in the evening, write a few more sentences to describe how your day went. There is no need to dwell on the outcome or judge yourself; quickly jot down a few lines to reference in the future. You'll be surprised to see how a weekly review of your notes lets you quickly discover how you have aligned your life. I recommend a weekly review because it's a relatively short period but long enough to see patterns in your life.

A review does not mean that you should keep reliving the past. It is simply a tool to assist you in remembering at what level of energy you are at most of the time. If you notice that your notes bring you feelings of Love, Peace and Light, it confirms that you are using your gifts in alignment with your Original Source Agreement. If you see a pattern of Fear-based thoughts and actions throughout the day, you will quickly understand that you are misaligned. If this is the case for you, shift your energy and get back on track without judgment.

The fantastic lesson or take away from journaling is how quickly you realize how many times Love conquers Fear in daily life. You will soon see that by simply making a small shift in your energy vibration, Love can dominate your life. This pattern recognition is critical to observe because you are naturally loving, but the ego still tends to interrupt or short-circuit your natural loving nature.

Another way to remember the power of Love is to practice compassion for others experiencing negativity in their lives. Being compassionate is a powerful way to bring more Love to the surface of any life situation. And, by embracing others in this way, you begin to understand Love is your natural choice for an abundant life.

As a Physically aligned human, you program yourself to be fearful. It's a lot of work to keep this fear-based manipulation in check. Just know that you are more than the Physical Body, and you will find that your actions will change when you are aligned fully with Love guiding you in each moment.

Why Do We Question Love

When Fear is the focal point of your life situations, the Super-ego finds ways to keep you anchored in that Fear. Believe it or not, it is true. The Super-ego is very clever and wants you to remain confused or clouded by its manipulation. The most powerful tool it uses in its arsenal of deception is the judgment of both yourself and others. When judgment is present, you will question the power of Love and lock yourself in the prison of a fear-based illusion.

Therefore, the reason you question Love and its Divine unity with the Source Energy it provides is still rooted in the Mental Body's core belief of Fear when you are misaligned. Yes, it still goes right back to the same false belief programmed into you ever since the birth of the body. A misaligned person will put Fear at the forefront of their life situations and believe themselves to be a so-called victims. This false belief is nothing more than a misaligned Mental

Body. When you align Spiritually, the false stories cease, and you find yourself taking action on only what is real.

When you finally realize once and for all that Love is the only path to the recollection of your Original Source Agreement, you will step into the Light of Source Energy; the Highest Self reality will become your everyday truth. You will stop attempting to reason with the Super-ego and will always follow the guidance from Source Energy – without question. You can accomplish this shift in a heartbeat, but it is necessary always to stay conscious of the manipulative ways of a fear-based society.

If you have not done so, surround yourself with like-spirited people who understand the meaning of Spiritual Body alignment. Shift your perspective to Love and instill a sense of this higher-energy vibration into the world. Rise above the duality of the limited Physical Body alignment and teach what you know is truth. People who embrace this way of living do not need the fear-based stories of misaligned Mental Bodies. The shift becomes permanent, and they see life for the beautiful dance of Love that it truly is.

You will be surprised to find how many people are embracing the shift from Fear to Love. Even though the mass consciousness of the world is still relatively low energy, a few high-energy people can bring about change. The only way to stop questioning what is real and false is by embracing the Highest Self within you. Nothing outside you can assist you in becoming the person you indeed are. Yes, you can be guided or influenced by others who may have been living the path of Love longer than you. However, only your Spirit can overcome the fear-based reality of a misaligned society.

When you focus on Love in every life situation, your whole perception of life shifts. Your life aligns with the Original Source Agreement you made before you arrived in the Physical Body. You embrace the beautiful dance that life truly is, and you begin receiving the Abundance of what you give out to the world back to you ten-fold.

This life is a fantastic dance, so go out and give of yourself to others. Center yourself in Love and provide all your gifts to the power of Oneness. We are all here to give to others as we unite on this beautiful journey called Life. Enjoy the ride!

Chapter 7 Suggestions - Aligning Through Love

Love is the basis for all Spiritual learning. Love is the Divine spark of Source Energy within you and the most dominant source of energy vibration you will experience at the Highest Self level of understanding. Love is your natural state of Being and is constantly with you in every moment. Love will never fail you. Love is the Light of a God-realized Being.

- When you align yourself with the power of Love, you instantly eliminate all Fear in your life. Because Love has no boundaries, it is the only way to experience life to its full potential. Love is the key to a life based upon positive outcomes, Spiritual Enlightenment and Abundance. When walking the path of Love, you find yourself entirely open for acceptance of what IS and naturally radiate the vibrational energy field of Love in every present moment.

- You have a choice; you can live based on the root emotion of Love or Fear – it's really that simple. Through Love, we excite the higher energies of compassion, guidance, awareness, Peace and Light. You can overcome negative thought patterns and experience life by aligning with Love energy.

- When your experience anchors in Love, your True Self shines through and dissolves any negativity that arises from the lower levels of understanding – you experience life from an Authentic Self perspective.

- It's important to remember that most of the world is still living in a state of Third Dimension, false reality, where a clever ego drives their choices through the manipulation of

Fear. However, in the Fourth Dimension or Spiritual Body alignment reality, the natural focus is always on Love. Spiritual alignment is where free will results in actions taken from a loving perspective. The Highest Self awareness action is centered far beyond the limitations of the Third Dimension.

- Love has always been the solution to all unrest in the world. However, the politics of Fear have been so deeply anchored into the subconscious mind that it takes work to escape its grasp, and most people are not willing to leave their comfort zones to purge this false reality.

- Love is easy because it is your natural state of Being and can only bring about the Highest Self reality into your life. The experience of fulfilling your Original Source Agreement or Life Purpose Plan is only possible by Spiritual action focused on Love. This natural state is void of Fear and only understands the greater purpose in store for you. By keeping the higher vibration of Love in the forefront of each action, you naturally accept what is rather than fight each moment.

- A life focused on love energy is a powerful existence. It is a continual vortex of Kundalini Energy flowing through you. Love energy never diminishes. The truth of this reality is complicated for a misaligned person to understand as it is beyond the scope of their Mental Body reality. When Kundalini Energy flows through your Chakras unrestricted, the flow of Love is always the dominant factor.

- Love conquers all unrest in the world, and Love brings about the Highest Self reality of Oneness into our daily lives. When we feel connected in the Oneness of the Universe, we transmit loving energy to everyone around us. This awakening is walking the path of Spiritual Enlightenment. A Spiritually Enlightened person does not subscribe to the absurdity of Fear, because they know all Fear is nothing more than the illusion of a misaligned Four Body System.

Remember, Fear is nothing more than the illusion of doubt programmed into your subconscious mind. Doubt controls you. It brings you to question what you already know as truth. Then, the misaligned Mental Body produces a story that aligns with the doubt. You start to slide back down the energy ladder and manifest fearful outcomes in a circle of confusion.

It only takes an instant to slip, but the deeper you slip back into the emotion of Fear, the more challenging it becomes to realign yourself with Spirit. The Super-ego will take this fearful attitude and build a wall or smokescreen around your Spirit. If the outcome in your life situation has not yet brought you the rewards you are moving towards, the Super-ego could be stagnating your Spiritual Growth. Don't fall for this clever trick of the Super-ego. Just because your energy vibration has increased does not mean your resultant life situation will change instantaneously. BE PATIENT!

Chapter 8

Giving and Receiving

What Is the Power Behind Giving and Receiving

When aligned with Source Energy, we fully understand the power of giving to receive. We realize the Universe's natural balance aligns by giving to others. When we give, we are in balance with the Highest Self and solutions to challenging life situations appear as if by magic. The power of Love is behind life's Abundance and centers on giving and receiving.

By now, you should realize that you are here to assist humanity in understanding the Divine power of Love. To fully understand how giving provides the key to tapping into this unique Love Energy, you must dedicate part of your life to recollecting your Original Source Agreement. This sacred agreement brings the power of giving at the Highest Self level of reality. If you still lack the energy vibration to bring this wisdom to Light, you should consider spending more time in silence and again review Book One in this series, *Consciously Live What You Feel*. You will find what you seek in the silence of connection with Source Energy. There is no other place to align fully with your True Purpose for being here than the silence of non-thought.

Focus on the intention of Being the Spiritual Personality you are. Please don't bother with the rest of the form-based trivial matters of your life situation; they will all fall in place as you grow spiritually. Align yourself with the Harmony of the Universe, which means with the true meaning of Oneness. Accept the guidance that comes through you from Source Energy immediately and bring Knowing to the forefront of each action. Yes, if you are to reach the subsequent rewards of giving to others, this takes a leap of faith on your part.

Source Energy constantly speaks to you, but you must vibrate at a frequency high enough to understand the Divine language transmitted. In the silent moments of non-thought, you will hear the Source Energy guidance with Conscious Clarity. It would be best if you embraced the actions necessary to fulfill what you are directed to accomplish. Wayne Dyer explained it this way, "Don't die with your music still in you." You have a beautiful song to sing, and only you know the lyrics. Bring the vision you feel during the silent moments to the surface of life situations, and you will experience a different outcome.

Giving will bring you closer to Oneness with everyone around you because you are both the student and teacher. Balancing the two is part of a Spiritually driven life. When you focus your attention on your gifts, you will experience times of quantum leaps in energy vibration. These gifts will send you on a journey you could never experience if you stay anchored in a Physical Body belief structure where other egos manipulate you.

By opening yourself up entirely to the power of giving your gifts to others, you will be in Harmony with others who have shifted to Spiritual Body alignment. People will show up exactly when you need them to assist you in fulfilling your Original Source Agreement. Sometimes, the most straightforward idea will show up as a recommendation by someone else. Also, you will feel an energy shift when you harmonize with those sent to help you. By giving yourself first, you will become the catalyst for manifesting a life of Abundance for everyone around you. Rewards will be tenfold.

Nothing in life happens by accident. There is a Divine plan for everything, and you are the thread that holds the fabric of this fantastic woven Cosmic Energy together. The power of the Universe is within your grasp. All you need do is step outside your comfort zone to experience what greatness is truly in store for you.

Give of yourself as never before and you will bring Spiritual wisdom to Light!

Why Should We Give First Before Receiving

Giving is your natural state of Being when your life flows through the Divine power of Love. You *Consciously Embrace Your True Personality* by giving to everyone who flows with you on your life path. Sharing the Highest Self realization with everyone else is an enriching experience. You find that by being there for those who come to you for guidance, there is a natural feeling of compassion for everyone, and you experience a mirror image of the Love you are giving out.

If you are self-centered and only think of yourself, or what you will get if you give to someone else, the results will not be the same. It would be best to fully embrace the Divine power of giving without thoughts like "What's in it for me?" – That's old, Third Dimension thinking. Remember, you are here to serve.

When you give from a Spiritual perspective, you focus on "how may I serve?" Each thought aligns with the Highest Self realization, and your life evolves from a much higher state of consciousness. There's no way to explain the feelings of living life from the Highest Self realization of this perspective; you must BE the experience.

When aligned with the flow of sharing your Highest Self with the world, you experience being a natural leader. You will find that the more you give of yourself, the more you want to give. You could call it a "natural high" because the power of giving driven by Love Energy is like nothing else you will ever experience. When you are vibrating at this extremely high energy vibration, all life's challenges disappear, and you see the good in everyone. You become more compassionate and even become a better listener.

Many people equate giving to material or form-based "things" only. With this perspective in mind, you will never honestly give of yourself. Giving of yourself means your Spiritual Self first – Your Highest Self, not form-based possessions.

Your life path is a sacred journey blessed with the resultant effects of a Spiritually Purpose-driven Life. Bringing this vision to the forefront of every action is the equivalent of embracing the power of Love with every breath. You naturally breathe in oxygen to fuel the Physical Body; by embracing Love, you naturally fuel the Soul. "Share the Love" is not just a cute expression; it's the Spiritual Mantra of the Soul.

When you align yourself with giving first, you become more aware of your power. You will find that many people will benefit by simply sharing the gifts you brought to this Earth school. Why not step it up a level right now and dedicate yourself to bringing the power of giving to your daily life situations?

You will feel the power of Oneness grow in energy vibration the more you give of yourself!

What Is Your Natural State of Being

Your natural state of Being mirrors the realization that you are a Spiritual Being having a human experience. When you live your daily life based on this reality, you focus on Love as your primary emotional embrace. Everything you do in each life situation involves compassion and sharing your Spiritual Knowledge with others. All self-centered thinking stops and you become at Peace with your Spiritual life.

Keeping the Spiritual Body at the forefront of every action guides you toward further Spiritual Growth and makes an exceptional difference in how your life evolves. This realization is not just a trumped-up reality of a Super-ego attempting to trick you into its clever manipulations. The reality of your genuine identity becomes deeply embedded in your daily life situations, and your perception of what IS moves you forward in a way that the mind will never understand from a Physical Body perspective.

Your fundamental choice is straightforward; you can live your life from a Spiritual or Physical Body perspective. This choice means Love-based or Fear-based, as you discovered earlier in the *Conscious Clarity Energy Process*™. You say Yes to Spiritual Growth and continue to increase your energy vibration, or you stay stuck where you are and carry on as most of humanity does, lost in a Physical Body reality.

For some people, keeping up the momentum of Spiritual Growth is too challenging. I've experienced people moving forward in energy vibration quickly, but then they reach a plateau and stop – they are in a comfort zone, a Super-ego control mechanism. They place a timeframe on Spiritual Growth, and if they do not achieve a particular goal in a set period, they settle for where they are in the moment. Then, Super-ego takes complete control of their actions.

If you still do not recollect your Original Source Agreement, you have possibly reached a point in Spiritual Growth where you are comfortable with where you are. That's amazing; you have come a long way, but be cautious of your perception at this level of Spiritual Awareness. This comfort zone is equivalent to going to college and quitting a few classes short of receiving your final diploma. You have a lot of awareness, but you are not at the level of understanding where you live each moment for Spiritual Growth or the level of Love, Peace and Light that you could be.

There is unquestionably a point of comfort in the realization that you are a Spiritual Being having a human experience. However, the momentum you have built over the discourse of the *Conscious Clarity Energy Process*™ to increase your energy vibration can be very confusing if you have not shifted entirely to Spiritual Body alignment. The Super-ego can be very convincing at this point of Spiritual Enlightenment.

Be at Peace and *Consciously Embrace Your True Personality*, but never fail to continue your Spiritual Growth discourse. You are now at a tipping point and will never return to a certain extent, but you have a long way to go to reach true Spiritual Enlightenment.

Do You Live Your Life Based Upon Rules

There is a certain tipping point in Spiritual Growth where you no longer live your Earthly lifetime based upon only adhering to society's rules. You know that you have grown beyond the ego-controlled dogma. You break away from the drama of everyday life situations happening around you. You discover that you can keep a low profile about where you are heading and stop taking the rules of a low-vibrating society so seriously.

This shift occurs at different times in your lifetime but always in Harmony with your Original Source Agreement. "There must be something more to this life than what is seen on the surface" becomes more relevant once you shift entirely. You understand that it is unnecessary to follow the pack, and you become more of a leader each moment. You know change is coming, and you stay anchored in Cosmic Intelligence rather than mindlessly following society's rules.

As a small child, I remember constantly questioning society's rules. This questioning was especially true during the times of my Catholic childhood training. I would ask the priests and nuns how they knew what they professed as Truth. The answer was always the same; "Truth written in the Bible." My answer to this was always, "The Bible was written by man and based upon the perception of man's beliefs of what Jesus said. Therefore, how do you know that it's not just a reference? If you have not personally experienced the words of Jesus, you do not know the Bible to be true. You believe the referenced option of others that may or may not have experienced the reality." I can tell you this did not go over well with the religious leaders and is probably ruffling some feathers with some of you.

We all have experiences in life that bring about beliefs on the surface of a lifetime. However, the more profound knowledge of Spiritual Knowing radiates at the Highest Self-understanding level. The Super-ego will continue to bring beliefs back into your daily life and free will choices. If a set of man-made rules controls your beliefs, observe the energy vibration level of those who created the rules for you to follow. Have these rule makers grown to a level where they understand the Highest Self reality? Are they in Harmony with Love, Peace and Light energies?

Concerning the governing leaders, the mass consciousness of the world has not reached a point of Spiritual Growth. Most people in government are still just politicians, not Spiritual Leaders. If they are not living at least from a Higher Self perspective of life – why do you follow them and their rules so freely?

Are You in Touch with Your Highest Self

Your Higher Self is the Soul within the Physical Body, but your Highest Self is the God-realization of who you are. When you are consciously experiencing life from the exceptional Joy within you, believing in anything outside yourself becomes unnecessary. This God-realization is where the confusing part comes into play in the dance of everyday life.

When you live in the Knowing of Highest Self reality, you can discern the subtle change necessary to evolve to the Highest Self guidance available. Now that you have fully merged the ego and Soul as ONE, you can easily live each day from this blissful assemblage point by simply paying attention to your feelings. When you check in with your Highest Self reality as the normal function of your experiences in life, everything begins to make a lot more sense.

No one is better at Knowing what's best for you than the Higher Self personality guided by the Highest Self energy. You will never escape its tender, loving hand as you grow spiritually. The depth of knowledge within you is dynamic; it can overpower any outside interferences attempting to block its energy flow. If you follow the path of the Highest Self guidance daily, your life will be as planned at the higher energy levels of your Original Source Agreement.

The more you give of yourself to others from a Spiritual perspective, the more you will increase your energy vibration and, therefore, increase Abundance in your life. By stepping up to your Spiritual greatness, you open the door to an increased Light to guide your path. You cannot plan or set up this doorway as a goal. This doorway is your natural path found by surrendering entirely to the guidance of the Highest Self. Nothing outside you can even come close to the feelings you will experience when your life is in Harmony with the Highest Self reality.

As you become more adept at bringing your Spiritual visions to the forefront of your reality, you will discover what giving means. You will understand that you are here to assist others in Spiritual Growth, and the levels of understanding you will experience for yourself will grow exponentially. As your energy level increases, you will realize just how powerful your Highest Self truly is. Enjoy your journey into the upper levels of Self-realization and branch out to your community to share your gifts.

The rewards will blow your mind!

Does Giving Only Help Others

When you give yourself to others, you manifest the energies of Love, Peace, and Light to true potential. Many of the great experiences in life come from simple random acts of kindness from one person to another. By helping others, you are creating energy streams that will ripple effect many lives. You may not realize it now, but you certainly will experience the effects of living this reality of Oneness connection.

I love the movie, "Pay It Forward", because it brings this vision of assisting others in life to the forefront of our consciousness. In the film, no unique talents are necessary to bring about change to enhance another person's life; it is just a matter of exchanging energy in a way that uses Love to assist others.

Have you ever thought of your effect on other people simply by expressing an interest in who they are and what they are attempting to accomplish in life? If not, pay close attention to what is presented to you each moment. When you become a better listener, you will discover a completely different world patiently waiting for you to evolve to this level of understanding. This understanding has nothing to do with what you think, believe or trust. It is simply a shared energy at the Highest Self level of reality and can bring about lasting change in the world.

When I say become a better listener, it does not mean only from a Physical Body perspective; it means listening to the Source Energy guidance that comes through you after someone has shared what's on their mind. When you remove your self-interest from the situation, your perspective evolves to Oneness, which means you move beyond separation. By living in constant meditative action, the world around you will increase its mass consciousness energy level. It's a shift that is not noticed by many at our current level of mass consciousness awareness, but it is growing in energy vibration each moment.

Yes, you have the power to increase the mass consciousness of the world. You can choose to be a messenger of Love, Peace and Light or continue on a lower energy path and follow the unconscious patterns of ego-based reality.

Your feelings are a roadmap to achieving greatness for yourself and those surrounding you. Feelings will always provide accurate feedback when you consciously pay attention to the level of Kundalini Energy that is constantly flowing through your Chakra Energy System. As you continue to consciously increase your energy vibration, bring full attention to the intention of Consciously recording your feelings. Keep your journal updated as you continue on the Spiritual Growth path until you feel completely in touch with your Original Source Agreement.

How Do You Feel When You Give

When you feel tranquil or in bliss, you embrace your natural Being. You can BE in this beautiful energy all day if you bring the powers of Love, Peace and Light to every action you take. Giving is one of the most beneficial aspects of life. It produces high-energy feelings for both the giver and receiver. When we anchor in the realities of the feelings experienced through the power of giving, it changes our perspective as we grow Spiritually. We no longer care about what's in it for ourselves. We dance through life with an awareness that only comes from the understanding that we are all One.

When we give of ourselves, we open limitless possibilities for mass consciousness and Spiritual Growth. Spiritual Transformative Education focuses on the root power of giving to others from an energy position of pure Love. When you finally truly understand that every action you take in life has a ripple effect on humanity, you will be ready to receive the rewards that are the natural result of a giving lifestyle.

Most people equate giving to some form of giving material things, such as money or the "things" money can buy. Although giving material things you possess is a beautiful gesture, it's not nearly as beneficial in the big picture of life as giving of yourself. Rather than giving material things, how would you feel if you gave what you know through teaching?

For example, does it do a person better to eat fish that you give them, or does it do more for their overall growth to teach them how to fish? Yes, giving a fish satisfies the immediate requirement for food, but once the food is gone, the person will still require additional handouts if they do not know how to provide fish.

Massive corporations falsely restrict People's lives by providing all the necessities of living that they no longer know how to provide for themselves. Another example of this is general, everyday food. How many of you have a garden to offer rich, nutritious food for the table? Have you ever even attempted to grow a garden, or do you rely on everyone else to provide food for you daily? What would you do if food was suddenly unavailable from a grocery store? Could you grow your vegetables, and could you catch your fish? These may seem trivial, especially in Western cultures where food is abundant, but they are simply part of daily life for many people worldwide.

The point here is that you have certain natural gifts to cultivate in this lifetime. Sharing your gifts with others increases the energy vibration or potential for developing them so humanity benefits.

The feelings generated in energy vibration by giving yourself to others also enhance the mass consciousness of the immediate community and the world. The ripple effects of sharing yourself with others transcend anything the egoistic mind could ever do without Spiritual Guidance.

How Do You Feel When You Receive

How do you feel when you receive from others? Do you experience an inner feeling of Joy and acceptance for whatever you have received? Or are you nervous and wonder what they will expect in return? Does their generosity humble you, or are you thinking about what it means only for you in the exchange? From the natural Spiritual perspective of receiving, the feelings can be somewhat different than if ego drives the feelings.

Many people do not feel worthy of receiving from others and insist on a payment in return. This belief is mainly due to how their programming throughout life. When we receive, we ultimately thank the Universe for balancing the other side of the giving equation. This statement may contradict the lessons taught, especially the myth that "it is better to give than receive." Source Energy never intended you to provide everything for yourself; we are all here to assist one another. The Universe has a Divine balance that the mind cannot comprehend.

If you consciously monitor your life, you will quickly see a natural progression of receiving based on how you use your gifts to benefit Oneness. By experiencing the natural process of receiving, our feelings grow in Harmony with the balance of the Universe.

Imagine a world without currency – yes, there's no money to purchase any products or necessities for living. Could you revert to bartering, using only your gifts or knowledge to exchange equal value? Could you even start to discuss how to receive what is needed to live life to your most significant potential? If you answered no, you are living in the mental control mechanism of money in exchange for a product.

From a Spiritual perspective, money is nothing more than "green energy", and receiving it has nothing to do with material things. It concerns an even energy exchange between others based upon equality. Opening yourself up to Oneness and having balance in all your dealings in life may sound far-fetched to most of you. However, the natural state of Being in Oneness is the intent. Feel the energy of Oneness throughout your day. Accept the provided exchange. Do so without questioning it unconsciously. Feel that energy momentarily and then consciously develop it to its full potential.

By increasing the energy level of receiving with Oneness in mind, you open yourself up to an abundant lifestyle. You bring feelings of Joy and Harmony to those around you and genuinely understand what it means to be with the balance of the Universe.

Imagine how you would feel if you truly understood that sharing yourself is the catalyst to a balanced life where the feeling of Joy is always present, no matter the situation. Giving and receiving are of equal Spiritual value.

Why Is It Important to Feel the Same Both Giving and Receiving

Helping others is the stepping stone to the higher vibration of Spiritual Enlightenment. Helping others is the natural energy rooted in the Cosmic Intelligence of all Spiritual Beings. Helping others is intended to be the direct link to understanding the value of Oneness reality. Everything in the Universe balances through the Divine power of giving and receiving. In that case, there is no need to have separation based upon monetary judgment of perceived success rooted in the false, egoistic belief that you are better than someone else if you have an excess of money. You instantly become successful when you realize that you are part of the totality of life itself.

When you finally accept that you are a Spiritual Being having a human experience, you stop competing in daily life and begin to share in the dance of what is truly important. The separation disappears, and you become aware of the natural progression of moving through life from the Highest Self perspective. The Highest Self does not understand duality or the concept of cause and effect. The Highest Self only understands Love Energy and the core Knowing of its Divine Cosmic Intelligence.

Love Energy multiples when you have a Spiritual Body perspective of life. You feel the same whether you are giving or receiving. From this Spiritual perspective, unity is simply a natural state of being, and you give of yourself freely. In this Spiritual state of consciousness, the perceived need to receive when you give is gone. You share more of yourself for the simple purpose of helping others to achieve a higher energy vibration in life.

The discussion of helping others brings to mind an example of giving I experienced with my friend, Marianne Williamson, a few years ago. For those of you who do not know Marianne, she is an internationally acclaimed Spiritual Author of multiple books and online programs and a sought-after public speaker. Most recently, Marianne is running a campaign for President of the United States. At the time of my example, Marianne was the head minister of Renaissance Unity Church in Warren, Michigan.

I was a volunteer at the Veterans Hospital in Ann Arbor, Michigan, where part of my volunteer service was walking around the hospital, interacting with the Veterans, and bringing the high energy of Joy to the forefront of people's lives in any way possible. Many of the patients, especially those in the nursing home area of the facility, were very depressed. They seemed to have nothing to look forward to, and it was a deficient, vibrating energy to be around. I thought bringing some additional high-vibrating Spiritual energy into their lives would be a good idea.

Therefore, I invited Marianne Williamson to join me at the Ann Arbor Veterans Hospital to spend the day and speak with some of the patients and staff. However, lovingly, she said, "Rather than speaking to only a few people, why don't we arrange a full-blow speaking engagement for the entire Veterans Hospital facility so that I can fully provide my gifts." Of course, I immediately agreed to this suggestion.

However, I told Marianne the hospital doesn't have a large budget for such events. I knew Marianne receives thousands of dollars per event to present keynote speeches internationally. Marianne decided to provide the service for "free" and even asked me, "Do you want me to drive us to the hospital?" Now, that's what I call bringing the power of "giving" to the forefront of one's reality. This selfless act of kindness will always be at the top of my list as an example of unconditional giving.

We all have a Divine set of gifts to share with the world, but it's through each random act of kindness that the mass consciousness of the world evolves. Even though our gifts directly link to our career of choice, where we receive a monetary reward, there's always an opportunity to volunteer your services to those who cannot pay. We are all equal, and I encourage you to share your gifts with everyone who crosses your path on life's beautiful journey.

Open your heart fully, share yourself like never before, and you will witness miracles happening around you daily!

Have You Tried Volunteering

We all have careers that we use to provide for all of our daily human needs. Yes, payment in some manner for our services is received, and hopefully, you are amongst the population that is using their Divine gifts entirely. You show up for work each day and bring forth your best effort to give of yourself and receive remuneration for the service you provide. However, there is also a place to share your Divine gifts with those who cannot afford to pay you for your services. When you fully open your heart to this beautiful journey, you will also find yourself volunteering. In some way, heal or remove "disease" from someone less fortunate. If you have not volunteered your services to the community in some way, you should seriously ask yourself why not.

Whether you believe it or not, you are here to assist in healing that part of you that is holding you back from realizing your full potential. You are a product of the Divine Cosmic Intelligence created to fulfill an enigma within the Universe. You committed to bringing your Divine gifts to the forefront of your Original Source Agreement by showing up here on Earth. Volunteering your services to others brings into balance the Divine purpose of giving and receiving.

There is no better way to achieve Harmony with Source Energy than to share your gifts with others, regardless of their ability to pay. When you understand the difference between wanting and needing, you already receive more than you need. The excess you receive in "green energy" or "money" is not meant to be wasted on unnecessary expenditures. Share your excess money with the world. Many nonprofits count on people with excess funds to share their wealth with the community.

Another way to share is to give of yourself through the power of volunteering. Bring your gifts to those who need them, but never turn anyone away who cannot afford to pay you for them. Gifting your services as a volunteer is another opportunity to "pay it forward."

You never know what you are achieving when you share yourself. You can assume that others will benefit from what you share with them, but you never really get to follow up on how your teachings have helped each person who crosses your path. There is always a ripple effect to whatever you share in life. The limited understanding of the Mental Body can never fully appreciate what you have done for someone until you consciously choose to follow up on your efforts. In the big picture, all you need to do is provide your services to everyone who shows up on your path, and you will be rewarded tenfold without any effort whatsoever.

At one time or another, we have all experienced the tithing process, typically based upon some rule-based, religious endeavor of the human experience. Tithing is usually a percentage (10%) of a salary you have earned; however, the part missing from the experience is that you need not use only funds paid to you. By volunteering your time to provide a service to others who cannot afford to pay you, you bring tithing to the energy vibration level in Harmony with the Universal power of Oneness.

How often you volunteer is not to be measured monetarily based on how much you could have made by only servicing those who can afford it. When you volunteer, you will find a completely different reward for your time, not measured by monetary gain. You will find a connection with others, one you could never realize from a "what's in it for me" perspective of giving. Pay close attention to the ripple effect of one random act of kindness by sharing your gifts with others – no matter the circumstances.

What Does Connection with Others Do for You

When I speak of connection with others, it's rooted in the Spiritual perspective of Oneness. This Oneness means every connection you make with someone through the power of giving brings greater acceptance to your Authentic Self. The ego merges more, and you begin to remember your Original Source Agreement in greater detail. This Divine connection felt at the Highest Self reality of life is a stepping stone for you to fulfill your True Purpose for being here.

The more you connect with other people at the level of Source Energy awareness, the more you become the person you always were meant to be. This connection awareness is a significant time in your learning, so pay close attention to everything around you. As you begin to give more of yourself through the power of giving unconditionally, you will find yourself dancing through life with a new sense of priority. The path you are on now is not for the weak but for strong, energized Spiritual Seekers who have grown far beyond the limited understanding of mortal man.

When you align your life with others connected to the Highest Self reality, you KNOW more and DO much less. This reality is the paradox you will find yourself, an energy vibration that not only provides more of what you need quickly or with little physical effort but also with the power of recollection of your Original Source Agreement. Your outlook on life changes and you begin to experience levels of understanding only available to those in Harmony with Cosmic Intelligence.

Even though you are truly here for everyone else, you will experience a profound understanding of how the whole process of giving and receiving balances your life. You walk with a Lighter step because the energy vibration surrounding you anchors into your subconscious. This shift is a significant acceptance of who you are – a Spiritual Being having a human experience. You understand that part of the totality of Oneness is in pure Harmony with Source Energy. This Highest Self realization is about the connections made in the Fourth and Fifth Dimensions of Life.

By accepting everything around you without judgment, you will step into the next level of Cosmic Intelligence or the Fifth Dimension of Life. You will no longer question why or who you are here at this energy-vibration level. You will anchor yourself on a path that brings about change for you and everyone you meet because you will be in Harmony with like-*spirited* people who understand the paradox of human understanding – more commonly known as duality.

Is It Really All About You or Everyone Else

Duality is a product of the human experience, which man has created to bring separation to a false reality. The ego needs duality to survive because it needs to be in control. Duality is taught even by those considered to be Spiritual leaders in the world. This enigma makes it difficult for us to break away from the control mechanisms of the Mental Body. Therefore, the Super-ego gains strength because the topic of duality provides talking points for discussion even in Spiritual communities. If you genuinely want to bring Oneness into your life at the Source Energy and Conscious Clarity of Self level, you must first understand that nothing other than Love is essential.

The limitless offerings from the Universe continue through Love, not the duality or yin and yang, which is a false understanding of life in the Physical Body. You must bring your energy vibration up to the level of consistent, Highest Self awareness to fully understand what is in store for you. Yes, this means you will be bucking the system of egoistic control. If you are to finally reach past the limited perspective of Mental Body control over you, you must make a conscious choice to shift your perspective.

When you finally understand that duality is a complete waste of form-based energy, you will shift your perspective entirely into Spiritual Body alignment and Harmony with your Original Source Agreement. Once this final shift occurs, you will "feel" the need to be there for others like never before. This awareness means the Truth about your life is revealed at the Highest Self level of Cosmic Intelligence and in Harmony with your Original Source Agreement.

Until you fully grasp the reality of Oneness, you will still function in a society that continues to control you for other egoistic control purposes. I urge you to believe in yourself and the gifts you have brought to this human experience. Your gifts are all you need to propel your Higher Self into the expanding power of the Universe. We have only just begun to realize the Truth of how we have been manipulated for centuries by those who would seek separation as a means to control us.

The human experience is blissful – that's the Truth! Therefore, break away from the limited power of duality, and you will feel the Divine power of Source Energy guidance. Source Energy is patiently waiting for you to become One with ALL THAT IS. When you only take action based on what is best for everyone, life evolves into an Oneness reality, where Love overcomes all unrest. Imagine yourself as a spark of energy that is part of the entire Universe, and you will start to see the big picture of what life is all about.

Being the "change that you want to see in the world" is not about what you are to receive or give. It's about the wholeness that unites us in the Harmony of Oneness. If you can grasp for even a moment the limitless possibilities available, you will never again question why you are here.

Many clues are provided to you each day to bring the insanity of duality to the forefront of your understanding. So, I ask you, "Are you ready to experience the true bliss of Life experience?" It's time to wrap your arms around the Divine power within you and never look back!

Can You Have Your Cake and Eat It Too

We live in a world controlled by duality, taught that "cause and effect" are the typical aspects of reality. However, there is only Light, and Divine Energy is Love, which endures all and does not require the comparison of duality.

The old saying, "You can't have your cake and eat it too", is nothing more than a figment of a misaligned Mental Body. If you align with the Physical Body at the forefront of your reality, you are simply experiencing life at a lower energy vibration than you deserve. You can realign your Four Body System at any moment; all you need do is accept that you are a Spiritual Being with a lower vibrating, human experience.

There's no need to believe everything you are told by those surrounding you who want to control your life.

All change comes first from a vision of what the future can hold. By accepting your Divine Energy transmitted through you from a Highest Self guidance perspective, you can break away from the control mechanism and use it to empower others to realize their greatness. Giving what you know to be Truth will increase the energy vibration of everyone who shares your life path.

The cake metaphor is nothing more than a false reality because you have Source Energy guiding your way. You can overcome the false references that most people believe are true and increase your energy level to be in Harmony with Source Energy. This shift is not as complicated as the ego would have you believe. So, stop believing the lies and bring your Highest Self to the forefront of every action you take from this moment forward.

Most people are not ready to increase their energy vibration to the level of Spiritual Body alignment because they are still fearful of what their limited mind can accept as Truth. They live in this paradox where they know there is something more to this life than what is seen on the surface, but they are not willing to grow past the belief of a manipulating system of "cause and effect".

When you finally increase your energy vibration to God-realization level, you will be ready to honestly share yourself completely. You will not understand the true power of "giving to receive" until you accept yourself for who you are.

Do You Live Your Life Based Upon Sharing

Your responsibility to Oneness is to share your gifts fully with the world. You have within you the most significant gifts the world has ever known, but you still view them as a minor aspect of Self. By the time you read the rest of this book, I hope you will have dropped the false belief system controlling your life to this point. The Truth is it takes work to bring your Highest Self to the forefront of each moment. However, most of you will not take up the task of Spiritual Growth as the most essential aspect of your life. Most of you will come to a standstill and live a comfortable lifetime because of what you have learned. Most will not utilize the Divine Power of giving to its full potential, which is required to step up to the Fifth Dimension of Life.

Whatever you decide to take action on will still create a comfortable life experience with the knowledge you have brought to Light thus far in the Fourth Dimension. It is your choice and only yours to move into the Fifth Dimension of reality. This Fifth Dimension is where all the Abundance thrives, and your rightful moment to receive the guidance necessary to achieve it is waiting there. Either continue to play small or increase your energy vibration to the Highest Self level of reality in the Fifth Dimension.

As we continue from this point forward, a false belief system will still randomly challenge you. However, it will serve you best if you shift your perspective away from the false reality of a Physical Being experience. What you choose is up to you, and only you can bring your Original Source Agreement to Light!

As we move forward in Spiritual Growth, the naysayers will be left behind, and those of you who truly understand the power you have within you will begin to take the quantum leaps necessary to achieve your Ultimate Destiny. You will now have the opportunity to shift your consciousness from the lower energy fields of duality to the Highest Self reality of Oneness.

There are amazing Universal Truths available to you, but you must be willing to do the work necessary to achieve the Spiritual Growth lessons from the Highest Self perspective. To experience all that is available, you must purge the lower energy level of the Physical Body alignment. One of the most exciting energies resonates in the Universal Laws of Attraction. Most of you have heard of these channeling messages, but only a few understand they are a stepping point in your Spiritual Enlightenment journey.

What is the Universal Law of Attraction

Many Cosmic Intelligence tools are available to utilize on your Spiritual Growth path. The Universal Law of Attraction is one of them. However, your energy vibration and Four Body System alignment will determine the outcome of your vision. With Love, Knowing, and an open-heart philosophy of life, you can enhance your life situation tenfold. However, to achieve the full potential of your power, you must shift your perception to a Spiritual phase of awareness. The mass consciousness of the world has not truly understood the power of Spiritual Transformative Education because most of those teachings still focus primarily on the Mental Body.

The Law of Attraction states that what you think about most will manifest in your life. This statement is absolute and cannot be changed no matter how hard you try. Unfortunately, most people limit themselves to Physical Body awareness when using the power of the Universal Law of Attraction. Yes, there is more to attraction than what only the Mental Body perceives on the surface of life. If you only view the Law of Attraction from a Physical Body alignment perspective, you minimize the outcome to manifesting only material- or form-based results. However, there is a way to increase energy to this extraordinary Divine power.

Transform your understanding beyond the limits of the mental body, and you will fully achieve your destiny. If you continue increasing your energy vibration daily, you will quickly understand that there is no limit to what you can achieve. By bringing your awareness to the level of Cosmic Intelligence that is genuinely available, you will start bringing in the energies that have eluded you thus far. These energies are where all the significant shifts happen, beyond the limited understanding of only Mental Body dogma.

By shifting your life situation perception to a Spiritual nature, you will see what you are truly capable of with Conscious Clarity. You will feel the energies increasing and begin to experience a life destined for you in your Original Source Agreement. This Spiritual path magnifies for a person with Spiritual Transformative Education at the forefront of every life occurrence. The path is not an easy one at first because the limited understanding of most people is so deeply rooted in what you think. You will continue repeatedly testing until you finally acknowledge the awareness found in feelings and the alignment of a Spiritual Body reality.

Most people misunderstand the power of the Law of Attraction because they are so deeply vested in their current energy vibration level. This mistake is to be understood, as it takes a powerful surge of energy to break the bonds of a Physical Body alignment perspective. However, once you acknowledge the power of permanently shifting your Four Body System to a Spiritual Body alignment, you will no longer shift back to the limited aspects of the Physical Body.

The Law of Attraction is not only a form-based endeavor. Once you finally realize this, you will attract only those aligned with your Original Source Agreement. Then, you will experience the Abundance of life that is your destiny and no longer focus on the limited understanding of a false belief system. The shift will bring Conscious Clarity to you from a completely different perspective, and Abundance will flow into every category of your life as never before.

Chapter 8 Suggestions - Giving and Receiving

By now, you should realize that you are here to assist humanity in understanding the Divine power of Love. To fully understand how giving provides the key to tapping into this unique Love Energy, you must dedicate part of your life to recollecting your Original Source Agreement. This sacred agreement brings the power of giving at the Highest Self level of reality.

- When aligned with Source Energy, we fully understand the power of giving to receive. We realize the Universe's natural balance aligns by giving to others. When we give, we are in balance with the Highest Self and solutions to challenging life situations appear as if by magic. The power of Love is behind life's Abundance and centers on giving and receiving.

- Your natural state of Being mirrors the realization that you are a Spiritual Being having a human experience. When you live your daily life based on this reality, you focus on Love as your primary emotional embrace. Everything you do in each life situation involves compassion and sharing your Spiritual Knowledge with others. All self-centered thinking stops and you become at Peace with your Spiritual life.

- There is a certain tipping point in Spiritual Growth where you no longer live your Earthly lifetime based upon only adhering to society's rules. You know that you have grown beyond the ego-controlled dogma. You break away from the drama of everyday life situations happening around you. You discover that you can keep a low profile about where you are heading and stop taking the rules of a low-vibrating society so seriously.

- Concerning the governing leaders, the mass consciousness of the world has not reached a point of Spiritual Growth. Most people in government are still just politicians, not Spiritual Leaders. If they are not living at least from a Higher Self perspective of life – why do you follow them and their rules so freely?

- Your feelings are a roadmap to achieving greatness for yourself and those surrounding you. Feelings will always provide accurate feedback when you consciously pay attention to the level of Kundalini Energy that is constantly flowing through your Chakra Energy System. As you continue to consciously increase your energy vibration, bring full attention to the intention of Consciously recording your feelings. Keep your journal updated as you continue on the Spiritual Growth path until you feel completely in touch with your Original Source Agreement.

- Most people equate giving to some form of giving material things, such as money or the "things" money can buy. Although giving material things you possess is a beautiful gesture, it's not nearly as beneficial in the big picture of life as giving of yourself. Rather than giving material things, how would you feel if you gave what you know through teaching?

- How do you feel when you receive from others? Do you experience an inner feeling of Joy and acceptance for whatever you have received? Or are you nervous and wonder what they will expect in return? Does their generosity humble you, or are you thinking about what it means only for you in the exchange? From the natural Spiritual perspective of receiving, the feelings can be somewhat different than if ego drives the feelings.

- Imagine a world without currency – yes, there's no money to purchase any products or necessities for living. Could you revert to bartering, using only your gifts or knowledge to exchange equal value? Could you even start to discuss how to receive what is needed to live life to your most significant potential? If you answered no, you are living in the mental control mechanism of money in exchange for a product.

- Helping others is the stepping stone to the higher vibration of Spiritual Enlightenment. Helping others is the natural energy rooted in the Cosmic Intelligence of all Spiritual Beings. Helping others is intended to be the direct link to understanding the value of Oneness reality. Everything in the Universe balances through the Divine power of giving and receiving.

- When you finally accept that you are a Spiritual Being having a human experience, you stop competing in daily life and begin to share in the dance of what is truly important. The separation disappears, and you become aware of the natural progression of moving through life from the Highest Self perspective. The Highest Self does not understand duality or the concept of cause and effect. The Highest Self only understands Love Energy and the core Knowing of its Divine Cosmic Intelligence.

- Most people are not ready to increase their energy vibration to the level of Spiritual Body alignment because they are still fearful of what their limited mind can accept as Truth. They live in this paradox where they know there is something more to this life than what is seen on the surface, but they are not willing to grow past the belief of a manipulating system of "cause and effect".

- As we move forward in Spiritual Growth, the naysayers will be left behind, and those of you who truly understand the power you have within you will begin to take the quantum leaps necessary to achieve your Ultimate Destiny. You will now have the opportunity to shift your consciousness from the lower energy fields of duality to the Highest Self reality of Oneness.

Your responsibility to Oneness is to share your gifts fully with the world. You have within you the most significant gifts the world has ever known, but you still view them as a minor aspect of Self. By the time you read the rest of this book, I hope you will have dropped the false belief system controlling your life to this point. The Truth is it takes work to bring your Highest Self to the forefront of each moment. However, most of you will not take up the task of Spiritual Growth as the most essential aspect of your life. Most of you will come to a standstill and live a comfortable lifetime because of what you have learned. Most will not utilize the Divine Power of giving to its full potential, which is required to step up to the Fifth Dimension of Life.

Chapter 9
A Life of Abundance

Just What is Abundance

The definition of Abundance varies based on your Four Body System alignment. For a person who is Physically aligned, it typically means an Abundance of only material "things" that are manifest through the Mental Body to, in some way, pleasure the Physical Body. However, for a person who is aligned Spiritually, it means being in direct contact with the Highest Self reality and Spiritually aligned with one's Original Source Agreement.

When we shift our reality to having the Spiritual Body at the forefront of every decision and action, we open ourselves to the unlimited potential of achieving our Original Source Agreement here in this Earth school. The ego does not understand this shift because it reaches far beyond what it can comprehend. When you live a life based upon only the material or form-based perception of Life, you lose the complete understanding of what is available.

Many Spiritual Seekers get to a certain point of growth and then quit the necessary work to achieve full connection with Source Energy. Although they vibrate at very high frequencies, they manifest only a tiny portion of their Original Source Agreement into reality. This reality is why it is essential to understand that no matter how far advanced a person may "believe" they are Spiritual, each step is only a stepping stone into the abstract. And, of course, the ego has no direct recollection of the abstract found in the Original Source Agreement.

You discover what True Abundance is by bringing your Highest Self reality to the forefront of your daily Life and working your program to its fullest potential. When you begin to dismiss the clever urges and manipulations of the ego, you transform into a person who truly understands how to *Consciously Embrace Your True Personality*; you step away from all that is fearful and walk a path as one that has embraced the beauty of the Spiritual journey.

Typically, in the West, we are programmed to believe that all Abundance has to do with form-based manifestations of something we own or claim as ours. This mistake is again the misconception of a Physically aligned person. The reality of Life is that all that is truly important is found deep within our very Being. The biggest farce is the capitalistic idea that growth only concerns money and what it can buy. You are more than the money you earn! You already have the Abundance of the Universe within you, which will live on long after the Physical Body returns to its natural elements.

Can You Live a Life of Abundance without Money

The concept of "without" is a figment of the Mental Body blockage found in a Physically aligned person. It is the concept of duality at its deepest control level of reality. Most of these people are rooted in scarcity and only understand the entitlement of the egoistic mentality. This philosophy does not make them inferior to someone who has evolved to Spiritual Enlightenment. It simply means they are not vibrating at the level of the Highest Self reality and cannot truly thrive in the world.

When we stop the egoistic drive for more money, we purge the false conceptions of reality from our Four Body System and embrace the Spiritual Being within. From this "center" of understanding, we take different actions in every life situation. We no longer walk a path with duality or a false idea of what Life is all about. We remove the "Y" or fork in the road and bring Light to the understanding of a person walking a straight path to Spiritual Enlightenment. We achieve Abundance by dismissing the false beliefs that have imprisoned us for so long.

By living a life of Spiritual Abundance, you realize quickly that material possession is a "need" of the ego. The reality is that only that within you is accurate, and that which is outside you is an illusion. Yes, you still have to fit into society and the rules that govern this false reality, but you do so from a perspective that eliminates the form-based limits. You step away from the idea that material possessions are all important to determine your self-worth and begin to flow with the energies of your Original Source Agreement.

All Spiritual reality and Knowledge manifest in the silence of living a life of meditation. When you approach Life from this perspective, you quickly move beyond the idea that you are a servant of money and bring your true wisdom to Light. The Cosmic Intelligence of the Universe aligns with your Original Source Agreement – not the nonsense taught throughout your life situation to date.

If you are ready to thrive, stop working for money and bring your gifts forward to serve the world. When you free yourself from the shackles of a money-driven life, you will begin to understand that you are not what money can buy. *You are the essence of all manifestation in the limitless understanding of the formless reality.* Read that last part again and feel it deeply within your Soul.

Most People Are Shackled to Possessions, Are You

If your possessions define you, you are still living a life based upon form-based reality and a Physical Body alignment without even realizing it. Yes, most people mentally link to form-based material possessions in this life situation. However, you must genuinely understand that you will find your True Purpose for being here now without possessions. The formless reality you are is much more than what meets the eye on the surface of Life.

Once you are living based upon the Spiritual Body at the forefront of your reality, you come to a point in energy vibration where the possessions necessary to thrive in the Spiritual realm are always provided for you exactly when needed. This realm is not a reality even the Super-ego understands because when any form of ego stands in the way of your Spiritual Growth, you are not being your Authentic Highest Self.

Suppose you do not consciously spend moments defining your reality in the silence of the Source Energy connection. In that case, you will have difficulty relating to the happenings around you from a genuinely Spiritual perspective. You will continue to bounce back and forth from Spiritual Body to Physical Body alignment and sometimes feel stagnant in the middle of two realities. If this is the case for you, you will not be able to release material possessions peacefully if it is necessary to be in a Spiritual teaching position.

It is easy to become very comfortable with many possessions because it makes Life easier in a money-based society. However, it is more critical for your Spiritual Growth to experience both realms of reality so that you can be Joyful every moment, even without material or form-based possessions. Your Highest Self never questions the Spiritual Body reality of Life. Your Lower Self reality needs reassurances based on form-based reality that confuses you.

In a money-driven society, people are judged based on the material by-products of their environment. This judgment manifests at all levels of third-dimensional reality. The limited focus of a money-driven life will never replace the Abundance of a Spiritually-driven life. You must go deep within your Higher Self reality to bring Spiritual Enlightenment to the forefront of your Life.

When you genuinely understand what defines you, you will live with the "Highest Self" as your driving force for all available. By now, you should be vibrating at an energy level high enough to understand the identity that will serve you well, which, in turn, will bring True Abundance to your Life.

Do Your Possessions Define You

Spend some much-needed time in silence defining your identity. Use this time to evaluate your True Self and whether you serve Source Energy or Super-ego. You may still believe you can shift in and out of the Four Body System reality by moving from Spiritual Body to Physical Body alignment. I can assure you this is Super-ego being very clever to control the small portion of the false reality tied to possessions. Your True Personality defines itself by the Highest Self reality, not the lower energies that require possessions to define a life of Abundance.

Once you finally decide to take the road less traveled, you will understand that Joy is always with you and that you cannot be controlled by those who would have you stuck in the middle of an illusionary reality. It is important to remember that your Spiritual Growth is the only reason you are here on Earth. Furthermore, your Spiritual Growth defines itself by serving others and others seeking your guidance. This understanding will be the most challenging lesson on your path to Spiritual Enlightenment.

When you can let go of all your possessions and still feel the same Peace within your reality, you will be ready to become the Master Teacher. This position is not easy for the Super-ego to achieve because there may still be a small segment of your old belief system slightly controlling you. However, when the Highest Self finally takes over as the guiding Light of your reality, you will no longer have a "perceived need" for material possessions. You will still enjoy them, but the need will be gone.

All Spiritual Masters of Earth have either given up all their material possessions or have been willing to do so to achieve Spiritual Enlightenment. There is no more incredible feeling than the Joy within you to bring to your reality. This Joy is the driving Highest Self reality of Life, and you are never driven by what possessions you have. The path to this understanding can be very challenging, especially if you live where material possessions have been significant to you.

Always remember, all that is "needed" is already within you!

How Can You Minimize Stuff in Your Life

There is a unique, higher value to what you have within you than on the surface of your life situation. By accepting that you already have everything you need "within you", you learn to minimize the "stuff" or form-based possessions that merely symbolize your status in the world. No price expresses the higher value of the Knowledge that you are a Spiritual Being living a "temporary physical condition" called "being human". Yes, that is correct; you are not a Human Being but a *Spirit* "being human!"

Western society physically infects the population with the desire for monetary gain and the pursuit of possessions and power. This epidemic is not something to feel proud of because it diminishes our True Purpose for being here. We have the Spiritual guidance of Source Energy available to bring our Original Source Agreement to Light. However, most people are so busy attempting to acquire more money to purchase more "stuff" that the true path to happiness is nowhere to be found.

When society is judged by who has the most material possessions, it becomes a false illusion of reality; more effort achieving whatever symbol of success has the higher value. Usually, the measure of success focuses on what money can buy. It doesn't matter whether it's an education or another form-based tool for monetary gain. People work for money instead of having money work for themselves!

Governing bodies initially implemented Monetary Systems to enhance bartering between humans. When there is an established currency within a government, the actual worth of a material-based product is more straightforward to establish. However, with the increasing manipulation of companies to make more money to distribute to stockholders and executives, the whole idea of a simple monetary system has been high-jacked by a tiny percentage of the population. The entire system has become so complex that only a few clever individuals control it.

For our purposes here, we will stay focused on one's possessions. Just ask yourself how much stuff you have that sits in a corner or on a shelf without being used daily. Just list all your "stuff" and determine what you want to keep or what is needed to have a comfortable life. If you are honest during your evaluation, you will discover you can do without much of what you currently own. You will find that the only stuff you actually "need" to live a comfortable life is much less than you have in your current, form-based inventory.

Yes, having nice things is comfortable, but if you are honest with yourself, you will find that much of what you currently call your possessions is not actually "needed". Many people living in dire poverty today would appreciate having only a couple of the things you currently have in storage. Are you willing to part with some of this "stuff" to make someone else's situation easier, or are you brainwashed into believing you are more abundant with more form-based possessions?

Would You Consider Yourself Abundant with Less

Your definition of Self will determine whether you consider yourself abundant with less! If you focus on the Physical Body as the definition of the Self, you will see no logical reason to have fewer possessions. If you are aligned with the Spiritual Body and realize that you are a Spiritual Being, it will not matter to you how many form-based possessions you own. The Spirit (which is formless) has no conception of the perception of less. The Spiritual Body is limitless and, therefore, always lives in Abundance!

If you have been paying close attention, you will notice that no matter what the question or search for truth is, when the Spiritual Body is at the forefront of your Life – you understand that you are already fully abundant.

Four Body System alignment is the most crucial aspect of your Life. No matter the life situation of the human experience, you always bring your focus back to Spiritual Body alignment. Your reward is the Knowledge that you are a fully realized Being. You do not need possessions to bring Abundance to your Life. The concept of Abundance from a Spiritual perspective negates the need for "stuff". If you do not believe this, ask any person on their deathbed what they are taking with them when they transition fully back to Spirit.

Once you fully understand the Spiritual reality of Life, you will live your situation based upon serving others and participating in the Earth School from a completely different perspective than most mass consciousness. As you should know by now, the energy vibration of the mass consciousness is still very low, which ultimately means humanity still believes only in the Physical Body perspective of Life.

Less is an illusion of the Mental Body aligned with the Physical Body reality. If you truly understand that you are a Spiritual Being having a human experience, material possessions manifested in this life situation are meaningless. Your concept of less must shift if you are to understand the meaning of Abundance fully. By bringing your Spiritual vision to Light, you will no longer care whether or not you have unnecessary possessions. I urge you to sit with this understanding to anchor its vibrational powerfully.

Most people spend precious moments concerned with "having more stuff" when they could merely allow Life to flow with a conscious awareness of Self. If you are still worried about your stuff, your path will never be one of true Abundance.

How Much Time Do You Spend Worrying About Your Stuff

Worrying about losing your material possessions is a mind game of the physically aligned individual that vibrates at a very low-energy frequency. A Physically aligned person's form-based identity is always concerned with having more than others to express their limited understanding of self-worth. If you continue to bring possessions to the forefront of your Life, you will stay locked in the never-ending, unconscious world of false beliefs.

One of the miracles of living a Spiritually aligned Life is that you no longer spend any time concentrating on how you will acquire more possessions. Yes, more stuff will manifest in your Earth school experience, but it will not have any control over you. You will not think about how to get more stuff or how to keep your material possessions. You will find yourself giving away many of your earthly possessions in a loving manner. Redistributing some of your material possessions means you will be conscious of what others need and not have a mental block concerning keeping everything for yourself.

When you freely share your possessions, it becomes easy to understand that you will not take anything with you when you leave this incarnation. Why wait until the body is dead to share your form-based possessions? Do you believe you actually "own" anything currently in your possession? If you do, you have a long way to go to be considered Spiritually Enlightened.

The path to Spiritual Enlightenment can be challenging for a Physical Body aligned person because the form-based concept of reality vibrates at a much lower energy vibration than a Spiritual Body aligned person. Therefore, a Spiritually aligned person sees the lower energy vibration of form-based "stuff" as secondary to achieving the destiny of an Original Source Agreement. When your energy vibration increases, so will your concept of Abundance, which will ultimately bring you to the understanding that material possessions are only to be used to assist you in bringing spiritual transformative education to the world.

When you realize that the most crucial use of form-based material objects is to catalyze sharing, you will have joined the few who understand why you are here. As you grow Spiritually, you will focus on bringing new meaning to how your Earthly possessions are used. You will no longer purchase that which does not serve your Spiritual Growth and will begin to share more of what you have with those on your path. You will justify your material possessions from a new perspective.

Can You Justify Every Material Possession Honestly

The physicality of form-based products vibrates a very dense energy. Dense energy is the lowest energy found on this planet and can only manifest at the lower vibrations of the physical plane of reference. In other words, that manifested in material form is dense and will be left behind when you leave your human form. Therefore, you should be able to discern or justify your material possessions from a Spiritual perspective if you are to share their benefits with the world. The Spiritual philosophy is not very clear for a Physically aligned person. Why? Because they genuinely believe that what they own is, in some small way, part of who they are. They allow their possessions to define who they are.

By shifting your perspective to the Spiritual realm of material ownership, you identify those possessions as tools to enhance Spiritual Growth. Spiritual perspective means before something is purchased, the question is asked, "How will this serve my Spiritual Growth and others?" If a purchase is made, the reason for having the form-based possession has a higher vibrating intention for the purchase.

As an example, consider the purchase of a second home:

Let's say a second home is a vacation home you use infrequently. Do you allow that home to sit empty when you are not using it? Or do you rent it when you are not using it so others can enjoy it, too? Your initial response to this question will help you to discern your current Four Body System alignment.

You may be surprised to learn how many people have multiple homes worldwide because they have achieved massive monetary gain, only to have those homes sit idle when they are not using them personally. From a Physical Body perspective, they feel they earned the right to keep these homes to themselves. However, if you shift the perspective to a Spiritual reality, it is desirable to have the homes to use when they want to use them while renting them during periods of non-usage for others to enjoy. When you focus on bringing Joy to others, a natural, abundant resultant factor is achieved, and additional income for the owners can be donated to a worthy cause.

Sharing material purchases with others brings about Conscious Oneness. Oneness reality is True Abundance when you understand that your endeavors bring happiness to others and yourself. If you are in a position to share your good fortune with others, why would you not do so freely? If you have shifted your perception to the idea that you are only here to serve the Spiritual Growth of yourself and others, you would understand that you can bring Joyful experiences to many without any effort whatsoever. This is True Abundance - the whole concept of equally sharing what is form and formless.

When we bring our possessions to the service of Spiritual Transformative Education, we find a different reason for purchasing form-based products in the first place. We no longer shop for the pleasure of having some*thing* new. We shop with the understanding that whatever it is that we purchase can be of benefit to many and is only with us temporarily. Furthermore, we understand that we can enjoy material possessions but not at the risk of believing they are only for one's pleasure.

Ask yourself how you may be able to share your possessions today. Can you see how much Joy can come from watching someone else benefit from your Abundance?

Have You Ever Given Away Something You Love

We all have cherished possessions with some formless, inspired value or meaning. It could be something handed down by a Loved One from the past or purchased as a tool for Spiritual Growth. Whatever meaning this possession has provides a Joyful feeling, or you could say you Love it. The point is this cherished possession is very significant to us.

Now, picture yourself giving this cherished possession to someone else.

The benefit of giving your cherished possession away for someone else to enjoy is witnessing the outcome. A feeling of pure bliss comes with parting with something that has been a happiness tool for you. No words can explain the Joy that comes from providing something of inspired value to someone else. It would be best if you experienced it to gain the full benefit from the action.

As you grow Spiritually, you will discover that the meaning behind giving away a material possession is genuinely a significant step in increasing energy vibration. When you shift from the idea that you own anything form-based to the truth that all material possessions will be left behind, you will understand how much power you truly have. You will live from the Highest Self reality of Life and no longer "need" that many material possessions.

The Spiritual path is pure Love and aligns with feelings of a very high energy vibration. Many of you are on your way to living in Harmony with the Oneness of the Universe. The more time you spend in the silence of the Cosmic Intelligence genuinely guiding your way, the more you will become comfortable with your temporary life situation. The Highest Self does not need material things. However, that doesn't mean using material possessions can't benefit Spiritual Growth.

When you live your Life from a Spiritual perspective, you understand the difference between a Physical or Spiritual Body alignment perspective and choose different actions and possessions. You follow *Knowing* rather than mental beliefs and stay aligned with your Original Source Agreement as a resultant factor. You find Abundance in even the most minor cherished possessions and have a completely different perspective on Life.

This state of understanding, outside happiness, comes from the inner Joy only found in the formless realm of reality.

Does Having a Lot of Material Items Make You Happy

The vibration of a material item will bring about feelings that are in Harmony with its energy vibration. If the item vibrates at low energy, you will feel it at a denser level and no higher. The only way to increase the energy of your feelings about owning the material item is by creating a story about the item and its effect on you. By keeping this in mind, take a few moments to list all the current material things you have that seem to provide you with happy feelings. Don't think about it too much; feel the emotions that surface as you visualize the material possessions you hold dear to your heart.

After you complete your list of material possessions, take a few minutes to rank their importance to you; assign a number based upon priority from 1-10, with 10 being the highest value. Once you have all the items numbered, take another few minutes to justify why you numbered them accordingly. Just make a few notes describing what you feel about each item. You may be surprised at what you feel about each item. You will find that you were probably more excited about some than others before purchasing your material possessions. You will also find that the story you attached to each item will vary and result from the number value. This result is natural from a Physical Body perspective, but from a Spiritual Body perspective, all the items should have equal emotional value.

Remember, everything in your current situation has an energy vibration, with no exceptions. The denser the item is, the lower it will be vibrating. Then, it increases perceived value if an emotional thinking story resonates with the possession. This perceived increase can be very confusing because some of the anticipated excitement of owning the possession starts to wear off as it ages. The item hasn't changed, but your story about the item does. That doesn't make the item any less, but it does vibrate lower when you change your mind about its importance because you have emotionally decreased its value. From a Physical Body alignment perspective, you can see how an item may lose its value as it ages. The happiness you feel about the item drops in energy because of your emotional attachment.

Now, spend a few moments putting your material into categories linked directly to the "Categories of Life" outlined in the *Conscious Clarity Energy Process*™. You will see some interesting patterns. The lower vibrating energy categories will harmonize with the dense material possessions. Therefore, there will only be a temporary emotional attachment to the perceived happiness level. A Physically aligned person cannot see the reality of what is happening here because they only understand the concept of reaction to feelings as a result of a story assigned to possessions.

However, from a Spiritually aligned perspective, there is no change in the vibration of the material item. It is a material possession of equal value to all other material possessions, and it is equally enjoyed once it is gone because feelings remain the same.

The Joy from within the Spirit matters in Life – not the material items.

How Does the Cycle of Money Work for You

Money is no different than any other material possession; it has its energy vibration. Therefore, you could call it "green energy". You will not take any money with you once you leave the Physical Body and fully transition back to the Spiritual Self. Therefore, while you are in human form, how you cycle your money in this Earth school will determine the meaning you place on it.

If you work strictly for monetary reward, you will be one of those people who is a prisoner of money. However, if you develop the gifts you brought with you and choose a career that aligns with your Original Source Agreement – you will never work "for money". Source Energy will always provide you with all the resources needed to fulfill your True Life Purpose. This realization is one of the most challenging realities for a Physical body-aligned person. The whole concept of money flowing to you loses its meaning in the physical "need" to acquire it.

In truth, money is only to be used as a tool for you to have an easier time bartering in your current life situation. It has no value other than what society places on it. Money is an established currency used to acquire necessary, Earthly possessions without bartering using other temporarily owned possessions. In the world economy, the currency becomes worthless if the governing body no longer recognizes it. Therefore, being a good steward of the money you already have is essential. If you do this, the Universe will reward you with more to recycle into the world.

In Book 1, *Consciously Live What You Feel* of the "Life's Little Secrets Book Series", a complete blueprint or system was outlined for you that teaches how to be a good steward of the money that flows through your Life. It is a detailed understanding of how you can achieve financial security so that you never have to think about how to acquire more money in a form-based world. It is a system that works automatically – providing you follow its guidelines. Please spend some time reviewing that system now so that you can bring its awareness back to Light. This review will help you to focus on how money works for you rather than how you need to work for money.

All money cycles in the world markets; therefore, it is nothing more than a means to function in the illusionary life situation before you physically. While you are here developing your Spiritual Growth, be aware of the many ways you can achieve financial freedom. Let the money paid for your services grow in a "green energy" perspective as you do with any other category of this life situation. The more you recycle this "green energy" with others, the more it will grow exponentially.

This recycling is all part of the Universal Law of Attraction – What you focus on most will grow in energy vibration. Therefore, be sure to have money work for you rather than you working for money. Be willing to give first, and then watch the miraculous way receiving all that is needed flows into your Life.

Do You Believe in Giving and Receiving

How you answer the question, "Do You Believe in Giving and Receiving?" indicates how your Four Body System is aligned. If you are aligned based upon the natural state of Love and sharing, you are living your Life in Harmony with the Highest Self power of Knowing. However, if you are aligned based upon the false reality and limited understanding of scarcity, your Life is in Harmony with the Lower Self energy of Beliefs. If you are still watching out only for yourself, it will be difficult for you to comprehend the difference.

Previously, we spent much time on giving and receiving. During those lessons, I asked you to rethink your understanding of what comes first in a Spiritually aligned person. Then, I presented them to form an understanding within yourself of how to shift your perspective to true Abundance. The whole idea of Abundance is rooted in the power of giving to receive. When you truly understand that you are here to serve, you will fully understand the power you have within you to live an abundant life.

Just as the mind is the servant of the Physical Body, the sum totals of the two are the servants of the Spiritual Body or Soul. A misaligned personality traps you in the mindset of scarcity without ever understanding it. One of the most valuable assists you have at your immediate disposal is the unlimited power of Love and sharing. How you perceive this incredible energy will determine your next steps in the *Conscious Clarity Energy Process*™ coursework.

Continuing to limit your greatness is a form of scarcity. You are not living a life of Abundance by locking yourself in the limited possibilities of only a Physically aligned person. Some of you may have amassed significant sums of money, but you will not live a joyous life. If you are still locked in the idea of "me first, and only then, I will give some to others", you unknowingly limit yourself to a life that will never be truly abundant. Many of you will not fully understand what you currently lack until you have some events in your life that trigger you into reality.

The Universe perfectly aligns with Cosmic Intelligence; everything you have experienced in Life thus far has been on purpose, nothing is unnoticed, and ironically, you agreed to it all before you stepped into human form. Whether you believe this or not, it speaks volumes about your energy vibration at this current moment. Your definition of Abundance will determine how you move forward from here, and you will undoubtedly begin to understand how giving and receiving are part of how well you Know your purpose for being here in your body today.

Can You Equate Purpose with Possessions

Why you came here is the most critical question you can ever ask yourself! If you are conscious of your life's true purpose, you bypass some uncomfortable experiences or tests by learning about Yourself. If you truly understand that you are a Spiritual Being having a human experience, you will be using your possessions as tools for the Spiritual Growth of yourself and all others who cross your path. You will have stepped into the Spiritual realm of True Abundance when equating purpose and possessions equally.

Those of you still searching for answers will face many challenges on the journey to Spiritual Enlightenment. You will continue to "play small" and experience many tests or challenges while, slowly but surely, learning about the Highest Self. You agreed upon this path before you came here into this Earth school. The ego does not understand the reasons for the tests, but the Spirit accepts them because it Knows there is a Divine reason for every experience in Life.

Nobody can guide you to Spiritual Enlightenment other than your Highest Self. This reality is a Universal fact requiring acceptance to shift your perception from the Physical Body to Spiritual Body alignment. You have been brainwashed all your Life into believing the Physical Body is the driving force for your Life. However, you can shift from this delusion to Spiritual Body alignment and a life of true Abundance. The decision is only a heartbeat away for you to take a quantum leap into the realm of Pure Joy. Once you have fully decided to *Consciously Embrace Your True Personality*, you will experience the Pure Joy you have always wanted.

When you bring the vision of your Original Source Agreement to the forefront of your Life by the recollection of the Highest Self, there will be no turning back to your old Lower Self perceptions. Old paradigms will constantly trigger you until you reach that Divine energy vibration level. You may even fall upon some tough times to fully experience what is left to discover when material possessions disappear from your life situation. This eradication of possessions can be an enlightening experience and deep despair.

However, when you finally surrender to the bottomless Love of Oneness you share with all other Spiritual Beings, you will begin to understand just how much Divine power you have. By connecting with Source Energy, you will experience what it truly means to Love unconditionally and the purpose of material possessions in your Life.

Are You Happier with Love or Material Things

If you still identify with the material possessions you currently own and are asking for True Love, be prepared to leave all of those material possessions behind. You will eventually share all of the assets you own with others when the death of the Physical Body occurs. Four Body System alignment will determine whether you do this voluntarily or are relieved of the assets via a test. The why behind this sharing process is revealed to each person differently, but it will happen, and there is nothing that you can do to avoid it.

If you ask anyone on their deathbed what they wish they had more, the answer is never money or material possessions. It is always some of the Highest Self understanding of Love and what Unconditional Love offers. Everyone will eventually transition fully to the Spiritual realm on their deathbed, but it doesn't have to be this way. You can transition before you leave the Physical Body by living the Spiritual Life you have always been meant to experience. You can live the Pure Joy of a blissful life by surrendering to the Divine power of the Highest Self energy in a heartbeat!

When you Know deep within yourself that you are part of the fantastic Abundance of Oneness in the Universe, you will have a deeper understanding of the purpose of the material things in your Life. You will experience the Abundance of a Spiritually aligned Being and forever look at Life differently. Unconditional Love is the answer to fully understanding this perspective of Life. Love is an eternal blessing that can never be exhausted by external means.

Love does not provide the external emotion of happiness; it gives the inner blissful reality of Joy.

Pause for a moment, read that again and feel it. Happiness can only provide the form-based, external emotional illusion of a physically aligned perspective or false reality. Furthermore, material possessions can be gone in a heartbeat and ultimately will be when the Physical Body dies. If you do not believe these truths while living in this situation, be ready to experience significant material loss.

The false reality of happiness is found everywhere throughout the planet. We are programmed since the birth of the body to believe that only that which is outside us in the form-based world, which the Mental Body creates, is real. Therefore, most people seek happiness outside themselves rather than simply experiencing the Joy they already have within. This illusion is further falsely enabled by the misconception that form-based possessions somehow define who you are. This manipulation is the greatest hoax ever perpetrated on humanity, as it separates us rather than uniting us in Oneness of Self. It feeds on the needs of the ego and drives a mental block into the reality of who we are.

If you live in this low-energy vibration long enough, you begin to believe that it is accurate, and you will make up a story about your life based upon those false beliefs and an unreal concept of what Wealth truly is.

How Does Your Life Blueprint Determine Your Wealth

We are each provided with a Life Plan, which I refer to as your Original Source Agreement, based upon living Life at the Highest Self reality of Life. It is an entirely balanced plan that leaves nothing out and aligns with a Spiritual Body perspective of Life. It is an actual Life Blueprint that you can follow to bring you to the State of Unlimited Wealth. However, you must be willing to leave behind all the false illusions of the ego to fully remember this incredible plan you created for yourself before you showed up on this planet.

The misconception that Wealth is some form-based monetary or possessions gain is all based upon the ego's false reality. Therefore, most of humanity seeks more possessions to demonstrate great Wealth. The entire world relies upon this false reality, controlled by the stock markets around the world. This market thrives on a small number of people manipulating the money markets based on a fear-based reality. This illusion has existed for so long that most humanity has accepted it. It is reinforced by labeling society as upper, middle and lower class, with the lower classes serving the upper class.

Therefore, if you place yourself in one of these classes, you conform to the illusion that only monetary measurement determines who you are. You believe that Wealth is some form-based measurement of your worth, and you allow yourself to be manipulated by the small percentage of people labeled as upper class. The whole basis of how our current government operates follows this false reality. It is structured so those with the most political influence control the population's middle and lower-class segments. Furthermore, it is all based upon an egoist mentality that has no moral consideration for who we genuinely are – Spiritual Beings having a human experience.

However, the good news is that the mass consciousness of the world is increasing its vibration level as more and more people awaken to how to change this illusion back to Spiritual reality. Source Energy programmed us to use the Spiritual Wealth we brought to bring about change. When we begin listening to Source Energy guidance rather than the monarchs of the world, we begin to recollect our Original Source Agreement plan for Abundance. A Spiritually aligned person understands how manipulation by governing bodies has brainwashed us into believing we are only form-based human beings.

Yes, a Spiritual uprising is taking place, providing the Wealth of Abundance measured only through Spiritual means. Until you rise above the low energy vibration of the controlled masses, you will stay imprisoned in the duality control mechanism of the third-dimensional world. In truth, we are all equal, which ultimately means duality must be eradicated from our perceptive reality if the human race is to thrive rather than survive the manipulations of an egoistic-ruled society.

Remember, you are not only the Physical Body; until you fully understand this Universal Truth, you will not understand the concept of Oneness or the Body-of-One mentality of Abundance.

Charter 9 Suggestions - A Life of Abundance

    The definition of Abundance varies based on your Four Body System alignment. For a person who is Physically aligned, it typically means an Abundance of only material "things" that are manifest through the Mental Body to, in some way, pleasure the Physical Body. However, for a person who is aligned Spiritually, it means being in direct contact with the Highest Self reality and Spiritually aligned with one's Original Source Agreement.

- Typically, in the West, we are programmed to believe that all Abundance has to do with form-based manifestations of something we own or claim as ours. This mistake is again the misconception of a Physically aligned person. The reality of Life is that all that is truly important is found deep within our very Being.

- Less is an illusion of the Mental Body aligned with the Physical Body reality. If you truly understand that you are a Spiritual Being having a human experience, material possessions manifested in this life situation are meaningless. Your concept of less must shift if you are to understand the meaning of Abundance fully. By bringing your Spiritual vision to Light, you will no longer care whether or not you have unnecessary possessions. I urge you to sit with this understanding to anchor its vibrational powerfully.

- Sharing material purchases with others brings about Conscious Oneness. Oneness reality is True Abundance when you understand that your endeavors bring happiness to others and yourself. If you are in a position to share your good fortune with others, why would you not do so freely? If you have shifted your perception to the idea that you are only here to serve the Spiritual Growth of yourself and others, you would understand that you can bring Joyful experiences to many without any effort whatsoever. This is True Abundance - the whole concept of equally sharing what is form and formless.

- The vibration of a material item will bring about feelings that are in Harmony with its energy vibration. If the item vibrates at low energy, you will feel it at a denser level and no higher. The only way to increase the energy of your feelings about owning the material item is by creating a story about the item and its effect on you. By keeping this in mind, take a few moments to list all the current material things you have that seem to provide you with happy feelings. Don't think about it too much; feel the emotions that surface as you visualize the material possessions you hold dear to your heart.

- Money is no different than any other material possession; it has its energy vibration. Therefore, you could call it "green energy". You will not take any money with you once you leave the Physical Body and fully transition back to the Spiritual Self. Therefore, while you are in human form, how you cycle your money in this Earth school will determine the meaning you place on it.

- Why you came here is the most critical question you can ever ask yourself! If you are conscious of your life's true purpose, you bypass some uncomfortable experiences or tests by learning about yourself. If you truly understand that you are a Spiritual Being having a human experience, you will be using your possessions as tools for the Spiritual Growth of yourself and all others who cross your path. You will have stepped into the Spiritual realm of True Abundance when equating purpose and possessions equally.

- When you finally surrender to the bottomless Love of Oneness you share with all other Spiritual Beings, you will begin to understand just how much Divine power you have. By connecting with Source Energy, you will experience what it truly means to Love unconditionally and the purpose of material possessions in your Life.

- If you ask anyone on their deathbed what they wish they had more, the answer is never money or material possessions. It is always some of the Highest Self understanding of Love and what Unconditional Love offers. Everyone will eventually transition fully to the Spiritual realm on their deathbed, but it doesn't have to be this way. You can transition before you leave the Physical Body by living the Spiritual Life you have always been meant to experience. You can live the Pure Joy of a blissful life by surrendering to the Divine power of the Highest Self energy in a heartbeat!

Love does not provide the external emotion of happiness; it gives the inner blissful reality of Joy.

- We are each provided with a Life Plan, which I refer to as your Original Source Agreement, based upon living Life at the Highest Self reality of Life. It is an entirely balanced plan that leaves nothing out and aligns with a Spiritual Body perspective of Life. It is an actual Life Blueprint that you can follow to bring you to the State of Unlimited Wealth. However, you must be willing to leave behind all the false illusions of the ego to fully remember this incredible plan you created for yourself before you showed up on this planet.

The misconception that Wealth is some form-based monetary or possessions gain is all based upon the ego's false reality. Therefore, most of humanity seeks more possessions to demonstrate great Wealth. The entire world relies upon this false reality, controlled by the stock markets around the world. This market thrives on a small number of people manipulating the money markets based on a fear-based reality. This illusion has existed for so long that most humanity has accepted it. It is reinforced by labeling society as upper, middle and lower class, with the lower classes serving the upper class.

Remember, you are not only the Physical Body; until you fully understand this Universal Truth, you will not understand the concept of Oneness or the Body-of-One mentality of Abundance.

Chapter 10

We Are a Body of ONE!

What Does - We Are a Body of One Mean

Knowing you connect with ALL THAT IS in the Universe is more than a belief of the Mental Body. As you have learned from previous chapters, miracles are commonplace when you live your Life based upon Love being at the forefront of every action. By understanding that you can increase your energy vibration to the level of the Highest Self reality, you become One with Source Energy and realize that *We are a Body of ONE*.

The concept of A Body of One or Oneness is not for the limited Mental Body, misaligned by the manipulations of egoistic behavior. Oneness is a Deep Knowing found in the unlimited Mental Body that follows guidance from the Highest Self or Source Energy guidance. Guidance communication is fully realized from a Spiritual Body aligned concept of who you are. When you finally accept that you are a droplet of the same ocean of Love that flows through the Universe, you will understand that you and Source Energy are the same Being.

Although the mass consciousness of the world is increasing, we still have a long way to go to *Consciously Embrace the True Personality* – the God-realized Being that we are. Why? Because we are brainwashed into believing we are separated from God as a whole. We are not yet vibrating at the energy level that naturally brings Oneness to the forefront of everyone's reality. The greatest gift we have to offer the world is our Spiritual understanding of being connected with the I-AM-Ness of ALL THAT IS. Unfortunately, the concept of being "equal" and "one" is still lost in most people of the old, third-dimensional mindset.

A Third Dimension society continues to rule the world by power-hungry people who keep separation and judgment alive with meaningless conflicts. This separation prevails through the low-energy vibration of fear-based tactics. Looking closely, you will find that most media coverage is fear-based. The focus is typically on separation because it generates more news, uncertainty and profits for a few large corporate enterprises. This separation is all based upon the idea that some people are less than others and are therefore not worthy of the concept of Oneness.

Furthermore, the few media outlets that are reporting this malignant manipulation of society are considered "fake news" sources by those in political power. The malignancy itself gains fuel from people centered on negativity. These negative people don't realize they are falling for this grandiose manipulation. These followers are vibrating at such a low frequency in the Third Dimension of reality that they close their eyes to the falsehoods presented to them.

When our governments classify people by categories rather than equality, the meaning of the Body of One is lost. When the "system" is governed by old, third-dimensional paradigms, there is no possibility of uniting the world. The control mechanisms of a few have been so deeply ingrained into our society that we are now seeing unmoral behaviors from government leaders accepted by society as natural. The depth of this brainwashing has reached a new tipping point, where we will either survive based upon entirely shifting into the Fourth Dimension of Spiritual reality, or Humanity will become extinct. This observation may sound like doom and gloom, but it is a reality constantly fueled with low-energy vibrations each day. This unmoral behavior was particularly true in the West when the Trump Administration attempted to alienate us from the rest of the free world and NATO.

As I have stated, one of my favorite quotes by Ralph Waldow Emerson is "When it's dark enough, you can see all the stars." We are at that tipping point where it is time to unite in Fourth Dimension reality. It's dark enough now, and every one of us has a responsibility to speak up for what is right-minded thinking and open-hearted feeling. The shift into

Spiritual Transformative Education is more important than ever before, and it is essential to evolve to the level of awareness that can accelerate Humanity forward. It is time for the old, third-dimensional paradigms of thinking to be purged from our reality. To survive, we must unite and increase our energy vibration to the Divine power of Oneness.

Does How We Think Make Us Who We Are

Change comes from increasing energy vibration, ultimately realigning our belief system with Knowing. Our inner thoughts drive our outer experience in Life, which is about who we think we are. You will stay in the old, third-dimensional dysfunction and separation paradigm if you have not yet shifted into the Spiritual Body alignment reality. Many older generations are stuck in this low-energy vibration and refuse to awaken to the truth. Many of these people are still controlling our government and are fighting every day for their survival while they still have the power to influence society. However, change is coming whether they like it or not. As these ridged-thinking individuals retire into their dysfunction, we will see a change in society based upon what is truly best for the mass consciousness of the world.

It will take some time to reverse the harm done. How we "think" will become even more critical in expanding the shift that is now gaining momentum in the Fourth Dimension; we need to finally bring Oneness to the forefront of society so that the mass consciousness level can continue to increase. Our Four Body System alignment has never been more critical today. As more and more Spirits are vibrating at a Higher Self level of understanding are brought into this human existence, we are experiencing a natural shift in birth energy vibration.

The Spirits taking new human forms today are coming into the Physical Body at a much higher energy vibration than ever before. It's natural for a child to say, "This doesn't feel right to me", instead of mindlessly following the crowd. Children are now speaking out like never before and questioning what is happening in the world based more on "feeling" than thinking. Our responsibility is to embrace our children and listen to what they say because they are our future leaders. When a family is united in Oneness reality, it becomes a stepping stone for change in the world. This change is why we must embrace our Highest Self reality in every household so that our children receive education beyond old, third-dimensional paradigms.

Our Evolution will shift in direct proportion to the level at which we increase our energy vibration – it's really that simple!

If you are unwilling to put old paradigms behind you to move forward, then maybe it is time for you to step aside and allow those who have seen the Light to step into their Greatness. The old saying, "You can't teach an old dog new tricks", is dissolving slowly but surely, but we have a long way to go. Change is here NOW, and everyone willing to step into our Greatness will thrive beyond the limited beliefs of a fear-based, dogmatic society.

The limitless possibilities available to a Fourth Dimension society manifest in a Body of One philosophy. Are you someone who is joining this Evolution, or are you attempting to hold Evolution back because you lack Spiritual awareness?

How Do You Fit into the Body of One Philosophy

Self-examination is the key to understanding the Mental Body separation of Oneness. A person with a misaligned Four Body System does not understand the Body of One philosophy. This misunderstanding is genuine because they vibrate at such a low energy that they feel fearful when Source Energy speaks. They lock themselves into the rigidity of third-dimensional "thinking" and the false stories that are a constant distraction, which, in turn, are based upon false beliefs deeply anchored into their subconscious minds. This false reality is simply an old paradigm fueled by the low-energy thoughts of fear-based ideology. The negative effect of living a life from this perspective generates more Fear and actions that are destructive to the well-being of society as a whole.

Each day, our choices impact the outcome of the next day because the actions we take in the present moment will bring about our future reality. This reality is why it is more important now than ever before for the human race to examine our moral compass to understand where we truly stand. Our journey today depends on our relationship with the Universal Intelligence of the Universe.

We can overcome the manipulative power of misguided individuals by simply speaking out and using our Spiritual guidance to dissolve the old, third-dimensional paradigm of egoistic control. The solution to all fear-based problems is found in the Body of One potential, safely anchored inside a Spiritually aligned Mental Body. The choice to place your attention on the intention of changing your Four Body System alignment is now as crucial to our Evolution as breath is to the Physical Body.

In a misaligned Four Body System, thoughts have power over the experience of Life because emotional disconnects with reality drive them. The misaligned Mental Body in a person fuels false past beliefs anchored deeply in the subconscious mind. The power this has over someone aligned in this manner is staggering. As Jesus said when taking his last human breath on the cross, "Forgive them for they know not what they do." We are at this same tipping point again but can change our actions in a heartbeat.

Everything changes once you focus on the intention of a Body of One philosophy of Life. You no longer place yourself first as you begin to visualize the ripple effects of your actions on Humanity. You shift from rigidity to a pleasant, loving person. You soften and no longer believe you are a victim of circumstances because you take control of your Life instead of allowing others to control you. This shift can be very confusing for a person still locked in the reality of egoistic beliefs and behaviors. It's not easy for everyone to make this shift. And that is why the ego still dominates the mass consciousness of the world. Most people are so locked into the false reality of Life that they cannot even contemplate the possibility that there is a higher vibrational way to live.

Through self-reflection, you can overcome any doubt that you may have about shifting your reality. Sitting in Silence will increase your energy vibration to the point where you can honestly evaluate where you stand today. Be patient with yourself and allow the guidance that comes in Silence to be your guiding Light.

Without Thinking, Can I Identify Myself As Being One with All

Living in a "Meditative State of Being" is just the opposite of "doing" a meditation practice. Eliminating unnecessary thoughts is the key to bringing this reality into your daily Life, and reaching this energy vibration level is not easy. Many of you will have difficulty answering the question, "Without thinking, can I identify myself as Being One with ALL?" because you have not retrained yourself to sit in Silence honestly. When I speak of sitting in Silence, I mean removing ALL thoughts from your consciousness. Sitting in non-thought is not accomplished overnight, as it is truly a connection with the Omni Source of all that is formless!

Connecting with Source Energy from a Conscious Clarity level takes an energy vibration in Harmony with Source Energy or in alignment with that which is formless. Connecting can be very confusing because most people cannot eliminate ALL thoughts instantaneously without actually 'thinking' about non-thought. Therefore, it may be more comfortable for you to start practicing meditation that slowly (but surely) will take you on a journey into non-thought. Before you understand and feel the reality of "Being in a Meditative State" genuinely in Harmony with Source Energy, you must discover how to eliminate ALL thoughts from your Mental Body. Rest assured, once you align yourself with this energy vibration level, you can immediately step into the reality of non-thought. The key once again is to align your Four Body System with the Spiritual Body at the forefront of your existence.

As you journey through your daily meditation practice, you will notice that it becomes easier to connect with the Highest Self if you practice each day sequentially. By sitting in Silence daily, you will find that you will soon miss your practice if you skip a day.

It can sometimes feel overwhelming when the Mental Body retrains to align with the Spiritual Body at the forefront of your journey. This feeling is natural, and you should not become discouraged if you feel out of sorts at the beginning of your meditation practice sessions. Allow whatever thoughts come and then softly dismiss them with Love. Give yourself plenty of space to reunite with the formless presence of Source Energy. You are discovering how to reconnect with your Highest Self. The time it takes to form this habit of consciously connecting is unimportant because "time" is an illusion of form-based reality.

You are re-learning how to, once again, become the Master of yourself – Your Highest Self. If you are still living your Life based upon the false reality that you are only the Physical Body, you are probably still lost between realities.

A Mental Body that has been programmed for years to believe it is a victim of the life situation you are now living will continue to place mental obstacles on your path. Remember, the ego will never cease in its attempt to retain the form-based control over you. Therefore, if you are not participating in the Silence of a meditative practice daily, you will remain confused and shift back and forth between the two alignment scenarios.

The ego will continue to bring duality into your Life until you finally surrender fully to the Spiritual Body. Before then, you will continue to have "moments" of Conscious Clarity but will not permanently stay aligned with the Spiritual Body. That is until you stop listening to the thoughts that permeate an ego-driven Mental Body.

Keep in mind that the whole reality of a Spiritually aligned Life is beyond the understanding of the typical human belief system. Therefore, if you truly understand what is available, you must remove all false beliefs from your Life. The permanent elimination of duality occurs when you are truly willing to step into your Greatness fully. Until you do so *entirely without question*, you will be in the seemingly never-ending cycle of a conflicted Mental Body.

Do You Believe in Letting Go and Letting God

The concept of "Letting Go and Letting God" catalyzes the understanding of Oneness. When you live your Life beyond the limited beliefs of the mind, you begin to experience a life beyond believing that God or Source Energy is some entity outside yourself that is to worship. Once you truly understand who you are, you stop the insanity of looking for happiness outside yourself and blossom into the Joy that is your natural state of Being within.

The simple act of surrendering fully to the concept of Oneness is the most essential action of your Life. While this may seem far-fetched to someone with a misaligned Four Body System, it is the only path to true Spiritual Enlightenment. When you permanently shift to the Spiritual Body alignment in the forefront of your Life, you stop asking, "Why did this happen to me?" and switch to "How can I use this to serve the Oneness of the Universe?"

Once you genuinely know that you are an intricate part of Source Energy, your actions in Life will align with the concept of Oneness, not separation. When you stop thinking for your benefit only, you awaken a part of you that can foresee the future with Conscious Clarity. All doubt is gone because you no longer think separation from that found in the Highest Self vibration of Life. All that is available to you radiates from a perspective of Knowing what is in store for you and those you serve. You no longer make as many detailed plans to achieve your Life Purpose because your path is through a lens open to unlimited possibilities. You understand that nothing is beyond the reach of a Spiritually aligned person.

As you shift open, sitting with a group of people once a week in a church to worship some deity outside yourself loses its power over you. You no longer need the reassurance of others that you are on the right path; instead, you "feel" what is best for you flowing through your Spiritual Body. This awakening to Oneness of Spirit is not outside you – it is found deep within the Spiritual Body reality of Life. Once you shift to the Cosmic Intelligence housed within your Highest Self, all past beliefs fade away as the necessary training to awaken you to Oneness reality.

As you spend more and more time sitting in Silence, you will discover all the *solutions* to any challenge you have manifested for your Spiritual Growth are in your immediate presence. You awaken to fully understanding how to *Consciously Embrace Your True Personality* and stop shifting in and out of Spiritual Body alignment. The concept of believing there is a greater power outside yourself shifts to an energy vibration that you can now truly understand.

Do You Believe There Is a Greater Power Than Yourself

The whole concept of there being a greater power beyond yourself is both true and false. Humanity has lived with this mystery since the "first breath" was taken on Earth. This issue is because of the limiting beliefs programmed into Humanity through societal influence.

Yesterday's old, third-dimensional paradigms are taught in typical religious and academic education systems today. Spiritual Transformative Education is too broad for the current education system to acknowledge as correct. The fact that you are both Co-creator and Creator is beyond the limited belief system of the mass consciousness of the world at this time. The fact that you are a God-realized Spiritual Being having a human experience is downplayed in society because saying you are God is blasphemy according to old paradigms.

In Oneness, we are all part of the whole, which includes the creator level of reality, where we embody the Source Energy responsible for all creation. If genuinely created in God's image, how can you possibly believe you are anything less than a co-creator of that same image? Through the *Conscious Clarity Energy Process™*, you are beginning to realize just how powerful you are. You are the co-creator of the Universe, which is ever-changing and evolving to the Highest Self reality. Therefore, as part of this Universal

Intelligence System, you are both a "droplet" of water in the sea of Life and the "totality" simultaneously.

When you chose to incarnate into the current Physical Body, you knew who you were exactly. However, through the constant bombardment of those surrounding you, telling you that you are less than you are, you lose your true identity. Now, you are seeking an answer to the never-ending programming of ego-based society that is vibrating so low that it can't even grasp the idea of there being "something greater to this life than what is seen on the surface." Humanity has slipped to this energy vibration level because we are duped into believing the stories meant to control us. It's not a conspiracy theory; it's a Spiritual Intelligence fact. Only Spiritual Transformative Education can correct the mass consciousness's wrong-thinking about this error in the world.

Because control mechanisms end when hearing the teachings, the egoistic society fears Spiritual Transformative Education. Duality or separation programmed into the Mental Body anchors into the mass consciousness. Until we step into the Greatness of the Highest Self reality, we as a species will continue to fall prisoner to this wrong-thinking philosophy. If you believe you are only the Physical Body, it's easy to manipulate you into following the old, third-dimensional paradigms of a low-vibrating society.

With this in mind, if you review the "Eight Categories of Life" detailed for you in Book 1 - *Consciously Live What You Feel*, you will understand how deeply the lower vibration programming embeds into a false belief system. You will see that six (6) of these categories, which are part of the control mechanism of the third-dimensional paradigm, are all part of keeping you locked into a negative belief system or the Physical Body alignment reality.

The choice is yours; you can stay locked in the Third Dimension or shift to the Fourth Dimension and beyond – through Spiritual Transformative Education. You can be a slave to an Egoistic Society or become a Master of the Universal Intelligence found within the Spiritual Body of Oneness.

How Do You Define Your True Self

It's time to stop playing small in Life. Life doesn't play small. By increasing your energy vibration to the level of Oneness found deep within your core, you can align with the Intelligence of the Universe to bring your True Self out of its dormant state. Cosmic forces are waiting to assist you, but you must deeply assess where you stand today to reach your True Spiritual Potential!

No more excuses for pretending you are merely a human being having a Physical Body experience. Your Physical, Mental and Emotional Bodies are simply part of the Four Body System available to serve your Spiritual Body reality. Until you bring this truth to the forefront of your Life experiences through Conscious Clarity of feelings, you will not grow to the energy vibration required to move into the Fifth Dimension of Life. If you genuinely want to increase your Spiritual Growth, you must take action on the tasks necessary to evolve into the Fifth Dimension.

How you define your True Self will determine how challenging your journey will be toward Spiritual Enlightenment. As you already know, once the Kundalini Energy begins stirring in your Four Body System, there is no apparent way to stop it. You ARE a Spiritual Being having a human experience. Suppose you are not willing to increase your energy vibration yourself. In that case, Source Energy will give you nudges or more intense experiences when you purposely attempt to block the Kundalini Energy flowing through your Physical Body.

Each day, you should be sitting in Silence and listening for the silent words of Source Energy manifested through feelings. If you have not made a Conscious Connection with Source Energy by this time, you still resist the total surrender necessary to achieve your True Purpose for being here. How you define who you are is the most essential assessment of your Life. It is more than just an act of "doing". It embodies Being in alignment with the Cosmic Life-force of ALL THAT IS. Without stepping up your energy vibration, you will limit yourself from achieving your full potential or Original Source Agreement in Life.

The *Consciously Embrace Your True Personality* discourse is about increasing your energy vibration level to the Fifth Dimension so that you can prepare yourself for living the Monadic Level of reality.

When you arrived in your current Physical body, you were innately aware of the Fifth Dimension energy vibration level. However, you are now programmed to a lower energy vibration level by those attempting to control you. Now is the appropriate time to reconnect with your essence and become the True Spiritual Personality you are.

Was There a Time You Felt Connected with Everything

Knowing that you are a Spiritual Being having a human experience is a powerful catalyst for shifting back to Spiritual Body alignment. This awareness brings back the truth of Knowing you connect with everything in the Universe. It's not a belief – It's a Deep Knowing or awareness rooted in the Silence of the Spiritually enriched Mental Body. Yes, non-thought is the key to understanding who you are and your unlimited power to manifest anything necessary to fulfill your True Life Purpose.

Before being programmed into the duality of a form-based reality of a Physical Body alignment, you were consciously aware of who you are. You could not speak the language of the culture of your physical birth, but you had a deep, silent understanding of your Spiritual reality. You had no doubts and trusted Source Energy for guidance without question. You were Spiritually aligned, deeply entrenched in Love energy rather than a manufactured belief structure rooted in Fear. As you explore the Highest Self, you will become more aware of the beauty of that innocence at your Conscious Center of Self.

As you continue the "meditation practice" needed to bring you back to Oneness, you will find that the connection with all that is will become more accessible. In this state of Meditative Bliss, you will recollect all you have promised to accomplish while you are here on Earth. It will be challenging at the beginning to release many form-based false needs. Still, after you increase your energy vibration to the level of Highest Self Awareness, you will BE in a continuous state of Knowing. Only you will KNOW when you reach this energy vibration level because the Highest Self comes from within you – not outside you!

At the Highest Self State of Awareness, you no longer rely on outside influences to experience happiness. You understand that you are more than the Physical Body or form-based reality. All that surrounds you radiate with Conscious Clarity, and you are grateful for each breath the body takes. There is a translucent glow to all you see, and your Life becomes rooted in the profound reality of Being a Spirit connected with Source Energy. Fewer words will be necessary to bring your Knowing to the surface of your Life, and you will find that you no longer live to satisfy the urges of the Super-ego.

Returning and remaining at this level of Spiritual understanding becomes your new reality, and you shift your actions to align with your Original Source Agreement promise. Many of your friends and family members, vibrating at lower energies, will misunderstand you, but you will no longer care what they think. You will allow their judgments and move on with your Life in a pure state of Love.

You will understand that "Meditation is not some "*thing*" you do; it is the experience of Being that which you are." You will KNOW the connection with everything that IS, WAS and ever will BE!

When Was the Last Time You Connected with Nature

The experience of non-thought is beyond the limited understanding of a misaligned Mental Body. Non-thought is in the depths of Spiritual Silence where outside interferences minimize separation. Returning to Nature is an excellent place to find this fantastic energy linked with Source Energy. When you are in Nature, all that is form-based can quickly silenced by the Spiritually aligned Mental Body. Genuinely connecting with Nature is an experience found within – it allows you to "feel" the words of Source Energy. In Nature, Source Energy vibrates through your Chakras without outside influences to distract from the Kundalini Energy flow.

Connecting with Nature doesn't mean simply going outside your home and sitting in your comfort zone. It means getting out of the city and finding a high-energy location where you can connect with the natural feelings, smells and vibrations of the unspoiled areas of the Earth. If you do live in a city surrounded by manufactured structures, especially dense concrete, escape from this hectic bustle of traffic that surrounds you. By bringing your Physical Body to an area devoid of these dense city structures, you will "feel" Nature in its most beautiful state of reality.

Many people conditioned to living in the city find it challenging to sit in Silence because they do not physically hear the dense, form-based, low-vibration noise they are accustomed to hearing. They may feel out of sorts when first returning to Nature. This chatter, what I call "background noise disconnect", can easily be overcome by slowly removing the low-energy distraction of the mind.

If you are one of the many who experience nervousness in Silence, you are experiencing the remnants of low-vibration chatter still embedded in your nervous system. It may take some time to release this low-energy pattern from your Physical Body. However, rest assured you can learn to remove and release this distraction over time.

We predominantly connect to the Astrological Elements of Fire, Earth, Air or Water. This connection is part of the Cosmic alignment of Nature. It is embedded in us at first breath and restored when we recollect our comforting feelings in Nature. Experiment with the Astrological Elements' different areas, and you will soon find the area you harmonize with the most.

In Book 3 of the Life's Little Secrets Series, *Consciously Live the Monadic Life*, you will find an in-depth explanation of Cosmic Energies. However, for now, you must understand you connect at a level of energy that harmonizes with this Cosmic Intelligence.

By sitting in Silence, our natural state of Being, we soon discover that the outside world of form-based reality is a mere fragment of the actual reality of Life. There is a whole Spiritual realm accessed at any time if you listen. By using the natural enhancement of Nature to bring this realization to the forefront of Life, we can achieve a higher energy vibration quickly. This natural state can be experienced by everyone – without exception. As you plunge deeper into the Highest Self realization, you will find many enhancements in Nature.

How Do You Feel When You Are in Nature

Your perspective of Life will determine how you feel in Nature. In truth, we are all connected with Nature at the energy vibration level we live in now. If you are Physical Body aligned, you will experience Nature from that perspective. If you are Spiritual Body aligned, you experience Nature from that higher vibrating perspective. Therefore, your experience is a paradox understood from your level of connection with the consciousness generated by your personal experience. If you know that you are One with ALL THAT IS, sitting in the stillness of Nature will only enhance your experience of Life. Suppose you still believe you are only the Physical Body. In that case, you will experience Nature through the five senses and limit your understanding to the lower energy vibration of a Physical Body aligned person.

When do you feel the best - in Nature or surrounded by the creations of the human species? As you learn to experience Life from the Highest Self perspective, your answer will be rooted in the energy vibration of the Cosmic Intelligence of the Universe. Do you believe your gifts connect to Nature? By bringing into play the beauty of your gifts before you arrive on this planet, you will have a fully understood experience if you use those gifts to benefit Spiritual Growth. The natural connection with Source Energy is the key to "feeling" connected with everything. Have you considered the duality of the mind in your answer to the question, "How Do You Feel When You Are in Nature?"

To *Consciously Embrace Your True Personality,* you must decide to stay Spiritual Body aligned. When you are Spiritually aligned, your observation of Nature will differ entirely from someone out of alignment. Suppose you are still struggling with the concept that you are a Spiritual Being having a human experience. In that case, you have not yet allowed yourself to see Life through the "feelings" you have when placed in different environments.

You should feel the same, whether in Nature or the middle of the city. The difference is only in the perception you bring to the experience. Sitting in Nature eliminates outside influences of the Physical realm or Physical Body aligned person. This paradox can confuse the spiritual seeker shifting in and out of Spiritual Body alignment. Whether you choose to admit it or not, if you are still dancing to the whims of a form-based reality, you are still allowing ego to control you in some manner. This challenge is all part of the Spiritual Enlightenment process. This example is why you must align yourself with the Spiritual Body at the forefront of your reality. There is a reason this discourse is called the Conscious Clarity Energy Process™, and the more you increase your energy vibration, the more apparent it will become for you.

Yes, there is a higher energy vibration found naturally in Nature. Still, you bring that energy to Light by increasing the Conscious Clarity of the Oneness at the Highest Self experience of Life. The distractions of the form-based world are constantly attempting to influence your perception of Life. However, you choose each moment to connect with Source Energy or not – it's really that simple!

Are There Simple Steps for Connecting with Source Energy

Although each person connects with Source Energy in their own way, there are three simple steps I recommend to enhance your experience:

Step 1 – Live Beyond Ego

You already know the ego will do whatever it can to keep your mind active with a constant flow of thought, opposite to the Conscious Clarity Energy Process™ teachings. Therefore, keeping the ego aligned to merge with the Spiritual essence of your Being is mandatory. In Book 1, *Consciously Live What You Feel*, you discover how to bring Spirit and ego together so that you can begin to *Consciously Embrace Your True Personality*. It is necessary to realign your Four Body System so that the Spiritual Body is at the forefront of all actions taken in Life. Once you are aligned Spiritually, the ego becomes the servant of the Soul or Spiritual Body.

When you have the Spiritual Body at the forefront of every vision, thought, and action, your Life evolves to the state of Bliss of BEING. You no longer think about being a victim of the circumstances surrounding you and become very aware of all you are. You begin to experience a life filled with Joyous feelings and increase your energy vibration tenfold. This new way of living brings a synchronistic chain of events that aligns perfectly with your Original Source Agreement. The spiritual knowledge you bring to each life situation increases daily, and you discover that you can experience a Joyful life each moment.

Therefore, living your daily Life beyond ego is essential to connecting with Source Energy.

Step 2 – Stop Thinking

The most challenging part for most people is to stop thinking. We live in a world where most people follow the pack unconsciously. This "group think" pack philosophy follows many outside influences and perpetuates a mentality enamored with fear-based propaganda. However, once you shift your Four Body System alignment, these influences have little or no effect on your consciousness. This shift is because you no longer see yourself as a victim of circumstances. You have grown beyond the control of the ego and, therefore, are living Life based upon Love, Peace and Light, where you *Consciously Embrace Your True Personality*. You have conquered the ego, and your true Authentic Self guides your actions.

Consequently, your thoughts are no longer Fear-based, and you live Life based upon what you FEEL rather than what you think. The limited energy vibration of the ego-based thoughts that once drove your actions shifts with a Loving connection with everyone around you. By aligning with Love, Peace and Light, your life experience only uses thought as a positive interaction with Spirit. You resurrect your True Personality and act based on the Spiritual Body guiding your Life.

Therefore, it becomes effortless to instantly remove all "thoughts" from your consciousness because your new thoughts align with the Spirit in the forefront. This shift makes it very easy to stop thinking and surrender to the beautiful energy level of pure Silence.

Step 3 – Listen to the Silence

As you immerse yourself in the beauty of Silence, you experience the energy level of conscious connection with Source Energy. Once you begin to experience this energy vibration, you will no longer need to revert to your old level of understanding. This process is not something you DO; it is the experience of *Being that which you are*. This surge is the natural flow of energy you were always meant to experience. It's this concept of Silence that will bring about the level of understanding that is in alignment with Source Energy guidance.

When you bring your Highest Self into the conversation with Source Energy, you can feel the messages communicated. Silence is the key to all spiritual growth, and you are the only one with the power to experience it to its fullest potential. Spending more time in Silence each day will develop a pattern within your consciousness that is always actively aligned with Source Energy communication.

There is no way for you to misinterpret the messages that come directly from Source Energy because they deliver a Conscious Clarity like you have never experienced before. You will KNOW when you are in Conscious contact with Source Energy – no one can describe its beauty adequately – you must experience it firsthand!

Do You Believe in Life after Earth Lifetime

Your energy vibration will determine how you answer this question; if it is form-based, it will be a different answer than Spirit-based. Nobody is ready to move up the path of energy vibration if they still align with the Physical Body at the forefront of their Life. That is not a judgment but a Spiritual Awareness fact.

If you are still functioning from a Physical Body perspective of Life, you will not begin to understand the messages sent to you now. You will continue to be absorbed in the form-based reality of Life and the low-energy vibration of beliefs rather than the essence of who you are. This observation is the Universal Law of Conscious Clarity. You cannot discern the possibilities of Life after the body's death if you align with the Physical Body at the forefront of your Life.

You have work to do if you are still misaligned, especially at this juncture of awareness. I know some of you are questioning the truth about how to *Consciously Embrace Your True Personality* because you are still struggling with the concept of eternal Life as a Spiritual Being. The way you embrace each moment is a direct reflection of how you are aligned. This alignment will always be the most essential step to Spiritual Enlightenment. If you are still seeking rather than KNOWING, you will continue to question all the Cosmic Intelligence of Source Energy that is coming to you at each moment.

The Physical realm vibrates far below that of the Spiritual realm, and only your Highest Self can bring you to the level of understanding that will once and for all stop the questioning. You must now finish your work as a Physical Body to transform into the next level of your existence. Creating a life in Harmony with your Original Source Agreement would be best. If you refuse to align with this unique path or destiny, I suggest you stop playing small and open yourself up to the possibilities of Spiritual Enlightenment. This shift is not a level of energy for the faint of heart but an energy open to the unlimited facets of your existence. Yes, you can be all you are meant to be and still exist in the lower energy vibration of the Physical realm, but you must also be ready and willing to exit this meager existence at any moment.

You never know when the time of your Physical Body's death will come – but know with certainty that it will. You may have a general idea or feeling of the time frame for the end cycle. Still, the specific transition will only come when your work is fully completed based on your Original Source Agreement. Embrace the remaining Earth time you have left In-Spirit and Know where you are going next to understand how you arrived here in the first place.

Can You Explain How You Got Here

If you cannot explain how you got here, you should begin a quest to communicate with the Highest Self from a different perspective than you have in the past. By recollecting the lessons and discoveries you have learned thus far on your life journey, you can gain a new understanding of how powerful you are Spiritually. NOW is the time to pull out all the stops and *Consciously Embrace Your True Personality*. This part of you is waiting for you to step up your game to the level of the Highest Self realization of God-self reality.

Throughout the *Conscious Clarity Energy Process*™, I guide you to bring your true vision or Original Source Agreement to Light. This task means bringing your Highest Self into the forefront of your actions and never looking back at the lower energy existence you have experienced up to this moment. Yes, this sounds contradictory, but only from a Mental Body perspective that wants to judge based upon past beliefs and the dogma of groupthink mentality. You are more than your Mental Body could ever understand, and you are now on a path to fulfill your ultimate destiny.

You arrived here as a Spiritual Being and will depart this Earth school as a Spiritual Being. How you spend the rest of your time here will determine what new beliefs you choose and how you use them to enhance those around you. You did not show up to play small; you are here to shine brightly, and the only possible way you can do this now is to bring your True Personality to the forefront of your daily Life. This task means no more shifting in and out of consciousness and settling for less than your destiny. By the time you bring the awareness of how you got here to Light, you will have arrived at the tipping point of Spiritual Transformation of Self.

Bring your spiritual practice to everything you do from this point forward, and you will find that Life is always a Joyful miracle. The more you set your Mental Body in place to take action on the Spiritual Body guidance received from Source Energy, the more you will realize how Spiritually powerful you are. No one is exempt from transitioning fully back to Spirit. You came from Spirit when you arrived here and will remain in Spirit for eternity.

How you bring your Spiritual Body to the forefront of your Life will determine your path. You could stay exactly where you are and possibly be content with your Life, but why would you settle for this when there is so much more for you to experience – *at the Highest Self realized existence*? Do you now KNOW who you are? Do you now KNOW how you arrived here? Do you now KNOW where you are going? Let Silence be your guiding Light and bring your reality's true essence to all you achieve in each moment.

Use your KNOWING rather than thinking, and you will arrive at your destination.

You are the creator of your own Life, and you alone KNOW the power you have to bring a brighter Light to the world. Create the miracles of a Spiritual Being and bask in the beauty found only in the power of Love, Peace and Light. Believe in yourself as never before and *Consciously Embrace Your True Personality*!

Do You Believe in Miracles

Miracles are all around us and are the natural form of co-creation with Source Energy, which we are here to experience. All of Life is a miracle. Therefore, why wouldn't you *Consciously Embrace Your True Personality* to bring miraculous events to your Life daily? A misaligned Four Body System teaches that miracles are beyond what each person can achieve in everyday Life. This falsity is nothing more than another manipulation of the misaligned Mental Body driven by a fear-based societal influence. Don't fall for this egoistic trickery.

Once you truly understand and fully acknowledge who you are, you will no longer require the word "miracle" because you will KNOW that all of Life is a miracle and your natural state of Being. When you live the Life of a Spiritual Being having a human experience, the perception of what is normal shifts. You no longer compare yourself or anyone else to another person. You acknowledge the fact that there are varying levels of energy vibration. You understand that you can increase your energy vibration at any time. You know the manipulations of a lower vibrating society, and you bring your vision or True Purpose to Light for the whole world to see.

As you increase your energy vibration, you bring the co-creation process to the forefront of your activities. You quickly discover that focusing on actions that do not serve the Soul and the betterment of all of Humanity are limited, low-vibration efforts founded in a groupthink mentality at best. When your Spiritual Growth aligns with the level of the Fifth Dimension, you step away from those that would hold you back in Life, and you genuinely embrace your Highest Self existence. You *Consciously Embrace Your True Personality*!

The term Miracles is not defined as intended by society, and there is a low-energy mental body understanding of what they signify. *YOU are the miracle* – let that sink in for a while. Sit with that realization in Silence and accept the Universal Truth for what it means. The misaligned Mental Body does not understand this level of observation; it is too busy thinking about all the reasons you are not worthy to vibrate at this level of understanding.

In truth, all miracles manifest in the reality of Oneness and the I-AM-Ness of Life. You are not in any way separated by misrepresenting society usage based on duality. You are part of the Oneness of the Universe and continuously aligned with Source Energy and the Divine guidance available. When you spend your time committed to Spiritual Growth and the teachings of the Fifth Dimension reality, you quickly discover that you are in total control of your Life. This realization means you and you alone are responsible for how each moment unfolds.

It's time to acknowledge your I-AM-Ness and stop caring about what others think about your known Cosmic Intelligence reality!

You Are a Body of One

You are a thread deeply woven into the fabric of Life, and your input is more important than you could ever imagine at the human level of understanding. For you to continue to increase your energy vibration to the level of the Highest Self or Sixth Dimension of reality, you must first fully *Consciously Embrace Your True Personality* for a while. By doing so, you will discover that your Life Purpose shifts into high gear, and you will no longer accept anything less than Spiritual Growth as your driving power. You are readying yourself to change to the deeper understanding level – The Monadic Life!

The *Conscious Clarity Energy Process*™ is rooted in the final reality of Oneness. We are a Body of One and can create a harmonious life with Source Energy. You have grown Spiritually beyond that of the current mass consciousness of the world, and it is time for you to take on the responsibility of Master Teacher. Master Teacher is not a title but a level of living Life from the Highest Self perspective of reality. The journey thus far was fabricated to suit the needs of the ego and Super-ego based upon using a Mental Body that shifts back and forth from Physical to Spiritual Body alignment.

Now, it is time to fully embrace the Highest Self within you and bring all that you have discovered about yourself to others. You are now ready to be a *Master Teacher* to the lower vibrating populous of the world. It is time for you to use your gifts to enhance your teaching methodology. Only you know the direction you must now travel to continually increase your energy vibration and the vibration of those surrounding you. As part of the fabric of Life, you have always been responsible for shifting forward at a level of Evolution in Harmony with Source Energy. As you journey forward, your guide is at an even higher level of understanding – The Monadic level.

Acknowledge the reality of the God-realization within you, and you will experience Life in Harmony with everyone and everything in the Universe. A level of understanding is waiting for you that far exceeds what you have discovered about yourself thus far. You may feel Spiritually Enlightened to a certain level of understanding right now, but you have just touched the surface of the higher realms of Spiritual Conscious Clarity of Self.

As you continue your journey into the wonders of the Universe, always remember there are no limits to your understanding other than those you place upon yourself.

In Book 3 of the Life's Little Secrets Series, *Consciously Live the Monadic Life*, you will begin to discover your interconnection with the Cosmic Intelligence of the Universe. You will align with the Planetary understanding of the powers within this never-ending creation of Life and discover how to utilize the Body of One reality to its fullest potential.

Namaste' - The Spirit within me honors the Spirit within you!

You are on an incredible journey, and your Life will continue to evolve far beyond the limited levels of understanding you have outgrown from the past realities that you allowed to control you.

Prepare yourself now to *Consciously Live the Monadic Life* and to understand that we are a complete Spiritual creation of ONENESS!

Chapter 10 Suggestions - We Are A Body of ONE!

Knowing you connect with ALL THAT IS in the Universe is more than a belief of the Mental Body. As you have learned from previous chapters, miracles are commonplace when you live your Life based upon Love being at the forefront of every action. By understanding that you can increase your energy vibration to the level of the Highest Self reality, you become One with Source Energy and realize that *We are a Body of ONE*.

- Change comes from increasing energy vibration, ultimately realigning our belief system with Knowing.

- Our Evolution will shift in direct proportion to the level at which we increase our energy vibration – it's really that simple!

- The limitless possibilities available to a Fourth Dimension society manifest in a Body of One philosophy. Are you someone who is joining this Evolution, or are you attempting to hold Evolution back because you lack Spiritual awareness?

- In a misaligned Four Body System, thoughts have power over the experience of Life because emotional disconnects with reality drive them. The misaligned Mental Body in a person fuels false past beliefs anchored deeply in the subconscious mind. The power this has over someone aligned in this manner is staggering. As Jesus said when taking his last human breath on the cross, "Forgive them for they know not what they do." We are at this same tipping point again but can change our actions in a heartbeat.

- Through self-reflection, you can overcome any doubt that you may have about shifting your reality. Sitting in Silence will increase your energy vibration to the point where you can honestly evaluate where you stand today. Be patient with yourself and allow the guidance that comes in Silence to be your guiding Light.

- The whole reality of a Spiritually aligned Life is beyond the understanding of the typical human belief system. Therefore, if you truly understand what is available, you must remove all false beliefs from your Life. The permanent elimination of duality occurs when you are truly willing to step into your Greatness fully. Until you do so *entirely without question*, you will be in the seemingly never-ending cycle of a conflicted Mental Body.

- It's time to stop playing small in Life. Life doesn't play small. By increasing your energy vibration to the level of Oneness found deep within your core, you can align with the Intelligence of the Universe to bring your True Self out of its dormant state. Cosmic forces are waiting to assist you, but you must deeply assess where you stand today to reach your True Spiritual Potential!

- The *Consciously Embrace Your True Personality* discourse is about increasing your energy vibration level to the Fifth Dimension so that you can prepare yourself for living the Monadic Level of reality.

- Non-thought is the key to understanding who you are and your unlimited power to manifest anything necessary to fulfill your True Life Purpose. You will understand that "Meditation is not some "*thing*" you do; it is the experience of Being that which you are." You will KNOW the connection with everything that IS, WAS and ever will BE!

- In Book 3 of the Life's Little Secrets Series, *Consciously Live the Monadic Life*, you will find an in-depth explanation of Cosmic Energies. However, for now, you must understand you connect at a level of energy that harmonizes with this Cosmic Intelligence.

- Although each person connects with Source Energy in their own way, there are three simple steps I recommend to enhance your experience:

  Step 1 – Live Beyond Ego

  Step 2 – Stop Thinking

  Step 3 – Listen to the Silence

- How you bring your Spiritual Body to the forefront of your Life will determine your path. You could stay exactly where you are and possibly be content with your Life, but why would you settle for this when there is so much more for you to experience – *at the Highest Self realized existence*?

- Once you truly understand and fully acknowledge who you are, you will no longer require the word "miracle" because you will KNOW that all of Life is a miracle and your natural state of Being.

You are a thread deeply woven into the fabric of Life, and your input is more important than you could ever imagine at the human level of understanding. For you to continue to increase your energy vibration to the level of the Highest Self or Sixth Dimension of reality, you must first fully *Consciously Embrace Your True Personality* for a while. By doing so, you will discover that your Life Purpose shifts into high gear, and you will no longer accept anything less than Spiritual Growth as your driving power. You are readying yourself to change to the deeper understanding level – The Monadic Life!

Prepare yourself now; keep Spiritual Transformative Education in the forefront of your awareness by reading, *Consciously Live the Monadic Life* and completing the *Monadic* level of the *Conscious Clarity Energy Process*™ to understand that we are a complete Spiritual creation of ONENESS!

Namaste

Illustrations

Illustration A – Original Source Agreement

Illustration B – The Train of Life™

Illustration C – Energy Transformation

Illustration D – Life Plan Balance

Illustration E – Energy Vibration - Life Fuel Source

Illustration F – Kundalini Energy

Original Source Agreement

Source Energy

Spiritual Highest Self = Before Human Birth

Birth = Beginning of The Train of Life™

Engine/Engineer/Personality – Highest Self/Conductor/Inner Guidance
(Original Source Agreement)

First Breath — Always Meant to Be Connected — *Unconditional Love*

Engineer
Personality
Ego

Conductor
Inner Guidance
Higher Self

← Birth Path - Flow on The Train of Life™ – Linear Momentum
(Original Life Plan – Original Source Agreement)

The Train of Life™

Conscious Clarity Energy Process™

Illustration - A

Copyright © Terry Swejkoski - All Rights Reserved Worldwide

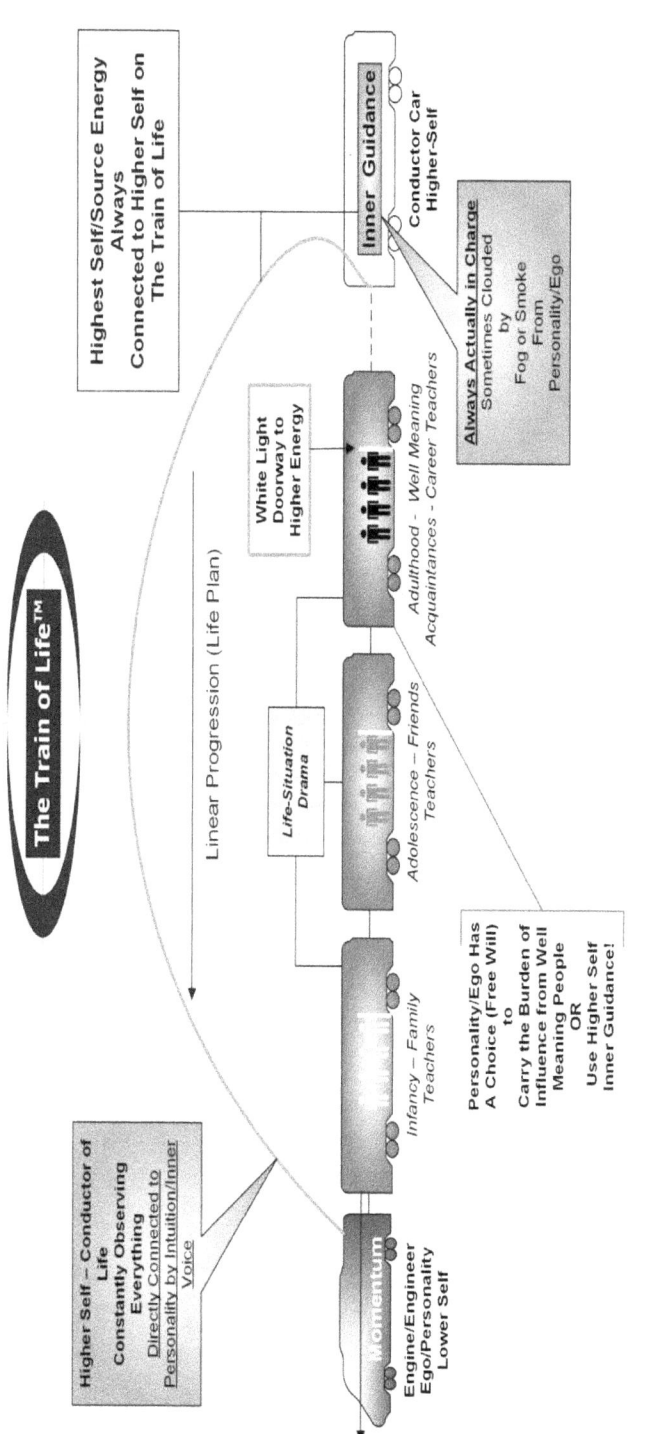

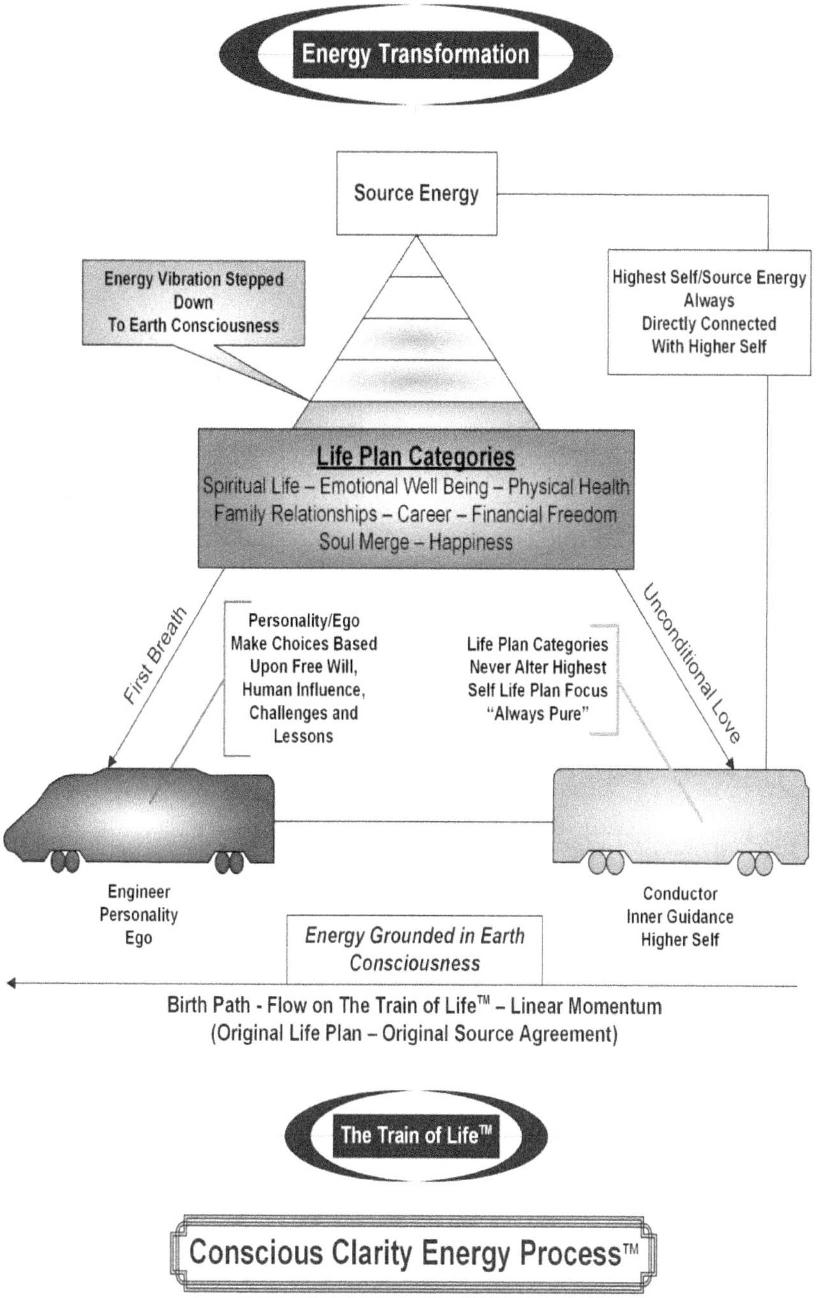

Energy Transformation

Source Energy

Energy Vibration Stepped Down To Earth Consciousness

Highest Self/Source Energy
Always
Directly Connected
With Higher Self

Life Plan Categories
Spiritual Life – Emotional Well Being – Physical Health
Family Relationships – Career – Financial Freedom
Soul Merge – Happiness

First Breath

Personality/Ego
Make Choices Based
Upon Free Will,
Human Influence,
Challenges and
Lessons

Life Plan Categories
Never Alter Highest
Self Life Plan Focus
"Always Pure"

Unconditional Love

Engineer
Personality
Ego

Energy Grounded in Earth Consciousness

Conductor
Inner Guidance
Higher Self

Birth Path - Flow on The Train of Life™ – Linear Momentum
(Original Life Plan – Original Source Agreement)

The Train of Life™

Illustration C

Copyright © Terry Swejkoski - All Rights Reserved Worldwide

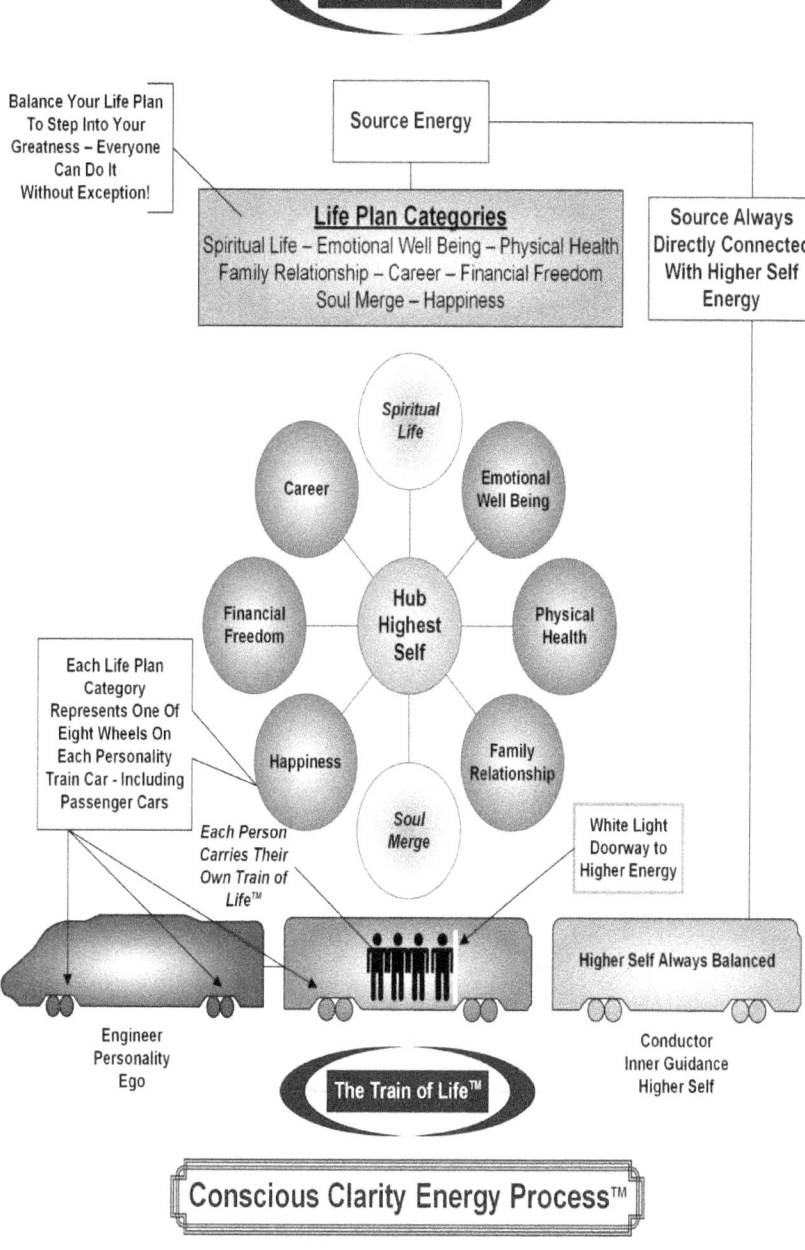

Illustration D

Copyright © Terry Swejkoski - All Rights Reserved Worldwide

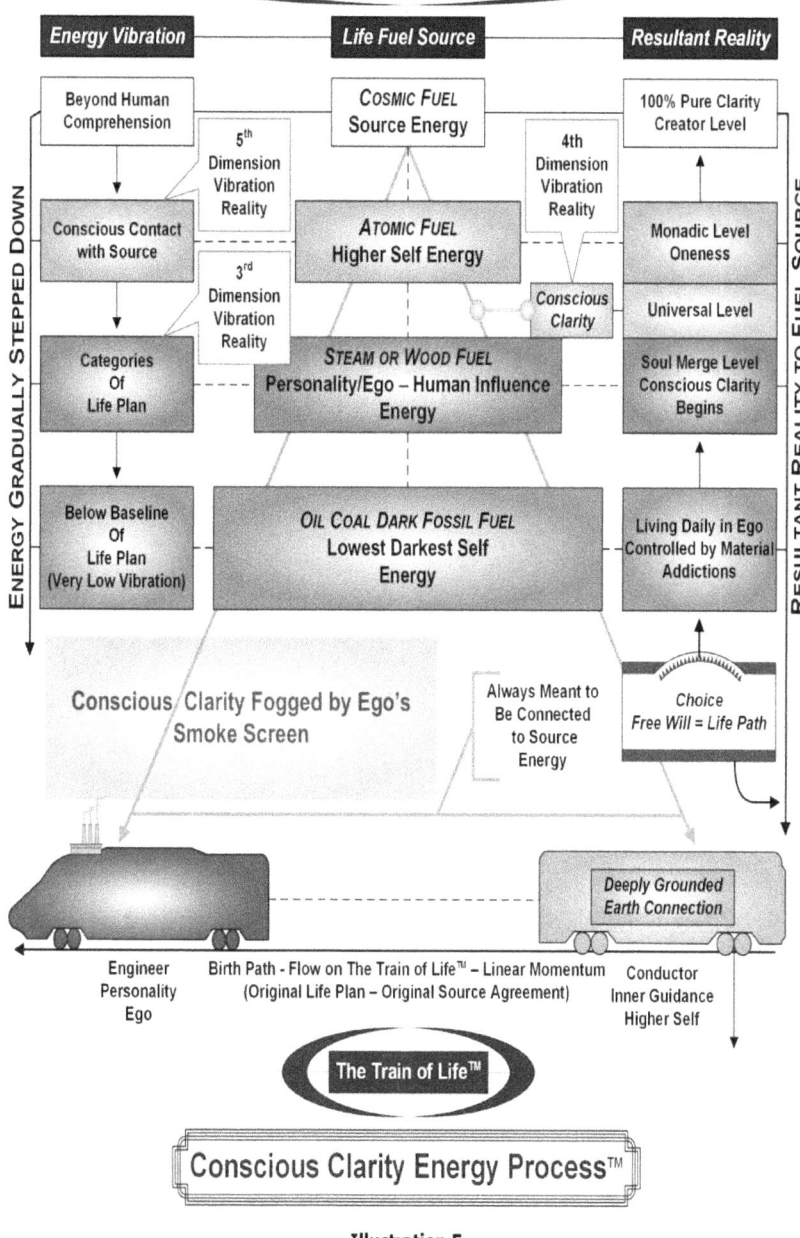

Illustration E

Copyright © Terry Swejkoski - All Rights Reserved Worldwide

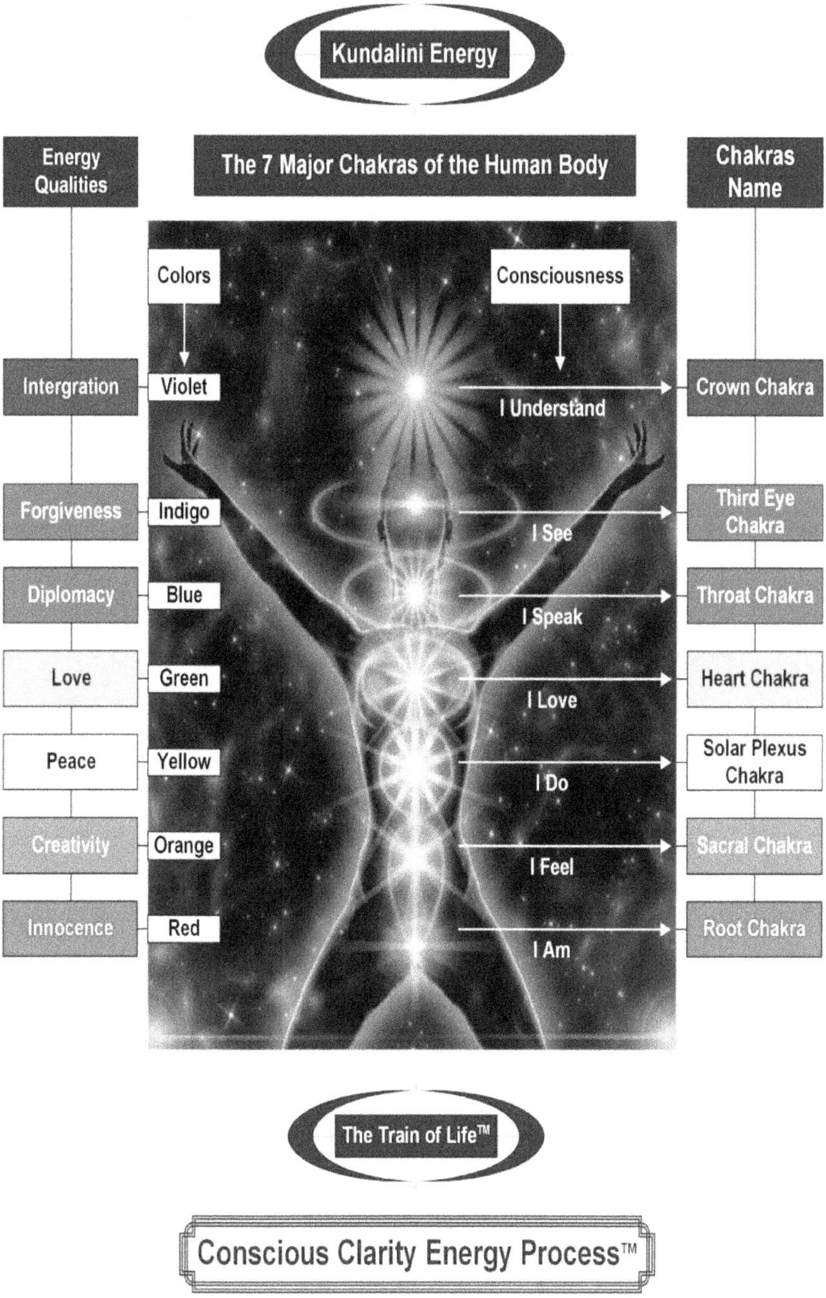

Illustration F

Copyright © Terry Swejkoski - All Rights Reserved Worldwide

www.ingramcontent.com/pod-product-compliance
Lightning Source LLC
Chambersburg PA
CBHW050336010526
44119CB00049B/574